THE SHORTER
NEW OXFORD BOOK OF
CAROLS

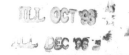

THE SHORTER
NEW OXFORD BOOK OF
CAROLS

EDITED BY

HUGH KEYTE

AND

ANDREW PARROTT

ASSOCIATE EDITOR

CLIFFORD BARTLETT

Music Department
OXFORD UNIVERSITY PRESS
Oxford   New York

Oxford University Press, Walton Street, Oxford OX2 6DP

Oxford New York Toronto
Delhi Bombay Calcutta Madras Karachi
Kuala Lumpur Singapore Hong Kong Tokyo
Nairobi Dar es Salaam Cape Town
Melbourne Auckland Madrid

and associated companies in
Berlin Ibadan

Oxford is a trade mark of Oxford University Press

Published in the United States
by Oxford University Press Inc., New York
200 Madison Avenue, NY 10016

Permission to perform the works in this anthology in public (except in the course of divine worship)
should normally be obtained from the Performing Right Society Ltd. (PRS), 29/33 Berners Street,
London W1P 4AA, or its affiliated Societies in each country throughout the world, unless the owner
or the occupier of the premises being used holds a licence from the Society.

Permission to make a recording must be obtained in advance from the Mechanical Copyright
Protection Society Ltd. (MCPS), Elgar House, 41 Streatham High Road, London SW16 1ER,
or its affiliated Societies in each country throughout the world.

British Library Cataloguing in Publication Data
Data available

Library of Congress Cataloging-in-Publication Data
Data available

3 5 7 9 10 8 6 4

ISBN 0–19–353327–8 (hardback)
ISBN 0–19–353324–3 (paperback)

Music and text origination by
Barnes Music Engraving Ltd., East Sussex,
and Hope Services (Abingdon) Ltd., Oxfordshire
Printed in Great Britain on acid-free paper by
The Bath Press Ltd., Bath, Avon

Items from this anthology are included on the EMI Classics
recordings 'The Carol Albums' (I and II) and 'The Christmas Album', performed
by the Taverner Consort, Choir, and Players, directed by Andrew Parrott

CONTENTS

PART II TRADITIONAL CAROLS

ENGLISH TRADITIONAL

INSTRUMENTAL MATERIAL

For the following items there is instrumental material available for hire from the publishers:

20:VII While shepherds watched their flocks by night; 21:I & II O remember Adam's fall/ Remember, O thou man; 25 En! natus est Emanuel; 26:I & III Puer natus in Bethlehem; 27:IV Joseph lieber, Joseph mein; 28 Quem pastores laudavere; 29:I & II In dulci jubilo; 30:I & II Vom Himmel hoch, da komm' ich her; 31:I Als ich bei meinen Schafen wacht'; 32 Vom Himmel hoch, o Engel, kommt!; 34 Es ist ein Roess entsprungen; 36 Adeste, fideles; 39 Joy to the world!; 40 Come, let us all with heart and voice; 45:I Stille Nacht! heilige Nacht!; 46 Rejoice, ye tenants of the earth; 47 Sound, sound your instruments of joy!; 48 Hark! the herald angels sing; 51:IV Angels, from the realms of glory; 61 Ding! dong! merrily on high; 79:II 'Nowell and nowell!'; 82:III A virgin most pure; 85:III God rest you merry, gentlemen

INTRODUCTION

This anthology is drawn entirely from the *New Oxford Book of Carols* (first published in 1992 and hereafter referred to as *NOBC*). We originally embarked on that book with the aim of compiling a single collection that presented the essential 'core' repertory of popular Christmas carols and hymns, in straightforward but characterful harmonizations with original foreign-language texts and English singing translations of a high standard. When we began work the huge scope of such a project became obvious, and a much broader scheme emerged.

Sadly, this put multiple purchase of the book beyond the resources of most choirs. It is with this in mind that we have now produced the *Shorter New Oxford Book of Carols*, designed to be used either independently or in conjunction with its parent volume (to which reference is freely made throughout). Selecting the contents of this smaller anthology was no easy task. Our guiding principle has been to include items of the broadest possible appeal, and there is a strong bias towards choral settings. All the most widely-known carols are included here—if not always in as many settings or versions as in *NOBC*—together with a good proportion of the less familiar repertory. Sometimes we have reluctantly had to omit material that might appeal primarily to more specialist groups and solo ensembles (e.g., many medieval songs and fifteenth-century English carols), though we have tried to include a representative sample of pieces from every historical period.

The historical notes on individual carols have been reduced to their essentials, and the present Introduction includes résumés of three substantial *NOBC* appendices (see below). Most of the performance suggestions that follow the historical notes on each carol in *NOBC* have been retained here, together with clarification of textual obscurities, but both are often best read in conjunction with the full *NOBC* notes. Where sources are not fully specified, details may be found in *NOBC*.

Items in the present book have been renumbered consecutively, but the *NOBC* number is given at the foot of the first page of each carol for cross-reference. The *NOBC* numbering has been retained, however, for individual settings within each carol, so that, for example, 4:ɪ and ɪɪɪ in this book correspond to *NOBC* 13:ɪ and ɪɪɪ, *NOBC* 13:ɪɪ having been omitted. The nature of the omitted items is usually described in the notes, and choral directors wishing to perform settings or texts given only in *NOBC* should apply to the publishers for permission to reproduce them. The layout of music and text in *NOBC* has in many cases been changed in the interests of the practicalities of performance, and this has sometimes resulted in other minor adjustments such as the renumbering of bars and footnotes.

The introduction to *NOBC* sets out our basic approach to the carol, but a summary may be useful here. The word 'carol' admits of many definitions. Our criteria for inclusion are broad but strict: the content must be narrative, contemplative, or cele-bratory, the spirit simple, the form strophic; but we have not been so doctrinaire as to exclude a few items that combine a quasi-strophic form and a carol-like modesty. Thus Darke's 'In the bleak mid-winter' (63:1) and Joubert's 'There is no rose of such virtue' (68) find a place, and the anonymous 'Swete was the song the Virgine soong' (18), though entirely through-composed, could hardly be denied.

Working on *NOBC*, we came to realize how restricted the current repertory has become. Whole genres which deserve to be widely known have been steadfastly ignored or laid aside, and in many individual cases a single 'standard' musical set-ting of a particular text has replaced former glorious diversity. Diversity is in many ways what we would most like to encourage: a disappointing feature of Christmas services is the stereotyped form of congregational song that has held sway for most of the twentieth century. It is with the hope of initiating change in this respect that we have described at length in Appendix 2 of *NOBC* some of the rich variety of neglected historical practices from the English and Germanic traditions that may profitably be revived or adapted to modern conditions. In the same spirit, we have produced such raw materials for fresh approaches as alternative settings and organ or instrumental symphonies and interludes, in the hope that some musicians will not only take them up but also absorb their implications and begin to amplify them from other printed sources and from their own improvisatory and compositional skills. We give no descants, but this is not because we are in any sense 'against' them. They need to be tailor-made for particular forces in a particular building; and, since even the best examples will grow stale with repeated use, they are best created afresh from time to time. We accordingly leave it to the individual user to supply them, if required.

In no sense is either *NOBC* or the present volume a self-contained repository of carols from which a 'New Oxford' version has merely to be passively selected: so far as financial and practical restraints have allowed, both collections have been envis-aged as greater and lesser cornucopias from the contents of which many different types of performance may be created.

Generous provision has been made for the kind of historically-based approach that performers are increasingly bringing to so much of the musical repertory, and, equally, for the corresponding use of folk (or folk-based) techniques in traditional music. But more conventional styles of performance have their own validity, and we have made a point of allowing for these too, wherever possible. True, many a tradi-tional tune requires no more than a single voice (and perhaps a drone) to bring it to life, but it is hardly to be withdrawn from congregational use for that reason. Nor would there be any automatic merit in providing medieval harmonies for a congre-gational performance of 'Veni, Emanuel' (6): the hymn is part of a living tradition, and is as validly presented with a freely modal organ accompaniment in early twen-tieth-century style as with the two-voice medieval setting that we also provide—the two might even alternate between choir (perhaps in Latin) and congregation.

With a very few exceptions, our editorial harmonizations have deliberately been kept to a maximum of four parts, and the ideal has always been to combine a carol-like simplicity with a historically appropriate manner. Where existing settings are used, we have generally avoided those that are too bland or too highly spiced for the tune, that ignore its implicit harmonies, or that are plain vulgar. Gruber's 'Stille

Nacht' (45) nevertheless finds a place in the debased setting (and form of the tune) in which it is known in the English-speaking countries, as well as in the patently superior original. In only a couple of instances have we deliberately suppressed a current form. One is the Mendelssohn tune for 'Hark! the herald angels sing' (48), where congregations will surely be quick to prefer and adapt to what the composer actually wrote. The other is 'Come, love we God' (17), where the single part given in the manuscript source is clearly an inner voice, rather than a true melody.

*   *   *   **

NOBC contains three substantial appendices which provide background information (much of it of a practical nature) for particularly crucial areas in our selection of carols. The five short sections which follow provide summaries of these.

The German Hymn Tradition

Vernacular congregational song was firmly established in the Germanic lands well before the Reformation, and was retained and developed by both Lutherans and Catholics. Pre-nineteenth-century practice in both Churches differed markedly from that of today, exploiting techniques that can usefully be revived or adapted for present-day use (and not only in hymns of the Germanic tradition). The performance notes of the relevant Germanic carols make frequent reference to such techniques, and the following gives the gist of the much longer Appendix 2 of *NOBC*; we hope that this section may help infuse a much-needed variety into carol- and hymn-singing at Christmas services and concerts. Restoration of some of the lost splendours of historical hymn performance could help raise what is too often mere mechanical repetition to a higher artistic level, so lessening the divide between choirs and congregations or carol-concert audiences, and drawing all concerned into a richer and more thoughtful relationship with the sung texts.

A congregation would normally be led by a cantor standing in its midst, and in a large town church it might be supported by a unison plainchant choir (*chorus choralis*). In Catholic churches a few cantors often fulfilled the same function, while among Lutherans the supporters might be the boys of the town Latin school with their master, or occasionally a mixed adult group from the congregation. These all sang entirely in unison, unaccompanied, and at a markedly slower pace than the polyphonic choir (*chorus musicus*), which also participated in hymns (though never, in the early days, simultaneously with the congregation). The *chorus choralis* seems to have become a rarity in Lutheran churches by the mid-seventeenth century, and the polyphonic choirs little by little took over the function of leading the congregation. But the old separation of choir and people in hymns probably still obtained in Leipzig, at least until Bach's death in 1750, and the division persisted in remote areas well into the nineteenth century.

In both Catholic and Lutheran traditions the polyphonic choir would typically be placed in a west-end organ gallery and be supported by instrumentalists. In the first golden age of Lutheran music, around 1600, the latter would often be supplemented by the town waits on important festivals, when groups of singers and players might be dispersed around the building to contrast and combine in a multiplicity of ways with each other and with the congregation, for hymns as well as for other music. A comparable variety was frequently obtained within the service as a whole, each hymn receiving an individual treatment according to its character and liturgical status: the solemnity of the pre-eminent gradual hymn, for example, might be marked at the main mass by starkly unison congregational singing (perhaps with an impressive organ introduction and organ verses) or by the most elaborate of choral sequences. Right from the early sixteenth-century, the Lutherans favoured combining the distinct congregational and choral forces in various ways, the most important of which are summarized below.

Congregational song in Catholic churches had much in common with the Lutheran tradition, but at Christmas there was a much greater emphasis on the carol (as distinct from the Christmas hymn), and countless new examples were still evolving or being composed in the nineteenth century. Most of those popular in the English-speaking world date from the seventeenth century, and were originally associated with the popular (non-ecclesiastical) shepherd dramas or with the custom of cradle-rocking at the midnight mass. They usually have triple-time tunes and include such maternal exclamations as 'Eya!' and 'Susani!'. (Cradle-rocking was also kept up by Lutherans before eighteenth-century rationalism put an end to all such ancient observances. The celebrant would rock an elaborate cradle on the altar, containing a figure of the Christ-child, in time to the music, while children in the nave might mimic his actions with a second cradle of their own: see notes to *NOBC* 55.) Such carols did not lend themselves to complex performance schemes, and where harmonizations are to be found in the early hymn-books they tend to be fairly characterless and associated with less appealing forms of the melodies: in most cases, therefore, we have taken text and tune from a particular book and (like the local directors of music) have provided our own harmonies.

The more formal chorale repertory is presented in the encyclopaedic printed collections of Michael Praetorius, which contain arrangements for every conceivable manner of performance current around 1600 and which were to be found in Lutheran churches of any size. Praetorius drew on both Lutheran and Catholic materials, complementing his own arrangements with those of the leading composers of the previous century. We have made considerable use of his deliberately straightforward settings in *Musae Sioniae VI* and *VII* (1609), which are suitable for both choral and congregational performance, and have selected the forms of the tunes best known in English-speaking countries. Pages 662–4 of *NOBC* Appendix 2 include suggestions for material elsewhere in Praetorius's collections that could be combined with, or substituted for, the harmonizations we give (including the note-against-note congregational settings in *Musae Sioniae VIII*, 1610) and some detailed performance schemes. The notes to individual carols in *NOBC* often mention suitable choral and organ settings by other composers, and, where appropriate, possible performance schemes are also included with the instrumental parts for the German hymns, available for hire from the publisher. What follows here is a brief summary of the most important techniques for the performance of hymns in the German tradition.

The organist would often introduce a hymn with a chorale prelude or a fantasia-like intonation in the Italian manner. Organ accompaniment for congregational singing, with simple, treble-tune harmonies, began to appear in the 1580s, and simultaneous singing by congregation and *chorus musicus* (with associated organ and instruments) began to spread from around the turn of the century; however, such manners of performance did not become the norm until the later eighteenth century. Inter-line interludes were common throughout the seventeenth and eighteenth centuries: at one extreme were simple formulae of standard length that followed each line and were identical in each verse, the one after the last line leading back to the first without a break; at the other were freer flourishes, often varying from verse to verse and usually concluding each one with extended 'cadencing' on the held last note. If inter-verse interludes or symphonies existed at all they were highly exceptional, but the organist would often substitute an idiomatic organ setting for one or more verses, as in medieval liturgical hymnody, or he might play an entire hymn in this manner (especially during the communion).

Various procedures were available when *chorus musicus* and congregation divided a hymn between them. The choir might sing in Latin, the congregation responding to each verse in the vernacular and (at least when unaccompanied) at its characteristic slower pace. Or (without tempo variation) the lines might be assigned to choir (often subdivided into groups) and congregation in the manner of *Wechselgesang* ('antiphonal song'), the same pattern always being retained for each verse. (Nos. 26 and 27 are classic examples of such *Wechselgesänge*.) The choir would often sing a particular hymn alone, and Praetorius gives extended verse-by-verse settings of several Christmas hymns, to be used complete or to be mined at will for more diverse schemes. These could also be combined with choral–congregational alternation (as above), and some of the grand motet-settings of opening and closing verses were to be used with simple congregational (or alternating choral–congregational) singing of the intervening verses. There are even polychoral settings of Christmas hymns in which the accompanied congregation forms one of the choirs—a technique pioneered in the court chapel at Kassel.

The English Urban Tradition

Organs (without pedals in the early days) were to be found in many eighteenth- and nineteenth-century London parish churches, usually alongside untrained choirs of children from the charity schools. In the chapels of certain institutions there was a high standard of singing by selected inmates, pre-eminent being the Methodist Lock Hospital, where John Madan preached and directed the music, providing sophisticated settings for two-part high voices and organ, with symphonies in the current secular manner between verses (see 38:II). In Anglican churches the organ played a much more prominent role than is now common, 'giving out' the tune (often in an elaborate 'chorale-prelude' manner), varying the accompaniment verse by verse, and supplying interludes between verses and/or short flourishes between the lines to allow the singers to draw breath. (Organ interludes are given with a number of hymns and carols in *NOBC*, and there is a list of published and manuscript sources for such material at the end of *NOBC* Appendix 2, following a more detailed consideration of the tradition.) In parts of the North of England, robed four-part choirs were to be found well before the Romantic Revival and the Oxford Movement of the early nineteenth century: like some choirs of Protestant Dublin, they seem often to have used organ accompaniment and to have favoured the conventional end of the wide spectrum of the 'gallery' style.

The English 'Gallery' Tradition

Hymns and carols found little place in parish churches following the Reformation, when the Calvinist rule that all sung texts should be of Biblical origin was enforced. Most of the few parish-church organs that survived the reformers were destroyed by Parliamentarians during the Civil War, so that the metrical psalms that were permitted in conjunction with (but rarely within) services were nearly everywhere sung in unaccompanied unison before the rise of west-gallery choirs in the eighteenth century. 'Gallery' singing might be in two, three, or four parts, and soon came to be instrumentally accompanied: a single bass instrument was common at least from the 1740s. Two parts can be surprisingly sonorous, and the soprano and alto parts were always optional in the tenor-tune era, when the tenor and bass parts were sometimes printed alone, leaving the user to supply upper parts if required.

In 1700 the first authorized Christmas hymn appeared—'While shepherds watched their flocks by night' (20), a paraphrase of Luke's account of the Nativity. This and the many non-Biblical carols that followed were designed to replace the metrical psalms before and after service on Christmas Day, and they were initially sung to familiar psalm-tunes of the same metre. The 'church tunes' in the tenor were doubled by some of the soprano voices at the higher octave, and the congregation (at least in theory) also sang the tune. Tenor tunes were also the rule in the original settings that soon began to appear, but from around the end of the eighteenth century there was a gradual change-over to the modern treble-tune format (without octave doubling), and the older settings were often updated by swapping round the tenor and soprano parts. (The same may easily be done for the tenor-tune settings that we give here, such as 20:v.) Many of the vast number of composers who provided country choirs with their settings wrote in a crude, home-grown style that knew little of academic part-writing. As a direct result, carols such as the nineteenth-century Cornish 'Sound, sound your instruments of joy!' (47) have a vigour and individuality rarely to be found in orthodox church music of the time. The same choir would often serve both the Methodist chapel and the local parish church, while many of the other nonconformist chapels had their own. This whole repertory was forgotten following the nineteenth-century introduction of barrel-organs, harmoniums, and chancel choirs, but it is now at last beginning to be taken seriously once more, and we have tried to include a representative selection of the best examples in *NOBC*.

The accompanying instruments were whatever lay to hand, almost invariably at treble or bass pitch. Flutes and bassoons were most common, and calculated combinations (such as the string band at Thomas Hardy's Stinsford) were very much the exception. In both tenor- and treble-tune settings the alto and tenor lines were invariably played at the higher octave; where possible, the treble was played at the higher octave and the bass at the lower. Where only three instruments were used, they probably supported treble, alto, and bass. At least in treble-tune settings, instrumental embellishment of the tune and bass would have been expected (see *NOBC* 89 and 96:iii for late, written-out examples). When the not-uncommon double bass was used, the bass line would sound entirely at the lower octave. Any additional instruments would double an appropriate part at pitch. The treble part (and tenor-tune doubling) was usually taken by boys, girls, or women indifferently, and the countertenor (alto) part by the same and/or by men, who were normally high tenors (as in the renaissance tradition) rather than falsettists. The singing ranged from a nasal 'folk-music' style to a relatively cultivated manner, but subtle dynamic gradation was quite unknown. Following eighteenth-century convention, 'soft' and 'loud' probably implied 'soli' (or semichorus) and 'full', and we have sometimes substituted the latter indications. The words were 'lined out' (recited) by the parish clerk or his nonconformist equivalent—at first line by line, eventually verse by verse—and the singing was usually led by a gallery tenor. The instruments would precede the singing by playing either the opening line(s) of the tune or a tiny pitch-setting formula. Many of the gallery singers were musically illiterate, and they (and members of congregations) were easily and frequently led astray by the octave-doubling instruments, so that many hybrid forms of the three upper parts flourished in the less well-regulated galleries, and new versions of melodies were constantly evolving (see 'The first "Nowell!"', 79, for a notable example).

The American 'Primitives'

The same tradition took root in New England later in the eighteenth century, though here 'complete' four-part settings were the rule and instruments were rarely used. (The frequent octave writing in William Billings's basses was a conscious device to make up for the lack of instrumental support.) There was a particular fondness for fuging tunes (in which one or more lines of the verse would be treated like a series of fugal entries). The change to treble-tune settings came in the years around 1800, a little later in the US than in England, and soon after this a vogue for 'correct' European music swept away the whole tradition. It had already spread to the South, however, where the shape-note composers developed it in a way that has no Old-World equivalent. They preferred three-part writing (treble, tenor, and bass) and an often starkly simple style, with much doubling of fifths and octaves, that derived from otherwise lost British traditions of improvised modal harmony (see 'Ye nations all', 42). Shape notes differed from conventional notation only in that the shape of the note-heads indicated the degree of the scale to be sung, enabling virtually anyone to sight-read and allowing any singer to take any part. Where the British and New England 'primitives' had doubled the tenor tune at the higher octave, shape-note singers doubled both treble and tenor at the contrary octave (see the carefully argued conclusions in Richard A. Crawford, *The Core Repertory of Early American Psalmody*, Madison [Wisconsin], 1984, p. xvi). An essential feature of shape-note singing is a steady 'jog-trot' pace and deadpan delivery.

The English Traditional Carol

The invaluable work of the Cornish antiquarians Davies Gilbert and William Sandys has long been the subject of some misunderstanding. It is accepted that their pioneering publications (*Some Ancient Christmas Carols*, 1822 and *Christmas Carols, Ancient and Modern*, 1833) are the earliest sources of many of the perennial modern favourites, and effectively saved the rapidly disappearing folk carol for posterity. But the mistaken notion that they concocted their own bass parts has blinded editors to the true nature of what Gilbert, in particular, preserved. He built up a large collection of Cornish carol manuscripts, and employed competent assistants to collect texts and notate tunes and settings. His impeccably engraved volume of 1822 (which he probably intended to follow up with a similar but much wider-ranging collection) is almost entirely drawn from gallery adaptations of traditional carols, evidently from a single Cornish location and by a single hand. The printing of only the (tenor-) tune and bass follows eighteenth-century practice, and we have provided upper parts in an appropriate idiom: the treble and tenor parts may be reversed, in line with later custom (see 'The English "Gallery" Tradition', above). Sandys, though a trained musician, was London-born, far less sympathetic to rustic music-making, and mainly interested in the texts. Whoever notated his amateurishly lithographed tunes seems sometimes to have drawn on gallery settings, sometimes to have transcribed as best he could from gallery performance, and perhaps to have devised some of the basses himself. Later editors smoothed out the roughnesses in the melodies of both Gilbert and Sandys, providing them with conventional harmonies and acclimatizing them to the middle-class drawing-room, the chancel, and the college hall. It is in this adapted form (rarely acknowledged) that most traditional carols have become generally known: we hope that the very different musical climate today will allow the grittier rustic originals to take their place alongside their assimilated urban cousins.

Such carols would also have been performed by the village waits of the eighteenth and nineteenth (and perhaps earlier) centuries as they visited each house in their parish on Christmas Night. Most other peripatetic carollers were 'luck visitors', calling down blessings on the household in return for gifts of money, food, or drink: wassailers (see 85–8), mummers (who often concluded with a carol), carriers of Advent Images (see notes, *NOBC* 131), poor women or children going 'gooding' (see notes, *NOBC* 154), groups of carol-singers in the modern sense (who existed at least from the mid-eighteenth century), and individuals, who often sang extended ballads on the Passion, the life of Christ (e.g., 84), or on legendary/apocryphal themes. Many groups undoubtedly sang in harmony, improvised or notated, as did the domestic carollers of Christmas Eve. Accompanying instruments must frequently have been used before the nineteenth century, though the possibility is often obscured by the survival of only the later and more rhapsodic forms of many of the old harmonically-based traditional tunes of the seventeenth and eighteenth centuries. Where appropriate, we have indicated chords above the music for simultaneous or alternative instrumental accompaniment, but in general the 'authentic' harmonization of traditional melodies is a chimera that we have resolutely not pursued, particularly because the SATB choir has no counterpart in traditional music-making. The existence of 'three-man songs' is well attested, however, with many known examples, and we have sometimes provided a rough setting of this type (which was not always confined to three individuals in performance) in addition to a more conventional harmonization.

EDITORIAL POLICY: TEXTS

We have normally chosen to base a text on a single source. Where a source is garbled, we have been as economical as possible in our emendations, which are usually noted. In a few instances, we have adapted more boldly: an editorial couplet has been added to 'Christians, awake!' (37), for example, so that (for the first time, to our knowledge) Byrom's poem may be sung complete.

An editor who begins to replace archaic words is setting foot on a dangerously slippery slope, for the process can all too easily lead to blandness: we have preferred to explain obscurities in footnotes. In the case of congregational hymns, however, we have been more flexible, and we generally follow the standard modern form of a text, where there is one.

Calculatedly offensive references to Jews have been removed or modified ('wicked Jews' becomes 'wicked men', for example) and the changes are noted. Marginal cases, such as the verse in a medieval *cantio* that calls on the 'wretched Jews' to convert to Christianity, are retained but marked with an asterisk (*) to indicate possible omission. We also asterisk verses for the usual purpose of indicating reasonable or conventional abbreviations of longer items, though without catering for those who, like a recent Anglican bishop, feel that the ideal hymn comprises 'two verses, one of which may be omitted'.

Orthography

Original spelling has been retained where desirable and practicable, but we have freely amended the spelling, punctuation, and layout of texts known to have been transcribed directly from a singer or a recording, noting only substantial changes.

The orthography of English medieval carols has not been updated, since we believe that the gains of retaining the original outweigh the losses: allusive, deliberately ambiguous, and regional spellings remain unobscured, and singers are encouraged to attempt a medieval pronunciation. Obsolete letters have, however, been replaced by their modern equivalents, and modern usage has been followed for i/j and u/v. Medieval Latin orthography is similarly retained, with no classicizing substitution of 't' for 'c' or 'ae/oe' for 'e' (thus *leticie* does not become 'laetitiae').

In early German carols and hymns we have sometimes given the Low German text; but when the carol is well known, and also in the many cases where this would be an odd match for the musical setting, we have felt free to substitute either a later version (using Praetorius's texts with his settings, for example) or modern High German.

When a modern composer has set an old text, we have nearly always followed his orthography. A rare exception is *Wither's Rocking Hymn* (64), where we have given the complete text in its original form in preference to the modernized selection of verses set by Vaughan Williams in the *Oxford Book of Carols*.

Punctuation

Punctuation in early sources tends either to be sparse or mainly rhetorical rather than syntactical. The conscientious editor may choose either to preserve the original indications or (as we have done) to provide modern syntactical punctuation that will make the grammatical structure, and thus the meaning, clear to the singer. This is particularly important in lyric verse, with its frequently elliptical grammar, and in traditional texts, where the syntax can often be very loose. (In a few folk carols there are passages that resist logical analysis, and here we have punctuated as helpfully as possible without imposing a spurious solution.) We have rarely modified the punctuation of recognized poets.

By the standards of modern prose we have chosen to over-punctuate, but this has been dictated by the special needs of singers, who may be sight-reading or coping with multitudes of unfamiliar verses; with such an editorial approach, a comma need not imply a hiatus of any kind. Singers' needs are normally greater in non-English texts, and we have treated these similarly (though German has its own rules). We have punctuated Latin as though it were English (see 'Quem pastores laudavere', 28, where a failure to punctuate often obscures the vital fact that lines 3 and 4 of verse 1 are direct speech).

Pronunciation

NOBC Appendix 1 provides a brief guide to fifteenth-century English pronunciation (carols 11–14), but we have not felt it appropriate to offer guidance for the wide range of other foreign, old, or dialect texts in this anthology. For the various historical pronunciations of Latin, see Harold Copeman's two related books, *Singing in Latin* and *The Pocket Singing in Latin* (Oxford, 1990).

Singing translations

In a simple, strophic form such as the Christmas carol the text has absolute primacy: however indissoluble text and tune may have become, it is the words that *are* the carol. This places a heavy responsibility on the translator, and one that is rarely taken sufficiently seriously. Even when the literal meaning of the original is adequately conveyed (and it is astonishing how cavalier translators can be), the rhyme scheme will often be ignored or bent wilfully out of true, as if it were a mere ornament to the verse. In reality, the counterpoint of verbal and musical rhyme is vital.

We have made determined efforts to find adequate translations, but for the most part have been compelled to do the job ourselves. This has involved original translation, the touching up of existing versions, and centonizing (a cento is 'a composition formed by joining scraps from other authors'—*OED*). We are only too aware of the shortcomings of the results, but they have, at least, the virtue of being accurate, low-key, and reasonably grateful to sing. It is also with the needs of singers in mind that we have favoured the kind of regularly stressed verse characteristic of many hymns: though this can be doggerel when spoken, it has a very different effect when sung. Where an original rhyme scheme is too tight for a strict English imitation, we have substituted one with a similar 'feel' (see, for example, 'Entre le bœuf et l'âne gris', 107).

In a few instances we have chosen not to provide a singing translation. We feel, for example, that no English version could do justice to the fusion of words and music in certain of the medieval *cantiones* (3–5), and have merely supplied literal prose translations. (Where an imitation or free translation is given it is usually accompanied by a literal prose version.)

EDITORIAL POLICY: MUSIC

The broad historical and geographical span of this collection has necessitated some flexibility in the editorial conventions we have adopted, and we have tried to strike a balance between the natural expectations of uniformity within the anthology as a whole and the different editorial conventions that are standard for particular repertories.

Ligatures and coloration are shown only in medieval and certain renaissance carols. They are indicated in the usual manner: by square brackets over the notes concerned, complete in the first case, broken in the second. Plainchant ligatures are shown by slurs.

Plicated notes in medieval music are printed small.

Preliminary staves, showing clefs, time signatures, and initial notes (omitting lengthy rests) are given when this is the most convenient way of indicating how the original notation has been changed. Elsewhere, changes of note values and notated pitch are mentioned in the notes.

Note values have usually been reduced in older carols so that crotchet/quarter-note movement prevails throughout the book.

Part ranges are generally given only when they are not obvious, and particularly when they do not conform to the normal SATB categories. They are shown by small solid noteheads between the key and time signatures.

Transposition. We have frequently adjusted the notated pitch in pre-nineteenth-century repertory, to allow for small differences from the modern standard of $a' = 440$ Hz and to bring the music to what we believe the intended pitch to have been. This will normally bring it within the most comfortable areas of the singers' ranges. The fifteenth-century English polyphonic carols (11–14) have been brought into ranges suitable for tenors and basses, but they may be retransposed to suit other groups.

Transposing treble clefs (𝄞) are used in the normal way to indicate that the part should be sung/played an octave lower than notated.

𝄞 indicates *either* that a part may be sung in the treble or tenor octave at will *or* that it is to be sung/played at both octaves simultaneously. Where the intention is not obvious from the context, it is explained in the performance note.

☞ indicates the melody line when it is not in the highest part throughout.

Accidentals are indicated in four ways: an accidental of normal size placed before a note is in the source; an accidental of normal size placed before a note but in round brackets is purely cautionary; an accidental of small size placed before a note would almost certainly have been supplied by performers as a matter of course; an accidental placed over a note and above the staff is an editorial suggestion.

Square brackets are used for various editorial additions.

Ornamentation by the performer was expected in many repertories, especially before the mid-nineteenth century. The subject is too varied and complex to be dealt with in detail here, though for some special cases see 89, 111, and *NOBC* Appendix 3. Cadential trills were routine in the eighteenth century, though sources are inconsistent in their indication and notation. In the interests of visual clarity, we have therefore omitted initial appoggiaturas and final terminations, but both are usually to be understood.

Beaming follows syllabification: notes sung to separate syllables are beamed separately and groups of notes sung to a single syllable are beamed together (or grouped by means of slurs if any are longer than quavers/eighth-notes). Exceptions to this have been made in the fifteenth-century English polyphonic carols, where beaming has been designed to clarify the rhythmic complexities, and slurs have not been used lest they give the impression that a legato style of performance is intended.

Performance notes are intended to suggest possibilities, but do not aim to be comprehensive. They are designed to guide and stimulate rather than to limit, and we have kept them concise by excluding general information on performance practice that is easily available elsewhere. Many carols would normally have been sung as a single melodic line, though we have not always specified this. 'Choir' is used in the conventional way to indicate groups with more than one voice per part or choir with or without congregation/audience. Thus a performance note reading '(*i*) choir; (*ii*) voices and organ' means '*either* choir singing in harmony, *or* any number of voices, in unison or harmony, with or without congregation/audience, and with organ'.

Superscript notation

Superscript rhythms are an economical and generally flexible device for dealing with the difficulty of fitting the words of later verses to the underlay of the first. This is a perennial problem, particularly in traditional carols, where the number of syllables in a line of text can vary considerably between verses and where the conventions for accommodating differences are not always those we might expect. The system is especially valuable for choirs; solo singers may prefer to go their own way, perhaps choosing to adapt the melodic line in some problem passages. (The written-out verses of the sixteenth-century carol 'Thys endere nyghth', 15, reflect this practice.)

The basic principle is that superscript note values indicate the *duration of a syllable* and not necessarily the rhythm to be sung. For example,

joyful

means that 'joy-' is to be sung to three beats and '-ful' to one, even if the melodic line has several notes in a context such as

joy - ful —

Superscript can also indicate where a single note (e.g., o) in verse 1 subsequently needs to be split into more than one note on the same pitch (e.g., ♩. ♪). This system means that in simple homophonic pieces such as carols the superscript can nearly always serve not just the tune but equally all the vocal parts.

The notation is normally used to mark departures from the way the first (underlaid) verse is sung. Where there are several texts (e.g., a text and its translation), the superscript notation always refers back to the first verse of the particular text or language being sung.

Small notes and dotted slurs in the music indicate the common deviations in later verses, besides any discrepancies caused by the simultaneous underlaying of more than one verse (or a verse and its translation) and such occasional irregularities as up-beat notes not sung in the first verse or other notes which must be substituted later for first-verse rests. Verses 3 and 8 of 'The Cherry Tree [Part I]' (73:1), given separately in our setting, are underlaid in example 1 (below) to show how they relate to the music.

Superscript slurs are used to indicate a natural elision of syllables (for instance, 'rev̑erently') and occasionally also as a less rigid alternative to superscript rhythms. Stylized superscript repeat marks (‖:‖) indicate the repetition of one or more words within a line, though they may not apply to all voices.

We have applied the superscript system with considerable flexibility, especially in cases where adherence to the letter of the law would lead to undue complexity or leave the sight-reader in doubt. In certain highly irregular carols, for instance, a greater amount of notation is given than is strictly necessary.

HUGH KEYTE
ANDREW PARROTT

March 1993

Example 1

1. Jo - seph was an old man, and an old__ man__ was__ he When

he wed - ded Ma - ry in the land of Ga - li - lee, *(etc.)*

3 Joseph and Mary walked through an orchard good,
Where was cherries and berries, so red as any blood.

3. Jo - seph and__ Ma - ry walked through an orch - ard__ good, Where was

cher - ries and ber - ries, so__ red as a - ny blood.

8 'Go to the tree, Mary, and it shall bow to thee,
And the highest branch of all shall bow to Mary's knee.'

8. 'Go to the tree,__ Ma - ry, and__ it shall bow__ to__ thee, And the

high-est branch of all_____ shall__ bow to Ma-ry's knee.'

ACKNOWLEDGEMENTS

The authors and Oxford University Press are grateful to those who have given permission for the use of copyright material in this anthology. Every effort has been made to trace copyright owners, and apologies are extended to anyone whose rights have inadvertently not been acknowledged. Any omissions or inaccuracies of copyright detail will be corrected in subsequent printings if notified to the publisher.

2:ɪɪ & ɪɪɪ. Latin and English texts, and prose rendering of the medieval English from *Medieval English Songs*, ed. E. J. Dobson and F. Ll. Harrison. Reproduced by permission.

22. Original R. Pring-Mill translation from *Now make we merthe*, book III. Used by permission of OUP.

33. Translation reproduced from *The Oxford Book of Carols* by permission of OUP.

51:ɪ. Arrangement reproduced from *The Oxford Book of Carols* by permission of OUP.

56:ɪ. Arrangement reproduced from the *English Hymnal* by permission of OUP.

62:ɪɪ. Music © 1923 B. Feldman and Co. Ltd., trading as H. Freeman and Co., London WC2H 0EA.

63:ɪ. Music © Stainer & Bell Ltd. Reproduced by permission of Stainer & Bell Ltd.

64. © Ralph Vaughan Williams 1928. Music reproduced from *The Oxford Book of Carols* by permission of OUP.

65. Music © Copyright 1952 Novello and Co. Ltd. © Renewed 1980. Reproduced by permission of Novello and Co. Ltd. Words reproduced from *The Oxford Book of Carols* by permission of OUP.

67. Music © Oxford University Press 1932. Reproduced by permission.

68. Music © Copyright 1954 Novello and Co. Ltd. © Renewed 1982. Reproduced by permission of Novello and Co. Ltd.

69. Music © Copyright 1957 Novello and Co. Ltd. © Renewed 1985. Reproduced by permission of Novello and Co. Ltd.

74:ɪ & ɪɪ. Melody © Stainer & Bell Ltd. Reproduced by permission.

74:ɪɪ. Arrangement reproduced from *The Oxford Book of Carols* by permission of OUP.

74:ɪɪɪ. Melody from *Folk Song in England*. Reproduced by permission of Lawrence & Wishart.

77:ɪ. Melody for 'Five gold rings' (added by Frederick Austin) © Copyright 1909 Novello and Co. Ltd. Reproduced by permission of Novello and Co. Ltd.

81:ɪɪ. Arrangement reproduced by permission of Stainer & Bell Ltd.

84:ɪɪ. Arrangement reproduced by permission of Stainer & Bell Ltd.

89:ɪ. Music and text reproduced from *The Wexford Carols*, © 1982, by permission of Diarmaid Ó Muirithe, editor.

90: Text reproduced from *The Wexford Carols*, © 1982, by permission of Diarmaid Ó Muirithe, editor.

91:ɪ & ɪɪ. Melody, Welsh text, and English translation from *National Songs of Wales*. © Copyright 1959 Boosey & Co. Reproduced by permission of Boosey & Hawkes Music Publishers Ltd.

95. Melody and text from *The Anglo-American Carol Study Book*. Copyright © 1948, 1949 (Renewed) G. Schirmer, Inc. International Copyright Secured. All Rights Reserved. Used by permission of G. Schirmer, Inc.

96. Melody and text from *Songs of the Hill-Folk*. Copyright © 1934 (Renewed) G. Schirmer, Inc. International Copyright Secured. All Rights Reserved. Used by permission of G. Schirmer, Inc.

102:I. English translation from *The International Book of Christmas Carols* by Walter Ehret and George Evans. Copyright holders Walter Ehret and George Evans. Used by permission.

103: Original English translation from *The International Book of Christmas Carols* by Walter Ehret and George Evans. Copyright holders Walter Ehret and George Evans. Used by permission.

104: English translation from *The International Book of Christmas Carols* by Walter Ehret and George Evans. Copyright holders Walter Ehret and George Evans. Used by permission.

113: Translation of vv. 1–3 reproduced by permission of Novello and Co. Ltd. Translation of v. 4 reproduced from *Carols for Choirs 2* by permission of OUP.

116:II. Arrangement © The Church Pension Fund. Reproduced from *The Hymnal*, 1982.

117:II. Arrangement © 1922 B. Feldman and Co. Ltd., trading as H. Freeman and Co., London WC2H 0EA.

118:II. Arrangement © 1954 B. Feldman and Co. Ltd., trading as H. Freeman and Co., London WC2H 0EA.

119: Original English translation of v. 3 from *The International Book of Christmas Carols* by Walter Ehret and George Evans. Copyright holders Walter Ehret and George Evans. Used by permission.

120: English translation from *The International Book of Christmas Carols* by Walter Ehret and George Evans. Copyright holders Walter Ehret and George Evans. Used by permission.

122: Original English translation from *The International Book of Christmas Carols* by Walter Ehret and George Evans. Copyright holders Walter Ehret and George Evans. Used by permission.

The authors would like to acknowledge the help of the following, inadvertently omitted from the Acknowledgements in *NOBC*: David Nutter; Guy Oldham; Michael Oliver; Nigel Osborne; Christopher Page; Maribeth Anderson Payne; Kathleen Pendar; Alan Pope; Susan Rankin; Anne Ridler; Jan Smaczny; Robert Spencer; Ian Spink; Charles Waetzig; John Ward; Clive Wearing; Henning Weber; Ingeborg Weber-Kellermann; Jeremy White; Alison Wray; David Wulstan; June Yakeley; Bennett Zon.

CAROLS

1

A solis ortus cardine
From lands that see the sun arise

(*Christmas*)

Sarum chant

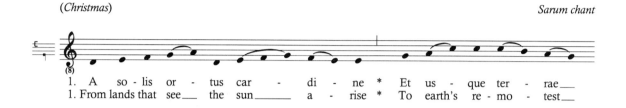

1. A so - lis or - tus car - di - ne * Et us - que ter - rae__
1. From lands that see__ the sun__ a - rise * To earth's re - mo - test__

li - mi-tem Chri-stum__ ca - na - mus__ Prin - ci - pem,_____
bound - a - ries Let ev - ery heart a - wake,_____ and__ sing_____

After doxology

Na - tum Ma - ri - a_____ Vir - gi - ne. A - men.____
The Son of Ma - ry,_____ Christ_____ the__ King.

2 Beatus Auctor seculi
   Servile corpus induit
   Ut, carne carnem liberans,
   Ne perderet quos condidit.

2 Behold, the world's Creator wears
   The form and fashion of a slave;
   Our very flesh our Maker shares,
   His fallen creature, man, to save.

3 Caste parentis viscera
   Celestis intrat gratia:
   Venter puelle baiulat
   Secreta, que non noverat.

3 For this, how wondrously he wrought!
   A maiden, in her lowly place,
   Became, in ways beyond all thought,
   The chosen vessel of his grace.

<table>
<tr><td>4</td><td>Domus pudici pectoris
Templum repente fit Dei
Intacta nesciens virum,
Verbo concepit Filium.</td><td>4</td><td>She bowed her to the angel's word
Declaring what the Father willed;
And suddenly the promised Lord
That pure and hallowed temple filled.</td></tr>
<tr><td>5</td><td>Enixa est puerpera
Quem Gabriel predixerat,
Quem matris alvo gestiens
Clausus Iohannes senserat.</td><td>5</td><td>That Son, that royal Son she bore,
Whom Gabriel announced before,
Whom, in his mother's womb concealed,
The unborn Baptist had revealed.</td></tr>
<tr><td>6</td><td>Feno iacere pertulit
Presepe non abhorruit
Parvoque lacte pastus est,
Per quem nec ales esurit.</td><td>6</td><td>He shrank not from the oxen's stall,
He lay within the manger-bed,
And he whose bounty feedeth all
At Mary's breast himself was fed.</td></tr>
<tr><td>7</td><td>Gaudet chorus celestium
Et angeli canunt Deo,
Palamque fit pastoribus
Pastor, Creator omnium.</td><td>7</td><td>And, while the angels in the sky
Sang praise above the silent field,
To shepherds poor the Lord most high,
The one great Shepherd, was revealed.</td></tr>
<tr><td>8</td><td>Gloria tibi, Domine,
Qui natus es de Virgine,
Cum Patre et Sancto Spiritu,
In sempiterna secula.
      Amen.</td><td>8</td><td>Eternal praise and glory be,
O Jesu, virgin-born, to thee,
With Father and with Holy Ghost,
From men and from the heavenly host.
      Amen.</td></tr>
</table>

Coelius Sedulius (fl. c.450)

vv. 1, 5, 8 tr. J. M. Neale (1818–66), adapted
vv. 2–4, 6, 7 tr. J. Ellerton (1826–93)

The Christmas-season hymn at lauds and vespers in the Sarum rite.

PERFORMANCE Choir, antiphonally, the first line (to *) sung by two soloists on the side that sings verse 1, the doxology full.

See *NOBC* for *Verbum supernum, prodiens* (no. 1), *Veni, Redemptor gencium* (no. 2), *Christe, Redemptor omnium* (no. 3), *Letabundus* (no. 5), *Festa dies agitur* (no. 6), and *Dieus soit en cheste maison* (no. 7).

2

Angelus ad Virginem

Gabriel, fram Heven-King

I

(Latin)

(*Annunciation; Christmas*)

Thirteenth-century
(Arundel MS)

1. An - ge - lus ad Vir - gi - nem Sub - in - trans in con -
2. 'Quo - mo - do con - ci - pe - rem Que vi - rum non cog -
3. Ad— hec— Vir - go no - bi - lis Res - pon - dens in - quit—

-cla - ve, Vir - gi - nis for - mi - di - nem De - mul - cens, in -
-no - vi? Qua - li - ter in - frin - ge - rem Quod fir - ma men -
e - i: 'An - cil - la sum hu - mi - lis Om - ni - po - ten -

-quit:— 'A - ve! A - ve Re - gi - na Vir - gi - num!
-te— vo - vi?' 'Spi - ri - tus— Sanc - ti gra - ci - a
-tis— De - i. Ti - bi, ce - le - sti nun - ci - o,

Ce - li Ter - re - que Do - mi - num Con - ci - pi - es, Et
Per - fi - ci - et— hec om - ni - a. Ne— ti - me - as, Sed
Tan - ti se - cre - ti con - sci - o, Con - sen - ci - ens Et

pa - ri - es In - tac - ta Sa - lu - tem ho - mi - num; Tu—
gau - de - as Se - cu - ra, Quod ca - sti - mo - ni - a Ma—
cu - pi - ens Vi - de - re Fac - tum quod au - di - o, Pa -

Por - ta— Ce - li— fac - ta, Me - de - la Cri - mi - num.'
-ne - bit— in te— pu - ra De - i— po - ten - ci - a!'
-ra - ta— sum pa - re - re De - i— con - si - li - o.'

4 Angelus disparuit
   Et statim puellaris
Uterus intumuit
   Vi partus salutaris.
Qui, circumdatus utero
Novem mensium numero,
Hinc exiit
Et iniit
   Conflictum,
Affigens humero
   Crucem, qua dedit ictum
Hosti mortifero.

5 Eya, Mater Domini,
   Que pacem reddidisti
Angelis et homini
   Cum Christum genuisti,
Tuum exora Filium
Ut se nobis propicium
Exhibeat
Et deleat
   Peccata,
Prestans auxilium
   Vita frui beata
Post hoc exilium.

Philip the Chancellor? (d. 1236)
(Arundel MS)

TRANSLATION   1 The angel, coming secretly to the Virgin, calming the Virgin's fear, said: 'Hail! hail, Queen of Virgins! You shall conceive the Lord of Heaven and Earth and give birth, remaining a virgin, to the Salvation of mankind; you, made the Gateway of Heaven, the cure for sin.'

2 'How shall I conceive, since I know not a man? How shall I break what I have resolutely vowed?' 'The grace of the Holy Spirit shall perform all this. Fear not, but rejoice, confident that chastity will remain pure in you by the power of God.'

3 At this, the noble Virgin, replying, said to him: 'I am the humble servant of almighty God. To you, heavenly messenger, who know so great a secret, I give my assent and desire to see done what I hear, and am ready to obey God's will.'

4 The angel disappeared, and at once the girl's womb swelled up by the power of the birth of Salvation. He, having been contained in the womb for nine months, came out from it and entered the conflict, taking on his shoulder the Cross, by which he gave the blow to the mortal enemy.

5 O Mother of the Lord, who restored peace to angels and men when you gave birth to Christ, beg of your Son that he may show himself favourable to us and wipe away our sins, offering help to enjoy the blessed life after this exile.

(tr. editors)

A Franciscan carol that was particularly popular in Britain. The English text is one of two paraphrases that were possibly written by peripatetic French friars, who may have brought the song to Britain. *NOBC* setting II (not included here) is from the mid-fourteenth-century Dublin Troper.

Verse 2, Latin: Mary lived as a temple virgin before the Annunciation, according to the *Protevangelium of James.*

PERFORMANCE   I, solo voice, with instrumental drone *ad lib.* We favour an 'isosyllabic' reading (each syllable occupying one beat) with a plainsong-like lengthening of the last note of each phrase. This brings out the ornamentation written into the music (the four-note group on '-li' of 'Celi' at the end of verse 1 is an elaboration of the two notes on the first syllable of 'intacta' in the previous phrase), it permits additional ornamentation, and it allows subsequent stanzas to be stressed naturally.

III (*i*) voice and instrument; (*ii*) two voices.

Both settings may be performed at any comfortable pitch. In the English text, *e/ed/es* final syllables are sounded except where elision is indicated.

I

(English)

(*Annunciation; Christmas*)

Thirteenth-century
(*Arundel MS*)

1. Ga - bri - el, fram He - ven - King Sent to__ the Mai - de____
2. Mil - de - lich him gan and - swere The mil - de Mai - de____
3. Wan the__ Maid - en un - der - stood And th'an - gels word - es____

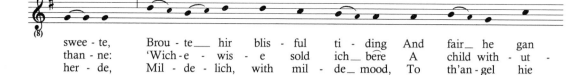

swee - te, Brou - te__ hir blis - ful ti - ding And fair__ he gan
than - ne: 'Wich - e - wis - e sold ich__ bere A child with - ut -
her - de, Mil - de - lich, with mil - de__ mood, To th'an - gel hie

hir____ gree - te: 'Heil__ be thu,__ ful__ of grace__ a - right!
-e____ man - ne?' Th'an - gel hir__ seid:__ 'Ne dred__ tee__ nout;
and - swer - de: 'U - re Lords thew - e maid__ i - wis

For__ God - es__ Son, this He - ven - Light, For__ man - nes love Wil
Thurw th'O - li - gast__ sal been i - wrout This il - che thing War -
Ich__ am, that__ heer__ a - bov - en__ is; A - nen - tis me Ful -

man bi - come And__ ta - ke Fles of__ thee, Mai - de bright, Man -
-of ti - ding Ich__ brin - ge; Al man - ken wurth i - bout Thurw
-fur - thed__ be Thi__ saw - e That ich,__ sith his__ wil is, A__

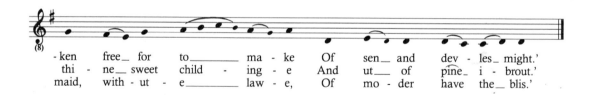

-ken free__ for to____ ma - ke Of sen__ and dev - les__ might.'
thi - ne__ sweet child - ing - e And ut__ of pine__ i - brout.'
maid, with - ut e____ law - e, Of mo - der have the__ blis.'

4 Th'angel went awei mid than
    Al ut of hire sighte;
  Hire womb arise gan
    Thurw th'Oligastes mighte.
  In hir wes Crist bilok anon,
  Sooth God, sooth man in fles and bon,
  And of hir fles
  Ibore wes
    At time,
  Warthurw us kam good won;
    He bout us ut of pine,
  And let him for us slon.

5 Maiden-Moder makeles,
    Of milce ful ibunde,
  Bid for us him that tee ches,
    At wam thu grace funde,
  That he forgive us sen and wrake,
  And clene of evri gelt us make,
  And heven-blis,
  Wan ur time is
    To sterve,
  Us give, for thine sake,
    Him so heer for to serve
  That he us to him take.

Thirteenth-century
(Arundel MS)

TRANSLATION 1 Gabriel, sent from the King of Heaven to the sweet Maiden, brought her happy news and greeted her courteously: 'Hail be thou, [who art] indeed full of grace! For God's Son, this Light of Heaven, for love of man will become man and take human form from thee, fair Maiden, to free mankind of sin and the devil's power.'

2 The gentle Maiden then gently answered him: 'In what manner should I bear a child without a husband?' The angel said to her: 'Fear nothing: through the Holy Ghost shall this very thing be done of which I bring news; all mankind will be redeemed by means of thy sweet child-bearing and brought out of torment.'

3 When the Maiden understood and heard the angel's words, she answered the angel gently, with gentle spirit: 'I am indeed the bond-maid of our Lord, who is above.

Concerning me may thy saying be fulfilled, that I, since it is his will, may as a maiden, contrary to natural law, have the joy of motherhood.'

4 With that, the angel went away, out of her sight; her womb began to swell through the power of the Holy Ghost. In her Christ was straightway enclosed, true God and true man in flesh and bone, and of her flesh was born in due time, whereby good hope came to us: he redeemed us from pain [of hell] and allowed himself to be slain for us.

5 Matchless Maiden-Mother, [who art] full of compassion, pray for us to him that chose thee, in whose sight you found grace, that he forgive us [our] sin and hostility and absolve us from all guilt, and, when our time comes to die, give us the bliss of heaven, for thy sake, so serving him here [below] that he take us to himself.

(tr. E. J. Dobson, adapted)

III

(*Annunciation; Christmas*)

Fourteenth-century
(Cotton Fragments)

1. An - ge - lus ad Vir - gi - nem Sub - in - trans in__ con - cla - ve, Vir - gi - nis for -
2. 'Quo - mo - do con - ci - pe - rem_ Que vi - rum non cog - no - vi? Qua - li - ter in -
1. Ga - bri - el, fram He - ven-King Sent to__ the Mai - de swee - te, Brou - te hir blis -
2. Mil - de-lich him gan and-swere The mil - de Mai - de than - ne: 'Wi-che-wi - se

-mi - di - nem_ De - mul - cens, in - quit: 'A - ve! A - ve Re - gi - na__
-frin - ge - rem_ Quod fir - ma men - te vo - vi?' 'Spi - ri - tus_ Sanc-ti__
-ful ti - ding_ And fair_ he gan_ hir gree - te: 'Heil_ be thu,_ ful of__
sold ich_ bere_ A_ child with-ut - e man - ne?' Th'an - gel hir_ seid: 'Ne_

Vir - gi - num! Ce - li Ter - re - que Do - mi - num Con - ci - pi - es, Et
gra - ci - a Per - fi - ci - et_ hec om - ni - a. Ne ti - me - as, Sed
grace_ a - right! For_ God-es_ Son, this He - ven-Light, For man - nes_ love Wil
dred_ tee_ nout; Thurw th'O-li - gast_ sal been i - wrout This il - che thing War -

pa - ri - es__ In - tac - ta Sa - lu - tem ho - mi-num; Tu__
gau - de - as__ Se - cu - ra, Quod ca - sti - mo - ni - a Ma -
man bi - come. And ta - ke Fles of___ thee, Mai - de bright, Man -
-of ti - ding_ Ich brin - ge; Al man - ken wurth i - bout Thurw

Por - ta Ce - li fac - ta, Me - de - la Cri - mi - num.'
- ne - bit in___ te pu - ra De - i po - ten - ci - a!'
- ken___ free for___ to ma - ke Of sen and dev - les might.'
thi - ne sweet_ chil - ding - e And ut of pine_ i - brout.'

3 Ad hec Virgo nobilis
   Respondens inquit ei:
'Ancilla sum humilis
   Omnipotentis Dei.
Tibi, celesti nuncio,
Tanti secreti conscio,
Consenciens
Et cupiens
   Videre
Factum quod audio,
   Parata sum parere
Dei consilio.'

4 Angelus disparuit
   Et statim puellaris
Uterus intumuit
   Vi partus salutaris.
Qui, circumdatus utero
Novem mensium numero,
Hinc exiit
Et iniit
   Conflictum,
Affigens humero
   Crucem, qua dedit ictum
Hosti mortifero.

5 Eya, Mater Domini,
   Que pacem reddidisti
Angelis et homini
   Cum Christum genuisti,
Tuum exora Filium
Ut se nobis propicium
Exhibeat
Et deleat
   Peccata,
Prestans auxilium
   Vita frui beata
Post hoc exilium.

Philip the Chancellor? (d. 1236) (Arundel MS)

3 Wan the Maiden understood
   And th'angels wordes herde,
Mildelich, with milde mood,
   To th'angel hie andswerde:
'Ure Lords thewe maid iwis
Ich am, that heer aboven is;
Anentis me
Fulfurthed be
   Thi sawe
That ich, sith his wil is,
   A maid, withute lawe,
Of moder have the blis.'

4 Th'angel went awei mid than
   Al ut of hire sighte;
Hire womb arise gan
   Thurw th'Oligastes mighte.
In hir wes Crist bilok anon,
Sooth God, sooth man in fles
   and bon,
And of hir fles
Ibore wes
   At time,
Warthurw us kam good won;
   He bout us ut of pine,
And let him for us slon.

5 Maiden-Moder makeles,
   Of milce ful ibunde,
Bid for us him that tee ches,
   At wam thu grace funde,
That he forgive us sen and wrake,
And clene of evri gelt us make,
And heven-blis,
Wan ur time is
   To sterve,
Us give, for thine sake,
   Him so heer for to serve
That he us to him take.

Thirteenth-century (Arundel MS)

See *NOBC* for *Procedenti Puero—Eya! novus annus est* · *Verbum caro factum est—Eya! novus annus est* (no. 9),
Ad cantus leticie (no. 10), and *Laudemus cum armonia* (no. 11).

3

Verbum caro factum est: Dies est leticie

(Christmas; New Year?)

Fourteenth-century
(Aosta MS 9–E–19)

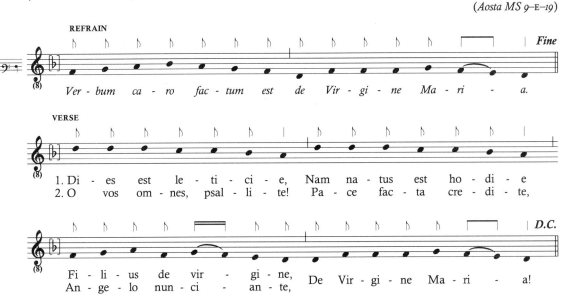

REFRAIN

Ver - bum ca - ro fac - tum est de Vir - gi - ne Ma - ri - a. *Fine*

VERSE

1. Di - es est le - ti - ci - e, Nam na - tus est ho - di - e
2. O vos om - nes, psal - li - te! Pa - ce fac - ta cre - di - te,

Fi - li - us de vir - gi - ne, De Vir - gi - ne Ma - ri - a! *D.C.*
An - ge - lo nun - ci - an - te,

3 Lux venit de Lumine
   In intacta Virgine;
     Noë! noë! dicite
       De Virgine Maria!

4 Portam clausam graditur,
   Qui alcio geritur:
     Deus homo nascitur
       De Virgine Maria.

5 Fatur a pastoribus,
   Dum natus est parvulus,
     Rex potens fortissimus,
       De Virgine Maria.

6 O Jesu, quem credimus,
   Da salutem omnibus
     Super in celestibus
       De Virgine Maria!

(Aosta MS 9–E–19)

TRANSLATION The Word is made flesh by the Virgin Mary.

1 This is a joyful day, for today a Son is born of a virgin, of the Virgin Mary.

2 Sing praises, everyone; believe that peace has come, through the message of an angel, by the Virgin Mary.

3 The Light [Christ] within a pure virgin comes from the Light [the Father]; sing Nowell! nowell! for the Virgin Mary.

4 He proceeds through the closed gate, he who is born from on high; God is born a man by the Virgin Mary.

5 It is told by the shepherds that a little Child is born; a great and mighty King is born of the Virgin Mary.

6 O Jesu, in whom we believe, grant us all salvation among those who dwell above in heaven, through the Virgin Mary.

One of four Latin carols that follow the cycle of Benedicamus song-tropes in the fourteenth-century Aosta manuscript. The 'closed gate' of verse 4 is the eastern portal of the city in Ezekiel's vision (Ezekiel 43:4; 44:2) which is traditionally associated with Mary's virginity: the King passes through it (i.e., Christ is born), after which it is sealed up for ever (Mary's perpetual virginity).

PERFORMANCE Refrain, choir; verse, solo voice(s). The opening refrain should probably be sung first by solo voice(s) and repeated full.

4

Verbum caro factum est: In hoc anni circulo

I

(New Year; Christmas)

(Jistebnice Cantional, 1420)

2 O beata femina,
  Cuius ventris Gloria
  Mundi lavat crimina
  De Virgine Maria.

3 Stella Solem protulit,
  Sol salutem contulit,
  Carnem veram abstulit
  De Virgine Maria.

4 Fons de suo rivulo
  Nascitur pro populo
  Quem tulit de vinculo
  De Virgine Maria.

Twelfth-century?
(Piae Cantiones, 1582)

III

(New Year; Christmas)

Fifteenth-century
(Trent MS)

2 O beata femina,
  Cuius ventris Gloria
  Mundi lavat crimina
  De Virgine Maria.

4 Fons de suo rivulo
  Nascitur pro populo
  Quem tulit de vinculo
  De Virgine Maria.

3 Stella Solem protulit,
  Sol salutem contulit,
  Carnem veram abstulit
  De Virgine Maria.

5 Laus, honor, virtus Domino
  Deo Patri et Filio,
  Sancto simul Paracleto
  De Virgine Maria.

Twelfth-century?
(Piae Cantiones, 1582)

TRANSLATION The Word was made flesh by the Virgin Mary.
1 In this rounding of the year life is given to the world; a little Boy is born to us by the Virgin Mary.
2 O blessed woman, the Glory of whose womb cleanses the sins of the world by the Virgin Mary.
3 A star brings forth the Sun, the Sun brings salvation, and takes unto itself very flesh by the Virgin Mary.
4 A Source from its own river is born for the people, whom it has brought from prison by the Virgin Mary.
5 Glory, honour, power be to the Lord God, Father and Son, and to the Holy Ghost, by the Virgin Mary.

One of the most popular of medieval carols. Only the two outer parts of III are notated, with the indication that the third is to be improvised in *fauxbourdon*. *NOBC* setting II (not included here) is from *Piae Cantiones* (1582).

PERFORMANCE I, refrain, choir; verse, two voices. Superscript repeat signs in the verses indicate the portion of text to be repeated at bar 15. III, three solo voices, perhaps with choral refrain.

See *NOBC* for *Verbum Patris hodie* (no. 14).

5

Verbum Patris umanatur

I

(New Year; Christmas) *(Moosburg Gradual, 1355–60)*

VERSE

1. Ver-bum Pa-tris u-ma-na-tur, O! O! Dum pu-el-la sa-lu-ta-tur, O! O! Sa-lu-
2. No-vus mo-dus ge-ni-tu-re, O! O! Sed ex-ce-dens vim na-tu-re, O! O! Dum u-

REFRAIN

-ta-ta fe-cun-da-tur vi-ri ne-sci-a.___ *Ey! ey! ey - a! no-va gau-di-a!*
-ni-tur cre-a-tu-re Cre-ans om-ni-a.___

3 Audi partum praeter morem, O! O!
  Virgo parit Salvatorem, O! O!
  Creatura Creatorem, Patrem filia.

4 In parente Salvatoris, O! O!
  Non est parens nostri moris, O! O!
  Virgo parit, nec pudoris marcent lilia.

5 Homo Deus nobis datur, O! O!
  Datus nobis demonstratur, O! O!
  Dum pax terris nuntiatur celis gloria.

Thirteenth-century
(Cambridge University MS)

TRANSLATION 1 The Word of the Father is made man, when a maiden is greeted; she, being greeted, conceives without knowledge of a man. Ey! ey! eya! new joys!

2 This is a new manner of birth, but exceeding the power of nature, when the Creator of all things is united with his creation [man].

3 Hear of an unexampled birth: a virgin has borne the Saviour, a creature the Creator, a daughter the Father.

4 In the Saviour's birth there is no parent of our kind; a virgin gives birth, but the lilies of her chastity do not wither.

5 God-made-man is given to us; this gift is shown to us, while peace on earth is announced with glory in the heavens.

This may have been written for the rumbustious festival of the subdeacons/lay brothers on New Year's Day.

PERFORMANCE I, verse, solo voice(s); refrain, choir. II, three voices.

II

Thirteenth-century
(Cambridge University MS)

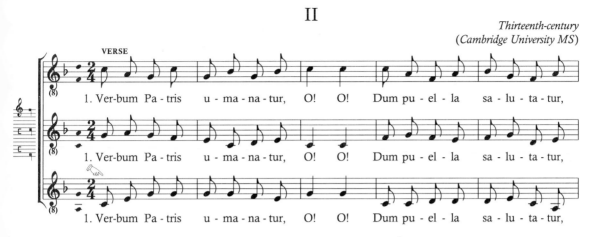

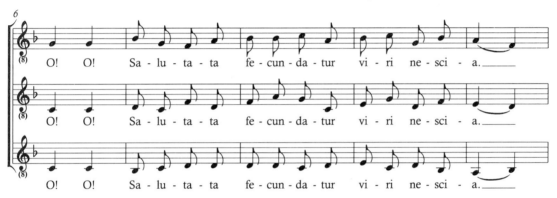

2 Novus modus geniture, O! O!
Sed excedens vim nature, O! O!
Dum unitur creature Creans omnia.

3 Audi partum praeter morem, O! O!
Virgo parit Salvatorem, O! O!
Creatura Creatorem, Patrem filia.

4 In parente Salvatoris, O! O!
Non est parens nostri moris, O! O!
Virgo parit, nec pudoris marcent lilia.

5 Homo Deus nobis datur, O! O!
Datus nobis demonstratur, O! O!
Dum pax terris nuntiatur celis gloria.

Thirteenth-century
(Cambridge University MS)

6

Veni, veni, Emanuel
O come, O come, Emmanuel!

I

Thirteenth-century?
(*Bibliothèque Nationale MS*)

(*Advent*)

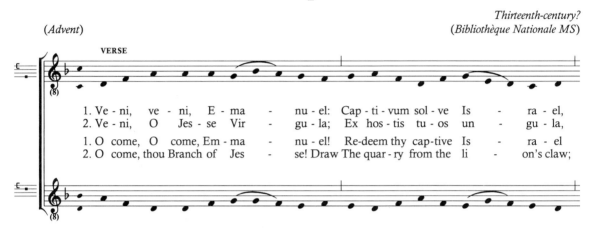

VERSE

1. Ve - ni, ve - ni, E - ma - nu - el: Cap - ti - vum sol - ve Is - ra - el,
2. Ve - ni, O Jes - se Vir - gu - la; Ex hos - tis tu - os un - gu - la,

1. O come, O come, Em - ma - nu - el! Re - deem thy cap-tive Is - ra - el
2. O come, thou Branch of Jes - se! Draw The quar - ry from the li - on's claw;

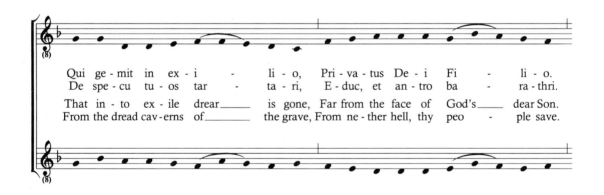

Qui ge - mit in ex - i - li - o, Pri - va - tus De - i Fi - li - o.
De spe - cu tu - os tar - ta - ri, E - duc, et an - tro ba - ra - thri.

That in - to ex - ile drear____ is gone, Far from the face of God's____ dear Son.
From the dread cav - erns of_____ the grave, From ne - ther hell, thy peo - ple save.

REFRAIN

Gau - de! gau - de! E - ma - nu - el Na - sce - tur pro te, Is - ra - el.
Re - joice! re - joice! Em - ma - nu - el Shall come to thee, O Is - ra - el.

3 Veni, veni, O Oriens;
   Solare nos adveniens;
   Noctis depelle nebulas,
   Dirasque noctis tenebras.

   Gaude! gaude! Emanuel
   Nascetur pro te, Israel.

3 O come, O come, thou Dayspring bright!
   Pour on our souls thy healing light;
   Dispel the long night's lingering gloom,
   And pierce the shadows of the tomb.

   Rejoice! rejoice! Emmanuel
   Shall come to thee, O Israel.

4 Veni, Clavis Davidica;
   Regna reclude celica;
   Fac iter tutum superum,
   Et claude vias inferum.

4 O come, thou Key of David, come,
   And open wide our heavenly home;
   Safeguard for us the heavenward road,
   And bar the way to death's abode.

5 Veni, veni, Adonaï,
   Qui populo in Sinaï
   Legem dedisti vertice
   In maiestate glorie.

5 O come, O come, Adonaï,
   Who in thy glorious majesty
   From Sinai's mountain, clothed in awe,
   Gavest thy folk the elder Law.

   Thirteenth-century?

   tr. J. M. Neale (1818–66)
   rev. T. A. Lacey (1853–1931), adapted

Alternative translation of verse 1:

1 O come, O come, Emmanuel!
   And ransom captive Israel
   That mourns in lonely exile here
   Until the Son of God appear.

   tr. J. M. Neale (1818–66)

II

Thirteenth-century?
(Bibliothèque Nationale MS, arr. editors)

1. Ve - ni, ve - ni, E - ma - nu - el: Cap - ti - vum sol - ve
1. O come, O come, Em - ma - nu - el! Re - deem thy cap - tive

Is - ra - el, Qui ge - mit in ex - i - li - o, Pri -
Is - ra - el That in - to ex - ile drear___ is gone, Far

-va - tus De - i Fi - li - o. *Gau - de! gau - de!* E -
from the face of God's___ dear Son. *Re - joice! re - joice!* Em -

-ma - nu - el Na - sce - tur pro te, Is - ra - el.
-ma - nu - el Shall come to thee, O Is - ra - el.

2 Veni, O Jesse Virgula;
　　Ex hostis tuos ungula,
　　De specu tuos tartari,
　　Educ, et antro barathri.

　　　Gaude! gaude! Emanuel
　　　Nascetur pro te, Israel.

3 Veni, veni, O Oriens;
　　Solare nos adveniens;
　　Noctis depelle nebulas,
　　Dirasque noctis tenebras.

4 Veni, Clavis Davidica;
　　Regna reclude celica;
　　Fac iter tutum superum,
　　Et claude vias inferum.

5 Veni, veni, Adonaï,
　　Qui populo in Sinaï
　　Legem dedisti vertice
　　In maiestate glorie.

　　　Thirteenth-century?

2 O come, thou Branch of Jesse! Draw
　　The quarry from the lion's claw;
　　From the dread caverns of the grave,
　　From nether hell, thy people save.

　　　Rejoice! rejoice! Emmanuel
　　　Shall come to thee, O Israel.

3 O come, O come, thou Dayspring bright!
　　Pour on our souls thy healing light;
　　Dispel the long night's lingering gloom,
　　And pierce the shadows of the tomb.

4 O come, thou Key of David, come,
　　And open wide our heavenly home;
　　Safeguard for us the heavenward road,
　　And bar the way to death's abode.

5 O come, O come, Adonaï,
　　Who in thy glorious majesty
　　From Sinai's mountain, clothed in awe,
　　Gavest thy folk the elder Law.

　　　tr. J. M. Neale (1818–66)
　　　rev. T. A. Lacey (1853–1931), adapted

Alternative translation of verse 1:

1　O come, O come, Emmanuel!
　　And ransom captive Israel
　　That mourns in lonely exile here
　　Until the Son of God appear.

　　　tr. J. M. Neale (1818–66)

The text is based on the series of 'O' antiphons sung at vespers on the days leading up to Christmas. The tune was first published by Helmore and Neale in 1854 from a lost source, and it is not known whether they found it set to this text. Suspicions that it might have been a Victorian invention were removed in the 1960s when Dr Mary Berry discovered a two-voice version (I), though with a different text, in a processional which was probably copied for a French nunnery.

'Emanuel' means 'God with us' (see Isaiah 7:14, quoted in Matthew 1:23). 'Israel' is used in the conventional sense of 'Christians', and the Babylonian exile is a metaphor for fallen man, banned from paradise.

The 'Branch of Jesse' (verse 2) refers to the messianic prophecy in Isaiah 11:1. The verse looks forward to the harrowing of hell by Christ before his resurrection, and the destruction of Satan's power over man.

'Oriens' (verse 3) is a light that rises over the horizon, whether the morning sun or the daystar, invoking Malachi 4:2.

The 'Key of David' (verse 4) refers to the messianic prophecy of Isaiah 22:22.

'Adonai' (verse 5) means 'Lord', and was one of the titles substituted by devout Jews for the unutterable Name of God. The rest of the verse concerns the giving of the Ten Commandments to Moses, the 'elder law' which is now to be interpreted in the light of further revelation: 'A new commandment give I unto you . . .' (John 13:34).

PERFORMANCE I (*i*) verse, two voices; refrain, choir; (*ii*) choir. II (*i*) voices and organ; (*ii*) choir.

7

Qui creavit celum

He who made the earth so fair
(Song of the Nuns of Chester)

(Christmas)

Thirteenth-/fourteenth-century?
(Huntington Library MS)

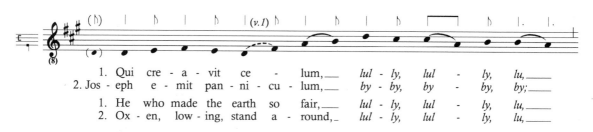

1. Qui cre - a - vit ce - lum, ___ *lul - ly, lul - ly, lu, ___*
2. Jos - eph e - mit pan - ni - cu - lum, ___ *by - by, by - by, by; ___*

1. He who made the earth so fair, ___ *lul - ly, lul - ly, lu, ___*
2. Ox - en, low - ing, stand a - round, _ *lul - ly, lul - ly, lu, ___*

Na - sci - tur in sta - bu - lo, *by - by, by - by, by, ___*
Ma - ter in - vol - vit Pu - er - um, *lul - ly, lul - ly, lu, ___*

Slum - bers in the sta - ble bare, *by - by, by - by, by, ___*
In the stall no o - ther sound, *by - by, by - by, by, ___*

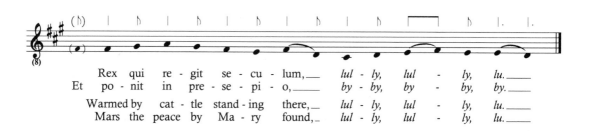

Rex qui re - git se - cu - lum, ___ *lul - ly, lul - ly, lu. ___*
Et po - nit in pre - se - pi - o, ___ *by - by, by - by, by. ___*

Warmed by cat - tle stand - ing there, _ *lul - ly, lul - ly, lu. ___*
Mars the peace by Ma - ry found, _ *lul - ly, lul - ly, lu. ___*

3 Inter animalia, *lully* . . .
 Iacent mundi gaudia, *by-by* . . .
 Dulcis super omnia, *lully* . . .

4 Lactat mater Domini, *by-by* . . .
 Osculatur parvulum, *lully* . . .
 Et adorat Dominum, *by-by* . . .

5 Roga, mater, Filium, *lully* . . .
 Ut det nobis gaudium, *by-by* . . .
 In perenni gloria, *lully* . . .

6 In sempiterna secula, *by-by* . . .
 In eternum et ultra, *lully, lully, lu,*
 Det nobis sua gaudia, *by-by* . . .

Thirteenth-//fourteenth-century?
(Huntington Library MS)

3 Joseph piles the soft, sweet hay, *lully* . . .
 Starlight drives the dark away, *by-by* . . .
 Angels sing a heavenly lay, *lully* . . .

4 Jesus sleeps in Mary's arm, *lully* . . .
 Sheltered there from rude alarm, *by-by* . . .
 None can do him ill or harm, *lully* . . .

5 See his mother o'er him bend, *lully* . . .
 Hers the joy to soothe and tend, *by-by* . . .
 Hers the bliss that knows no end, *lully* . . .

English version by Irene Gass, adapted

TRANSLATION 1 He who created the sky is born in a stable, the King who rules the age.
2 Joseph buys a tiny swaddling-cloth; the mother wraps the Child and places him in the manger.
3 Among the animals lie the world's joys, sweet above all things.
4 The Mother of the Lord gives milk, she kisses her Infant and worships the Lord.
5 Mother, ask your Child to grant us joy in eternal glory.
6 Throughout the ages, to eternity and beyond, may he give us his joys.

The carol survives in a fifteenth-century processional from the Benedictine nunnery of St Mary, Chester. It may have been part of a procession for the blessing of the crib. (See *NOBC* for the subsequent antiphon 'Hodie Christus natus est' and concluding chant.)

PERFORMANCE (*i*) Small solo group alternating with choir (*lully*, etc.); (*ii*) choir throughout.

See *NOBC* for *Dies est laeticiae* (no. 18).

8

Corde natus ex Parentis
Of the Father's heart begotten

I

(*Christmas*)   (*Piae Cantiones, 1582, arr. editors*)

1. Of the Fa - ther's heart be - got - ten Ere the world from cha - os rose, He is Al - pha and O - me - ga, He the Source and he the Close Of what - ev - er is, or has been, Or the fu - ture years dis -

Sae - cu - lo - rum sae - cu - lis.

After doxology

- close, Sae - cu - lo - rum, sae - cu - lo - rum sae - cu - lis. A - men.

'Saeculorum saeculis' = 'Unto the ages of ages' [eternity].

2 At his word was all created;
    He commanded, it was done:
  Earth, and heaven, and depths of ocean,
    In their threefold order one;
  All that grows beneath the shining
    Of the orbs of moon and sun
      Saeculorum saeculis.

3 He assumed this mortal body,
    Frail and feeble, doomed to die,
  That the race from dust created
    Might not perish utterly,
  Which the dreadful Law had sentenced
    In the depths of hell to lie

4 O that birth, for ever blessèd!
    When the Virgin, full of grace,
  By the Holy Ghost conceiving,
    Bore the Saviour of our race,
  And the Child, the world's Redeemer,
    First revealed his sacred face

5 O ye heights of heaven, adore him!
    Angel-hosts, his praises sing!
  Powers, dominions, bow before him,
    And extol your God and King!
  Let no tongue today be silent,
    Every voice in concert ring

6 This is he whom once the sibyls
    With united voice foretold,
  His the birth that faithful prophets
    In their pages did unfold;
  Let the world unite to praise him,
    Long-desired, foreseen of old

7 Hail, thou Judge of souls departed!
    Hail, thou King of them that thrive!
  On the Father's throne exalted
    None in might with thee may strive,
  Who at last, to judge returning,
    Sinners from thy face shall drive

8 O ye elders, lead the anthems:
    Laud your God in ancient lays!
  Youths and maidens, hymn his glory!
    Infants, bring your songs of praise!
  Guileless voices, in sweet concord
    Unto all the length of days,

9 Let the storm and summer sunshine,
    Gliding stream and sounding shore,
  Sea and forest, frost and zephyr,
    Night and day their Lord adore;
  All Creation joined to praise thee
    Through the ages evermore,

10 Christ, to thee, with God the Father,
    And, O Holy Ghost, to thee,
  High thanksgiving, endless praises,
    And eternal glory be;
  Honour, power, and all dominion,
    And eternal victory

*tr. editors, partly a cento after J. M. Neale (1818–66)
and Roby Furley Davis (1866–1937)*

Alternative translation of v. 1:

1 Of the Father's love begotten
    Ere the worlds began to be,
  He is Alpha and Omega,
    He the Source, the Ending he
  Of the things that are, that have been,
    And that future years shall see,
      Evermore and evermore.

tr. J. M. Neale (1818–66)

II

(Christmas)

(Piae Cantiones, 1582, adapted and arr. editors)

1. Of the Fa-ther's heart be-got - ten Ere the world from cha-os rose,

He is Al-pha and O-me-ga, He the Source and he___ the Close

Of what-ev-er is, or has____ been, Or the fu-ture

years dis-close, *Sae - cu - lo - rum, sae - cu - lo - rum sae - cu - lis.* A - men.

'Saeculorum saeculis' = 'Unto the ages of ages' [eternity].

2 At his word was all created;
       He commanded, it was done:
   Earth, and heaven, and depths of ocean,
       In their threefold order one;
   All that grows beneath the shining
       Of the orbs of moon and sun
           Saeculorum saeculis.

3 He assumed this mortal body,
       Frail and feeble, doomed to die,
   That the race from dust created
       Might not perish utterly,
   Which the dreadful Law had sentenced
       In the depths of hell to lie

4 O that birth, for ever blessèd!
       When the Virgin, full of grace,
   By the Holy Ghost conceiving,
       Bore the Saviour of our race,
   And the Child, the world's Redeemer,
       First revealed his sacred face

5 O ye heights of heaven, adore him!
       Angel-hosts, his praises sing!
   Powers, dominions, bow before him,
       And extol your God and King!
   Let no tongue today be silent,
       Every voice in concert ring

6 This is he whom once the sibyls
       With united voice foretold,
   His the birth that faithful prophets
       In their pages did unfold;
   Let the world unite to praise him,
       Long-desired, foreseen of old

7 Hail, thou Judge of souls departed!
       Hail, thou King of them that thrive!
   On the Father's throne exalted
       None in might with thee may strive,
   Who at last, to judge returning,
       Sinners from thy face shall drive

8 O ye elders, lead the anthems:
       Laud your God in ancient lays!
   Youths and maidens, hymn his glory!
       Infants, bring your songs of praise!
   Guileless voices, in sweet concord
       Unto all the length of days,

9 Let the storm and summer sunshine,
       Gliding stream and sounding shore,
   Sea and forest, frost and zephyr,
       Night and day their Lord adore;
   All Creation joined to praise thee
       Through the ages evermore,

10 Christ, to thee, with God the Father,
        And, O Holy Ghost, to thee,
    High thanksgiving, endless praises,
        And eternal glory be;
    Honour, power, and all dominion,
        And eternal victory

*tr. editors, partly a cento after J. M. Neale (1818–66)
and Roby Furley Davis (1866–1937)*

Alternative translation of v. 1:

1 Of the Father's love begotten
       Ere the worlds began to be,
   He is Alpha and Omega,
       He the Source, the Ending he
   Of the things that are, that have been,
       And that future years shall see,
           Evermore and evermore.

tr. J. M. Neale (1818–66)

III

(*Christmas*)   *York chant*

1. Cor - de na - tus ex Pa - ren - tis An - te mun - di ex - or - di - um,
2. Ip - se jus - sit et cre - a - ta, Dix - it ip - se et fac - ta sunt

Al-pha et O___ cog - no - mi - na - tus, Ip - se Fons et Clau - su - la___
Ter - ra, ce - lum, fos - sa pon - ti, Tri - na re - rum ma - chi - na,___

Om - ni - um que sunt, fu - e - runt, Que - que post fu - tu - ra sunt,
Que-que in his vi - gent sub al - to So - lis et lu - ne glo - bo,

After doxology

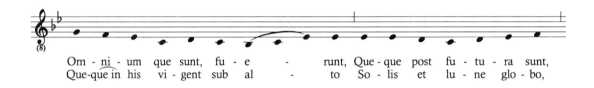

Se - cu - lo - rum se - cu - lis.   A - men.___

3   Corporis formam caduci,
    Membra morti obnoxia
    Induit, ne gens periret
    Primoplasti ex germine,
    Merserat quem Lex profundo
    Noxialis Tartaro
        Seculorum seculis.

4   O beatus ortus ille!
    Virgo cum puerpera
    Edidit nostram salutem
    Feta Sancto Spiritu,
    Et Puer, Redemptor Orbis,
    Os sacratum protulit
        Seculorum seculis.

5 Psallat altitudo celi,
   Psallite omnes angeli,
   Quidquid est virtutis usquam
   Psallat in laudem Dei!
   Nulla linguarum silescat,
   Vox et omnis consonet
      Seculorum seculis.

6 Ecce, quem vates vetustis
   Concinebant seculis,
   Quem prophetarum fideles
   Pagine spoponderant,
   Emicat promissus olim:
   Cuncta conlaudent eum
      Seculorum seculis.

7 Macte Judex mortuorum,
   Macte Rex viventium,
   Dexter in Parentis arce
   Qui cluis virtutibus,
   Omnium venturus inde
   Justus ultor criminum
      Seculorum seculis.

8 Te senes et te juventus,
   Parvulorum te chorus,
   Turba matrum virginumque,
   Simplices puellule,
   Voce concordes pudicis
   Perstrepant concentibus,
      Seculorum seculis.

9 Fluminum lapsus et unde,
   Litorum crepidines,
   Imber, estus, nix, pruina,
   Silva et aura, nox, dies
   Omnibus te concelebrent
   Seculorum seculis,
      Seculorum seculis.

10 Tibi, Christe, sit cum Patre
    Hagioque Pneumate,
    Hymnus, decus, laus perhennis,
    Gratiarum actio,
    Honor, virtus, victoria,
    Regnum eternaliter,
       Seculorum seculis. Amen.

vv. 1–9 Aurelius Clemens Prudentius (348–c.410)
v. 10 medieval

This adaptation from a hymn by the Romano–Spanish lawyer Prudentius was used in various ways in the liturgy. Tune III is the York version of the medieval melody. Neale's translation appeared in *Carols for Christmas-tide* (1853–4) to the melody of a Sanctus trope 'Divinum mysterium' from *Piae Cantiones*. The chant-like version (II) which is widely sung in the US has no historical source, but makes the mismatch of text and setting more easily assimilated.

PERFORMANCE   I, II: (*i*) unison voices; (*ii*) voices with organ; (*iii*) choir.
   III, voices.

9

Personent hodie
On this day earth shall ring

I

(*Christmas; Holy Innocents?*)   (*Piae Cantiones, 1582, arr. editors*)

1. Per - so - nent ho - di - e Vo - ces pu - e - ru - lae Lau -

Lau - dan - tes iu - cun - de
- dan - tes iu - cun - de Qui no - bis est na - tus,
Lau - dan - tes iu - cun - de Qui no - bis est na - tus,
Qui no - bis est na - tus,

Sum-mo De - o da - tus, Et de vir -, vir -, vir -, et de vir -,
Et de vir -, et
Sum-mo De - o da-tus, Et de vir -, vir -,vir -, et de vir -,
Sum-mo De - o da - tus, Et de vir -,

† 1   With the song children sing
To the Son, Christ the King,
Born on earth to save us;
Him the Father gave us.
Ideo, -o, -o, ideo, -o, -o,
Ideo gloria in excelsis Deo!

14 vir-, vir-, et de vir - gi - ne - o

de vir-, et de vir - gi - ne - o Ven-tre pro-cre - a - tus.

vir-, vir-, et de vir - gi - ne - o

et de vir-, et de vir - gi - ne - o

2 In mundo nascitur;
  Pannis involvitur;
  Praesepi ponitur
    Stabulo brutorum
    Rector supernorum;
  Perdidit spolia
    Princeps Infernorum.

2 His the doom, ours the mirth,
  When he came down to earth;
  Bethlehem saw his birth;
    Ox and ass, beside him,
    From the cold would hide him.
    Ideo gloria in excelsis Deo!

3 Magi tres venerunt;
  Munera offerunt;
  Parvulum inquirunt,
    Stellulam sequendo,
    Ipsum adorando,
  Aurum, thus et myrrham
    Ei offerendo.

3 God's bright star, o'er his head,
  Wise men three to him led;
  Kneel they low by his bed,
    Lay their gifts before him,
    Praise him and adore him.
    Ideo gloria in excelsis Deo!

4 Omnes clericuli,
  Pariter pueri,
  Cantent ut angeli:
    'Advenisti mundo:
    Laudes tibi fundo
  Ideo: Gloria
    In excelsis Deo.'

    (*Piae Cantiones, 1582*)

4 On this day angels sing;
  With their song earth shall ring,
  Praising Christ, heaven's King,
    Born on earth to save us;
    Peace and love he gave us.
    Ideo gloria in excelsis Deo!

    English version by
    Jane M. Joseph (1894–1929)

† The English version is best sung in unison. If sung in harmony, the alto and tenor underlay will need adjustment.

TRANSLATION 1 Let children's voices resound today, merrily praising him who has been born, sent by almighty God and brought forth from a virgin's womb.

2 He was born into the world, wrapped in swaddling clothes, and placed in the manger in a cattle shed, the Lord of the heavens, the Prince [who] destroyed the spoils of hell.

3 Three wise men appeared; they offered gifts and asked for a boy-child, following a star; they worshipped him, offering him gold, frankincense, and myrrh.

4 Let all the clerics, and likewise the boys, sing like the angels: 'You have come to the world; therefore I pour out praises to you: Glory to God in the highest!'

II

(*Piae Cantiones, 1582,*
arr. Gustav Holst, 1874–1934)

(Christmas; Holy Innocents?)

2 In mundo nascitur;
  Pannis involvitur;
  Praesepi ponitur
    Stabulo brutorum
    Rector supernorum;
  Perdidit spolia
    Princeps Infernorum.

2 His the doom, ours the mirth,
  When he came down to earth;
  Bethlehem saw his birth;
  Ox and ass, beside him,
  From the cold would hide him.
    Ideo gloria in excelsis Deo!

3 Magi tres venerunt;
  Munera offerunt;
  Parvulum inquirunt,
    Stellulam sequendo,
    Ipsum adorando,
  Aurum, thus et myrrham
    Ei offerendo.

3 God's bright star, o'er his head,
  Wise men three to him led;
  Kneel they low by his bed,
  Lay their gifts before him,
  Praise him and adore him.
    Ideo gloria in excelsis Deo!

4 Omnes clericuli,
  Pariter pueri,
  Cantent ut angeli:
    'Advenisti mundo:
    Laudes tibi fundo
  Ideo: Gloria
  In excelsis Deo.'

    (*Piae Cantiones, 1582*)

4 On this day angels sing;
  With their song earth shall ring,
  Praising Christ, heaven's King,
  Born on earth to save us;
  Peace and love he gave us.
    Ideo gloria in excelsis Deo!

English version by
Jane M. Joseph (1894–1929)

Probably written for the choirboys' feast in cathedrals on Holy Innocents' Day, when the choristers and their boy bishop ruled the choir and displaced the senior clergy from their stalls.

PERFORMANCE I (*i*) unison voices (omitting the editorial accidentals in bar 9 and perhaps also bar 17); (*ii*) choir.
  II, unison voices and piano or organ (or orchestra).

10

Puer nobis nascitur
Unto us is born a Son

I

(Christmas)

(Moosburg Gradual, 1355–60, arr. editors)

VERSES 1–3

1. Pu - er no - bis na - sci - tur,   Rec - tor an - ge - lo - rum;
2. In pre - se - pe po - ni - tur Sub fe - no a - si - no - rum;
3. Qui na - tus ex Ma - ri - a   Di - e ho - di - er - na:

In hoc mun - do pa - sci - tur Do - mi - nus Do - mi - no - rum.
Cog - no - ve - runt Do - mi - num Chri - stum, Re - gem Ce - lo - rum.
Per - duc nos cum gra - ci - a Ad gau - di - a su - per - na.

VERSES 4 & 5

4. O et O et O et O; O et O et O!
5. A et A et A et A; A et A et A!

O et O et O et O; Be - ne - di - ca - mus Do - mi - no.
A et A et A et A; De - o di - ca - mus gra - ci - as.

TRANSLATION 1 Unto us a Boy is born, the Ruler of the Angels; the Lord of Lords is nurtured in this world.

2 He is placed in a manger where asses feed; they recognized the Lord Christ, King of Heaven.

3 You who were born of Mary on this day: lead us joyfully to the highest joys [of paradise].

4 O and O, etc.; let us bless the Lord.

5 A and A, etc.; let us say 'Thanks be to God.'

These *Benedicamus* verses were widely sung throughout Europe, but the distinctive last-line repeat is peculiar to the *Piae Cantiones* version.

PERFORMANCE   I (*i*) (reflecting probable historical practice) a small group of voices (cantors in mid-quire), in unison until the two-/three-part final phrase of verse 4, a large group then, singing verse 5 in a similar manner; (*ii*) unison voices: verse 5 may be omitted, or sung in unison (to the top part in the last phrase) or in two or three parts.

II (*i*) unison voices; (*ii*) choir; (*iii*) unison voices and organ.

See *NOBC* for *Omnis mundus iucundetur* (no. 22), *Lullay, lullay: Als I lay on Yoolis night* (no. 23), and *Lullay, lullow: I saw a swete semly syght* (no. 24).

II

(*Christmas; Holy Innocents*)

(*Piae Cantiones, 1582, arr. editors*)

1. Pu - er no - bis na - sci - tur,   Rec - tor an - ge - lo - rum;   In hoc mun - do
1. Un - to us is born a Son,   King of choirs su - per - nal;   To this world he

pa - sci - tur Do - mi - nus Do - mi - no - rum, Do - mi - nus Do - mi - no - rum.
deigns to come Of lords the Lord e - ter - nal, of lords the Lord e - ter - nal.

2 In praesepe positum
    Sub foeno asinorum
    Cognoverunt Dominum
    Christum, Regem Coelorum.

*3 Hunc Herodes timuit
    Magno cum tremore;
    In infantes irruit
    Hos caedens in furore.

4 Qui natus ex Maria
    Die hodierna:
    Duc nos, tua gratia,
    Ad gaudia superna.

5 'Te salvator A et O,'
    Cantemus in choro;
    Cantemus in organo:
    'Benedicamus Domino.'

2 Lo! he lies within a stall
    Where cattle fed before him;
    King of heaven and Lord of all,
    They know him and adore him.

*3 Rage did Herod then impel,
    Whom fearful trembling fillèd;
    On the little boys he fell
    And every one he killèd.

4 Born of Mary on this day,
    By thy grace translate us
    To the realm above, we pray,
    Where endless joys await us.

5 Every voice in quire now blend
    To hymn our Saviour, Source and End;
    In sweet concord sing we so:
    Benedicamus Domino.

(*Piae Cantiones, 1582*)

v. 1 tr. G. R. Woodward, adapted
vv. 2–5 tr. editors

11

Nova! nova!

(*Annunciation; Christmas*)

Fifteenth-century
(*Hunterian Museum MS*)

REFRAIN / Fine

No - va! no - va! 'A - ve' fit ex 'E - va'.[1]

VERSE 1

1. Ga - bri - ell off hye de - gre, He___ cam down from Tri - ni - te To Na - za - reth in Ga - li - le. No - va! no - va!

D.C.

VERSE 2

2. He met a may - dn in a place, He kne - lyd down a - fore hir face, He seyd: 'Heile, Ma - ry, ful of grace!' No - va! no - va!

D.C.

VERSE 3

3. When the maiden herd tell off this Sche was full sore a - baschyd I - wys, And wened that sche had don a - mysse. No - va! no - va!

D.C.

[1] News! news! 'Ave' is made from 'Eva'.

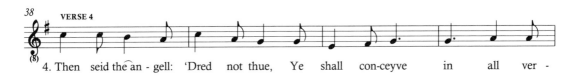

4. Then seid the an-gell: 'Dred not thue, Ye shall con-ceyve in all ver -

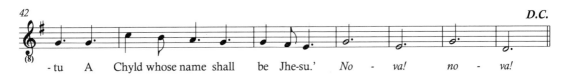

D.C.

-tu A Chyld whose name shall be Jhe-su.' No - va! no - va!

VERSE 5

5. 'It is not yit syx moneth a-goon Sen E - li - za - beth con-cey - ved

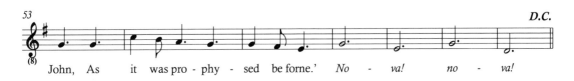

D.C.

John, As it was pro-phy - sed be forne.' No - va! no - va!

VERSE 6

6. Then seid the may - den ve - re - ly: 'I am youre ser - vaunt right tru - e -

D.C.

- ly. Ec - ce an-cil - la Do - mi-ni.'² No - va! no - va!

² Behold the handmaid of the Lord.

Most of the English medieval carols that survive are clearly written by and for professional musicians, but this one may have been sung more widely. The refrain embodies the popular medieval conceit that the Virgin Mary was the new Eve, the 'Ave Maria' of the Annunciation signalling the end of man's domination by Eve's sin.

PERFORMANCE Refrain, full; verse, solo (perhaps freely adapting the tune from verse 2 onwards). Some fifteenth-century carols begin with a solo refrain, repeated full, and this may be effective here. It is possible that all the Fs should be natural. For a guide to pronunciation see *NOBC* Appendix 1.

See *NOBC* for *Nowell: Tydynges trew ther be cum new* (no. 26).

12

Hayl, Mary, ful of grace

(Annunciation; Christmas)

Fifteenth-century
(Trinity roll)

26 D.C.

went[1] Whan the an - gel_____ seide 'A - ve'.
manne Thorw ver - tu and__ thorw dyng - ny - te.
bone, O[2] God in per - so - nys____ thre.

31 VERSES 4–6

*4. And the pro - phete Je - re - mye Told in his_____
5. Mo - che joye to us was graunt[3] And in er - the__
6. Ma - ry, graun - te us the blys Ther thy So - nys__

37

pro - phe - cie That the so - ne_____ of Ma -
pees_____ y - plaunte[4] Whan that born__ was_____ this__
won - ynge__ ys;[5] Of that we han y - done a -

That the so - ne of Ma -
Whan that born_____ was this
Of that we han y - done a -

42 D.C.

- rie Schuld deye for us on_____ ro - de_____ tre.[6]
faunte[7]__ In the londe of_____ Ga - li - le.
- mys[8]_____ Pray for us pur[9]_____ cha - ri - te.

[1] now has God entered thee [2] one [3] much joy was granted us [4] and peace planted on earth [5] where thy Son's dwelling is [6] the tree of the rood [7] infant [8] for what we have done amiss [9] through

Verses 1 and 2: it was believed that Mary conceived through the ear as she heard Gabriel's words. Verse 4, 'the prophete . . . told': he didn't.

PERFORMANCE Refrain, three voices or choir; verse, two voices. For a guide to pronunciation see *NOBC* Appendix 1.

13

Ther is no rose of swych vertu

(*Christmas*)

Fifteenth-century
(*Trinity roll*)

REFRAIN

Ther is no rose of swych¹ ver - tu

As is the rose that bare Jhe - su.

Fine

VERSES 1 & 2

1. Ther is no rose of swych ver -
2. For in this rose con - tey - nyd

- tu As is the rose that bare Jhe - su.
was He - ven and erthe in ly - tyl space,

¹ such

[2] a wonderful thing [3] by [4] leave [5] glory to God on high [6] of the same form [7] let us rejoice [8] let us go

The identification of Mary with the rose was a common medieval conceit. See 'There is no rose' (68) for a modern setting of this text by John Joubert.

PERFORMANCE Refrain, two or three voices, or choir; verse, two voices. Our added middle part in the refrain is of a kind that might have been improvised. For a guide to pronunciation see *NOBC* Appendix 1.

See *NOBC* for *Alleluya pro Virgine Maria* (no. 29), *Alleluya: A nywe werk is come on honde* (no. 30), *Make we joye nowe in this fest* (no. 31), and *What tydynges bryngest thou, messangere?* (no. 32).

14

Nowel: Owt of your slepe aryse

(*Christmas*)

Fifteenth-century
(*Selden MS*)

2 And thorwe a maide faire and wys[1]
  Now man is made of ful grete pris;[2]
  Now angelys knelen to mannys servys,
  And at this tyme[3] al this byfel.

3 Now man is bryghter than the sonne;
  Now man in heven an hye shal wone;[4]
  Blessyd be God this game is begonne,
  And his moder emperesse of helle.

[1] wise [2] worth [3] Christmas [4] now man shall live in heaven on high

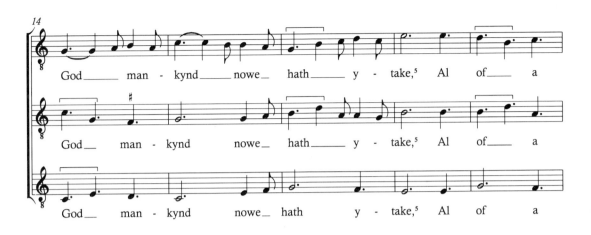

God____ man - kynd____ nowe__ hath____ y - take,[5] Al of____ a

God__ man - kynd nowe__ hath____ y - take,[5] Al of____ a

God__ man - kynd nowe__ hath y - take,[5] Al of a

mai - de with - out e - ny make;[6] Of al wo - men____ she

mai - de with - out____ e - ny make;[6] Of al____ wo - men she__

mai - de with - out____ e - ny make;[6] Of al____ wo - men____ she

4 That ever was thralle, now ys he fre;[7]
That ever was smalle, now grete is she;[8]
Now shal God deme[9] bothe the and me
Unto his blysse yf we do wel.[10]

*5 Now man may to heven wende;
Now heven and erthe to hym they bende;
He that was foo[11] now is oure frende;
This is no nay that Y yowe telle.[12]

6 Now, blessyd brother,[13] graunte us grace
A[14] domesday to se thy face
And in thy courte to have a place,
That we mow[15] there synge 'Nowel'.

Fifteenth-century
(Selden MS)

[5] for God has now taken on manhood   [6] husband   [7] he
[man] who was in thrall for ever is now free   [8] Mary
[9] judge   [10] act righteously   [11] foe   [12] there is no denying
what I tell you   [13] Christ   [14] at   [15] may

The text seems to have been inspired by a verse in Romans 12, which was read as an epistle in Advent: 'The night is far spent, the day is at hand: let us therefore cast off the works of darkness, and let us put on the armour of light.' 'Bereth the belle' (verse 1) implies leadership. Bells were hung on the lead horse of a team and on the leading sheep of a flock (the 'bell-wether'), and were awarded as the prize at country races.

The refrain is written monophonically in the source, but the refrain indications at the verse-end suggest that it is to be sung canonically; ours is one of several possible interpretations.

PERFORMANCE Refrain, choir or three voices; verse, three voices. For a guide to pronunciation see *NOBC* Appendix 1.

See *NOBC* for *Nowel syng we bothe al and som* (no. 34), *Synge we to this mery cumpane* (no. 35), *Nowell: Dieus wous garde, byewsser* (no. 36), *Nowell: The borys hede* (*The Exeter Boar's Head Carol*) (no. 37), and *Mervele noght, Josep* (no. 38).

15

Thys endere nyghth I saw a syghth

(*Christmas; Epiphany*)

Sixteenth-century
(*British Library MS*)

¹ the other night [a few nights ago]   ² pure   ³ rich

(*continued overleaf*)

VERSE 2

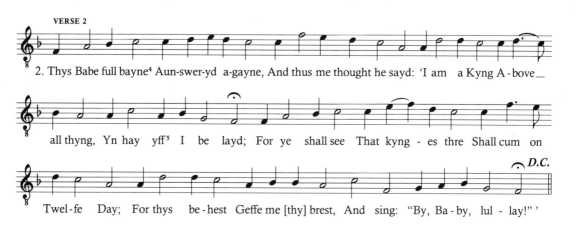

2. Thys Babe full bayne[4] Aun-swer-yd a-gayne, And thus me thought he sayd: 'I am a Kyng A-bove

all thyng, Yn hay yff[5] I be layd; For ye shall see That kyng - es thre Shall cum on

D.C.

Twel-fe Day; For thys be-hest Geffe me [thy] brest, And sing: "By, Ba-by, lul-lay!" '

VERSE 3

3. 'My Son, I say, Wyth-owt - tyn nay, Thow art my der-lyng der; I shall the kepe

Whyle thow dost slepe And make the goode chere; And all thy whylle[6] I wyll ful-fill,

D.C.

Thow wotyst hyt well, yn fay,[7] Yet more then thys, I wyll the kys And syng: "By, Ba-by, lul-lay!" '

VERSE 4

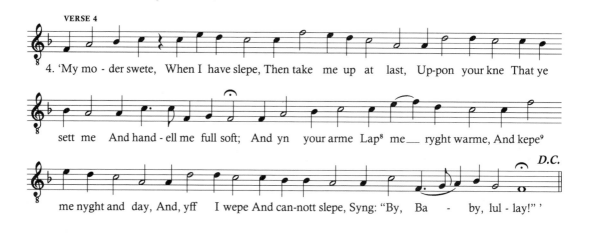

4. 'My mo - der swete, When I have slepe, Then take me up at last, Up-pon your kne That ye

sett me And hand - ell me full soft; And yn your arme Lap[8] me ryght warme, And kepe[9]

D.C.

me nyght and day, And, yff I wepe And can-nott slepe, Syng: "By, Ba - by, lul-lay!" '

4 disobedient   5 though   6 will   7 thou knowest it well, in faith   8 wrap   9 preserve

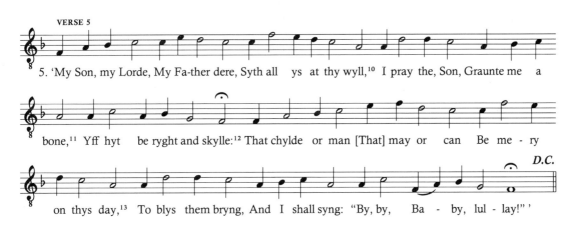

VERSE 5

5. 'My Son, my Lorde, My Fa-ther dere, Syth all ys at thy wyll,[10] I pray the, Son, Graunte me a

bone,[11] Yff hyt be ryght and skylle:[12] That chylde or man [That] may or can Be me - ry

on thys day,[13] To blys them bryng, And I shall syng: "By, by, Ba - by, lul - lay!" '

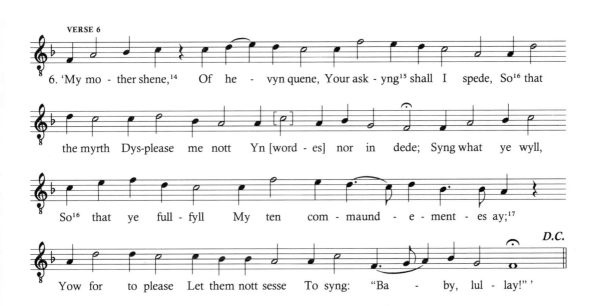

VERSE 6

6. 'My mo - ther shene,[14] Of he - vyn quene, Your ask - yng[15] shall I spede, So[16] that

the myrth Dys-please me nott Yn [word - es] nor in dede; Syng what ye wyll,

So[16] that ye full - fyll My ten com - maund - e - ment - es ay;[17]

Yow for to please Let them nott sesse To syng: "Ba - by, lul - lay!" '

[10] since all is at thy command   [11] boon   [12] reasonable
[13] Epiphany   [14] bright   [15] request   [16] provided
[17] always

A touching dialogue between the infant Jesus and his mother, on whose lap he sits. The references to the 'bright star' and the three kings mean that the carol was almost certainly written for the Epiphany (6 January). It is partly an apologia for merrymaking: the last six lines of verse 5 can be paraphrased as 'Whoever is merry on this [Epiphany] day, bring them to heavenly bliss, and I [in heaven] will sing [to you]: "By, by . . . ".' 'Them' in the final verse, line 9, refers to the merrymakers, including, of course, those who sing this carol. Mary refers to Christ as her Father (verses 1 and 5) because, as a co-equal member of the Trinity, he was creator of the universe.

PERFORMANCE Three voices. In the manuscript the 'middle' singer of the refrain takes the verses, which are probably to be sung in a flexible, text-led manner.

16

Lully, lulla, thow littel tyne child
(The Coventry Carol)

(*Holy Innocents*)

Sixteenth-century
(Sharp, 1825)

¹ two

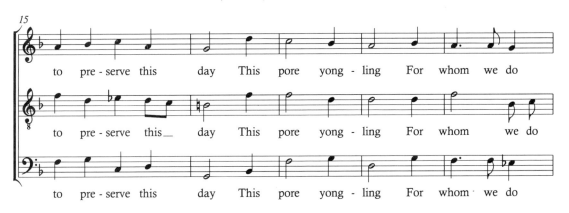

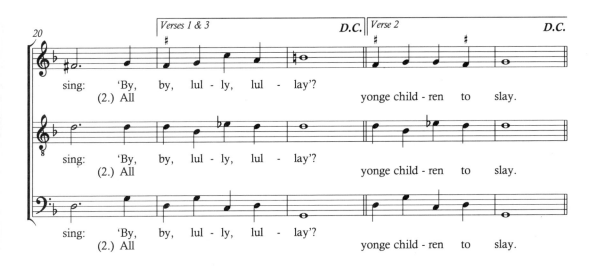

2 Herod the King

   In his raging

     Chargid he hath this day

   His men of might

   In his owne sight

     All yonge children to slay.

3 That wo is me,

   Pore child, for thee,

     And ever morne and say[2]

   For thi parting

   Nether say nor singe:

     'By, by, lully, lullay.'

Sixteenth-century
(Sharp, 1825)

[2] grieve and sigh

The song of the mothers of Bethlehem which precedes the murder of their children in the Pageant of the Shearmen and Taylors, one of the Coventry mystery plays. The only manuscript copy was destroyed in a fire in 1879 and all editions are based on a horrendously inaccurate engraving of 1825.

PERFORMANCE Three voices (probably originally a boy and two men).

See *NOBC* for *As I out rode this enderes night* (*The Coventry Shepherds' Carol*) (no. 41) and *We happy hirdes men* (no. 42).

17

Come, love we God!

(Epiphany; Christmas)

Sixteenth-century
(Shanne MS, arr. editors)

1. Come, love   we God! of might is most[1]   The Fa-ther, the Sonne, the Ho - lie Goost,
2. The   Fa-ther sent downe his one - lie Soune, Which of   a maide was man   be cum

Reg - nan - te   jam___ in   e - the - ra;[2]   The   which mayd man,   both more and lesse,[3]
Cum___   pu - ra   con - ti - nen - ti - a.[6]   In   Beth - lem,   Jui-de,[7] two beast be-tweene,

And cre - at   him   to his lick-nesse;[4]   O quan - ta,   O quan-ta   sunt_ hec o - pe-ra![5]
This Child   was borne, [that] I   of meane;[8] O no - va,   O no-va   stel - la lu - mi-na![9]

[1] the most mighty (Father, etc.)   [2] now reigning in heaven   [3] of higher and lower degree   [4] likeness   [5] O how many
are these works!   [6] with pure countenance   [7] Judah   [8] of whom I speak   [9] O light of a new star!

3 The hirdemen came with theyr offring,
   Ffor to present that pretie thinge[10]
      Cum summa reverentia.[11]
   They offred theyr giftes that Child untill;[12]
   They weere received with full good will;
      Quam grata sunt hec munera![13]

4 These kynges came from the east cuntrie,
   Which knewe then, by Astronomie
      Et Balam vaticenia,[14]
   That then was born the Kynge of Blisse;
   His mother a maid both was and is:
      O Dei mirabilia.[15]

5 To seeke that Babe they tooke the waie;
   They had good speede in theyr jurney,
      Stella micanta per via.[16]
   When they came wheere as Herod leay,
   The starr was hid that ledd the way
      Ob tetra regis crimina.[17]

6 Hee questioned them of theyr cunninge;[18]
   'What novells,'[19] he said, 'or what tydinge
      Vos fertis [ex Arabia]?'[20]
   They said was borne both God and man:
   'We will him worshipp as Soveraigne,
      Cum digna Deo latria.'[21]

7 'Come heare again!' Herod did saie;
   'Howe that ye speede[22] in youre jurney
      Mihi fiat notitia:[23]
   I will him worshipp'—he though[t] not so;
   He ment with fraud them for to sloo:[24]
      O ficta amicitia![25]

8 They past the towne; they saw the starre,
   Which ledd them till they found the barne,[26]
      Sugentem matris ubera;[27]
   They offred him gould, mirr, and sence;
   He tooke them with great diligence,[28]
      Quam digna est infancia.[29]

9 They tooke theyr leeve of that sweet thinge,[30]
   And thought to come by[31] Herod Kynge,
      Apparente voce angelica:[32]
   'Turne home,' he saith, 'leave Herodes will:
   He thinkes with fraud youe for to kyll,
      Per cauta homicidia.'[33]

10 They turnd againe full merilie,
   Ich[34] one into his owne cuntrie,
      Alacri terra tenera[35]
   They had heavens blisse at theyr endinge,[36]
   The which God graunt us, ould and younge,
      In clara poliregia.[37]

(*Shanne MS, 1611*)

---

[10] [to the Child]   [11] with great reverence   [12] unto
[13] how pleasing are these gifts!   [14] and the prophecy of
Balaam [Numbers 24: 17–18]   [15] O wonders of God!
[16] the star lighting their way   [17] because of the loathsome
crimes of the king   [18] knowledge   [19] news   [20] do you
bring [from Arabia]   [21] with worship worthy of God
[22] how did you fare   [23] tell me   [24] slay   [25] O feigned
friendship!   [26] bairn [child]   [27] suckling at his mother's
breast   [28] delight   [29] as befits a child   [30] [the Child]
[31] come to   [32] the angelic voice appearing   [33] by secret
murder   [34] each   [35] eager for his dear land   [36] death
[37] in the noble city of the King

From the commonplace book of the Roman Catholic
Shanne family of Methley, near Leeds, and headed 'A
Christmas carroll by Sir Richard Shanne priest'. Only the
tenor is given, perhaps under the misapprehension that it is
the melody, and our completion is editorial.

PERFORMANCE   (*i*) Solo, at any convenient pitch; (*ii*) three
voices; (*iii*) choir.

18

Swete was the song the Virgine soong

(Christmas)

Sixteenth-century
(arr. Thomas Hamond, d. 1662)

¹ also   ² deftly

This song has become well known through Geoffrey Shaw's arrangement in *The Oxford Book of Carols* (1928), which is good enough to have convinced many people that it was a genuine sixteenth-century setting. Hamond takes the treble and bass of a consort-song version, which may be the original. *NOBC* setting II (not included here) is for solo voice and accompaniment.

PERFORMANCE   Four voices, perhaps with lute and/or viols.

19

Thus angels sung
(The Angels' Song)

(*Christmas*)

Orlando Gibbons (*1583–1625*)
(*arr. editors*)

1. Thus an-gels sung, and thus sing we: 'To God on high all glo-rie bee! Let him on earth his peace be - stow And un-to men his fa-vours show.'

2 If angels sung at Jesus' birth
Then we have greater cause for mirth,[1]
For it was all for our poor sake
He did our human nature take.

3 Dear Christ, thou didst thyself abase
Thus to descend to human race
And leave thy Father's throne above:
Lord, what could move thee to such love?

4 Man, that was made out of the dust,
He found a paradise at first:
But see! the God of heaven and earth,
Laid in a manger at his birth.

5 Surely the manger where he lies
Doth figure forth his sacrifice;
And, by his birth, may all men see
A pattern of humility.

6 Stupendous Babe, my God and King!
Thy praises will I ever sing,
In joyful accents raise my voice,
And in the praise of God rejoice.

7 My soul, learn by thy Saviour's birth
For to abase thyself on earth,
That I may bee exalted high
To live with him eternally.

v. 1 George Wither (1588–1667)
vv. 2–7 anon. (Sandys, 1833, adapted)

[1] joy

The first verse, a paraphrase of Luke 2:14, is given in Wither's *The Hymnes and Songes of the Church* (1623), set to Gibbons's Song 34. Its heading concludes with an exhortation to 'joyne with them [the angels] in this Song, and sing it often to praise God, and quicken faith and charitie in our selves.' We have turned it into a Christmas hymn by adding six of the twelve stanzas of Sandys's version of 'Hark! hark what news the angels bring!' (*NOBC* no. 75). Gibbons provided only melody and bass.

PERFORMANCE (*i*) Unison voices and organ, with optional four-part choir; (*ii*) solo voice and continuo.

20

While shepherds watched their flocks by night

I

(*Christmas*)

after Christopher Tye (c.1500–73)
(arr. Richard Alison, fl. 1592–1606)

1. While shep - herds watched their flocks by night, All seat - ed__ on the ground,
2. 'Fear not,' said he (for might - y dread Had seized their_ trou - bled mind),

The an - gel of the_ Lord came down, And glo - ry__ shone a - round.
'Glad ti - dings of great joy I bring To you and_ all man - kind.

3 'To you in David's town this day
   Is born of David's line
The Saviour, who is Christ the Lord;
   And this shall be the sign:

4 'The heavenly Babe you there shall find
   To human view displayed,
All meanly wrapped in swathing bands,
   And in a manger laid.'

5 Thus spake the seraph; and forthwith
   Appeared a shining throng
Of angels, praising God, who thus
   Addressed their joyful song:

6 'All glory be to God on high,
   And to the earth be peace;
Good will henceforth from heaven to men
   Begin and never cease.'

Nahum Tate? (1652–1715)

This paraphrase of Luke 2: 8–14 appeared in Tate and Brady's Supplement (1700) to their *New Version of the Psalms of David*, and has traditionally been ascribed to Tate. It was the first (and for more than eighty years the only) Christmas hymn 'permitted to be used in [Anglican] churches', and was sung to any suitable psalm tune in common measure (8.6.8.6.). 'Winchester Old' (I) was included among seventy-five tunes in the sixth edition of the Supplement, but only with *Hymns Ancient and Modern* (1861) did it begin to oust the rich variety of melodies that the words had attracted over the previous century and a half. Tune II, widely sung in the US, derives from the aria 'Non vi piaque ingiusti dei' in Handel's opera *Siroe*. Tune V, 'Cranbrook',

now better known to the Yorkshire words 'On Ilkla Moor baht 'at', was written by a Kentish cobbler (and fine composer of hymn-tunes), Thomas Clark of Canterbury. 'Old Foster' (VII) was published in an orchestral setting with the words of Psalm 47, but circulated widely in the gallery repertory and in Yorkshire is always sung to 'While shepherds watched'.

NOBC Tunes III, IV, and VI (not included here) are, respectively, a major version of the tune commonly sung to 'God rest you merry, gentlemen' (85:1), an early fuging tune by Joseph Watts (1749), and a gallery setting from a manuscript of *c*.1830.

For performance note see p. 55.

II

after George Frideric Handel (1685–1759)

(Christmas)

V

Thomas Clark (1775–1859)

2 'Fear not,' said he (for mighty dread
  Had seized their troubled mind),
  'Glad tidings of great joy I bring
  To you and all mankind.

3 'To you in David's town this day
  Is born of David's line
  The Saviour, who is Christ the Lord;
  And this shall be the sign:

4 'The heavenly Babe you there shall find
  To human view displayed,
  All meanly wrapped in swathing bands,
  And in a manger laid.'

5 Thus spake the seraph; and forthwith
  Appeared a shining throng
  Of angels, praising God, who thus
  Addressed their joyful song:

6 'All glory be to God on high,
  And to the earth be peace;
  Good will henceforth from heaven to men
  Begin and never cease.'

Nahum Tate? (1652–1715)

PERFORMANCE   I (*i*) solo voice and lute, orpharion and/or cittern, with or without bass viol (tabulature parts are in *NOBC*); (*ii*) solo voice or four voices with mixed consort. Alison's setting is also suitable for congregation and organ, when it may be treated as a normal modern hymn-tune.

(Elizabethan congregations normally sang hymns in unison and unaccompanied.)
  II, voices and organ.
  V, voices, with instruments *ad lib.* (see Introduction).
  VII (*i*) choir and organ or piano; (*ii*) choir and orchestra.

VII

(*Christmas*)

John Foster (*1762–1822*)

1. While shep-herds watched their_ flocks by__ night, All seat - ed__ on the

21

O remember Adam's fall
Remember, O thou man

I

(Christmas)

Seventeenth-century?
(Bedford, 1733)

1. O re-mem-ber A-dam's fall, O thou man, O___ thou man! O re - mem-ber
2. O re-mem-ber, O thou man, O thou man, O___ thou man, O re - mem-ber,

A-dam's fall From_ heaven to hell! O re-mem-ber A-dam's fall, How we_ were con -
O thou man, Thy____ time mis-spent! O re-mem-ber, O thou man, How thou from thy

-dem-ned all In - to hell per - pe - tu - al, There for to dwell.
God didst run, And his pre-scence thou didst shun, There - fore re - pent!

3 O remember God's goodness,
   O thou man, O thou man!
   O remember God's goodness
     And promise made!
   O remember God's goodness,
   All our evil to redress
   (When we were remediless)
     And be our aid.

4 Oh, the angels all did sing,
   O thou man, O thou man!
   Oh, the angels all did sing,
     On heaven's high hill!
   Oh, the angels all did sing:
   'Praise be to our glorious King,
   And on earth, in ev'rything,
     To men good will!'

5 Oh, the shepherds startled were,
   O thou man, O thou man!
   Oh, the shepherds startled were
     At this strange thing!
   Oh, the shepherds startled were
   When near Bethlehem they did hear
   That Christ Jesus was born there
     To be our King!

6 To the stable they did go,
   O thou man, O thou man!
   To the stable they did go,
     This thing to see;
   To the stable they did go,
   Devoutly asking if 'twas so,
   If Christ had been born or no,
     To set us free.

7 In a stable he was born,
   O thou man, O thou man!
   In a stable he was born
     For lost man's sake;
   In a stable he was born:
   For us wretches, and forlorn,
   Our Redeemer thought no scorn
     Our flesh to take.

8 O give thanks to God alway,
   O thou man, O thou man!
   O give thanks to God alway,
     Joyfully!
   O give thanks to God alway
   For this, our happy day;
   Let all men sing and say:
     'Holy, holy!'

Sixteenth-century?
(vv. 1–7 Bedford, 1733
v. 8 Ravenscroft, 1611, adapted)

II

(*Christmas*)

Thomas Ravenscroft?
(*c.1582–c.1635*)

1. Re - mem - ber, O thou man, *O thou man, O thou man,* Re - mem - ber, O thou man, *Thy time is spent:* Re-mem-ber, O thou man, How thou art dead and gone, And I did what I can: *There - fore re - pent!*

† See performance note.

2 Remember Adam's fall,
    O thou man, O thou man,
    Remember Adam's fall
      From heaven to hell!
    Remember Adam's fall,
    How we were condemnèd all
    In hell perpetual,
      There for to dwell.

3 Remember God's goodnesse,
    O thou man, O thou man,
    Remember God's goodnesse,
      And his promise made!
    Remember God's goodnesse;
    How he sent his Sonne, doubtlesse,
    Our sinnes for to redresse:
      Be not affraid!

4 The angels all did sing,
O thou man, O thou man,
The angels all did sing
Upon the shepheards' hill;
The angels all did singe
Praises to our heavenly King,
And peace to man living
With a good will.

5 The shepheards amazèd was,
O thou man, O thou man,
The shepheards amazèd was
To heare the angels sing,
The shepheards amazèd was
How it should come to passe
That Christ our Messias
Should be our King.

6 To Bethlem did they goe,
O thou man, O thou man,
To Bethlem did they go
The shepheards three;
To Bethlem did they goe
To see whether it were so or no,
Whether Christ were borne or no
To set man free.

7 As the angels before did say,
O thou man, O thou man,
As the angels before did say,
So it came to passe;
As the angels before did say,
They found a Babe, whereas[1] it lay
In a manger, wrapt in hay,
So poore he was.

8 In Bethlem he was borne,
O thou man, O thou man,
In Bethlem he was borne,
For mankind's sake;
In Bethlem he was borne,
For us that were forlorne,
And therefore tooke no scorne
Our flesh to take.

9 Give thanks to God alway,
O thou man, O thou man,
Give thanks to God alway,
With heart most joyfully.
Give thanks to God alway
For this our happy day;
Let all men sing and say:
'Holy! holy!'

Sixteenth-century?
(Ravenscroft, 1611)

[1] where

Setting I may derive from the repertory of city waits. II, headed 'A Christmas Caroll' in the 'Country Pastimes' section of his *Melismata* (1611), is probably Ravenscroft's imitation of the procedures of rural carollers; it was still sung in Thomas Hardy's day and is the 'ancient and time-worn hymn' that the Mellstock choir sang to Fancy Day in *Under the Greenwood Tree* (1872).

PERFORMANCE I, voices, with optional doubling instruments in the full sections (see Introduction). Following contemporary convention, Bedford marks 'soft' and 'loud' merely to indicate 'soli' and 'full', which we have substituted. (This need not imply a choir.)

II (*i*) solo soprano, with three viols and perhaps continuo—lute, organ, etc.—with three lower voices joining in the 'refrains', printed in italic; (*ii*) four voices, singing throughout, with optional doubling/continuo instruments (see Introduction). When sung, the bass line in bars 1–2, 5–6, 9–12, and 14, and the alto in bars 12 and 14, should be performed in rhythmic unison with the other parts.

22

Riu, riu, chiu

(Immaculate Conception; Christmas)

Mateo Flecha the elder? (1481–1553)
(Villancicos de diversos autores, 1556)

27 **VERSE 1** [SOLO]

1. El lo-bo ra - bio-so La__ qui-so mor-der, Mas Dios po-de - ro-so La su-po de-fen-der;

35 **D.S.**

Qui-so-le ha - zer que No pu-die-sse pe-car, Ni aun o - ri-gi - nal Es-ta Vir-gen no tu - vie-ra.

43 **VERSE 2** [SOLO]

2. Es-te ques na - çi-do Es__ el gran Mo-nar-cha, Chris-to pa-tri - ar-ca De__ car-ne ves - ti-do;

51 **D.S.**

Ha-nos re-di - mi-do Con se ha-zer chi-qui-to: Aun-que e-ra in-fi - ni-to Fi - ni-to se hi - zie-ra.

59 **VERSE 3** [SOLO]

3. Mu-chas pro-fe - çi-as Lo han pro-fe-ti - za-do; Y aun en nues-tros di - as Lo he-mos al-can-ça-do.

67 **D.S.**

A Dios hu-ma - na-do Ve - mos en el sue-lo Y al hom-bre en el cie-lo Por-que el le qui-sie-ra.

75 **VERSE 4** [SOLO]

4. Yo vi mil gar - ço-nes Que an - da-van can-tan-do, Por a-qui bo - lan-do Ha - zien-do mil so-nes,

83 **D.S.**

Di-zien-do a gas - co-nes: 'Glo - ria sea en el çie-lo Y paz en el sue-lo, Pues__ Je-sus nas-çie-ra.'

91 **VERSE 5** [SOLO]

5. Es-te vie-ne a dar__ A__ los muer-tos vi-da Y vie-ne a re-par - ar De to - dos la ca - i-da.

99 **D.S.**

Es la Luz del Di - a A - que-ste mo-çue-lo; Es-te es el Cor - de - ro Que__ San Juan di - xe-ra.

(continued overleaf)

107 VERSE 6 [SOLO]

6. Mi- ra bien que os qua-dre, Que an-si-na lo o-ye-ra: Que Dios no pu - die-ra Ha-zer-la mas que ma-dre;

115   *D.S.*

El que er-a su Pa-dre Oy___ de-lla nas - çio   Y el que la cri - o Su hi - jo se di - xe - ra.

123 VERSE 7 [SOLO]

7. Pues que ya te - ne-mos Lo___ que des-se - a-mos, To-dos jun-tos va-mos, Pre - sen-tes lle - ve-mos;

131   *D.S.*

To-dos le da - re-mos Nues - tra vo-lun-tad,   Pues a se i-gua-lar Con el___ hom-bre vi - nie - ra.

Juan del Encina? (1468–1529/30)

TRANSLATION *Riu, riu, chiu*, the guard [shepherd] by the river: God protected our Ewe from the wolf.

1 The furious wolf tried to bite her, but almighty God protected her well: he made her in such a way that she could know no sin, a virgin unstained by our first father's [Adam's] fault.

2 This new-born Child is a mighty monarch, the patriarchal Christ clothed in flesh; he redeemed us by making himself tiny: he who was infinite became finite.

3 Many prophecies foretold his coming, and now in our time we have seen them fulfilled. God became man, we see him on earth, and we see man in heaven because he [God] loved him.

4 I saw a thousand young men [angels] singing as they flew, making a thousand sounds, chanting to Basques [all good Spaniards]: 'Glory be in the heavens, and peace on earth, now that Jesus is born!'

5 He comes to give life to the dead and to atone for man's fall: this very Babe is the Light of Day, the Lamb of whom St John spoke.

6 Look to it! it concerns you all: God made her [Mary] a mere mother; he who was her father was born of her today; and he who created her calls himself her son.

7 Now we have gained what we desired let us go together to present to him our gifts; let each resign his will to the God who was willing to come down to earth to become man's equal.

(tr. editors, after Robert Pring-Mill)

A vigorous imitation of peasant song, from the Valencian court of around 1530–50. 'Riu, riu, chiu' was a traditional call of Spanish shepherds when guarding their flocks in a riverside fold. Lines 3–4 of the refrain, together with verse 1, are built around the image of God the Father as shepherd: the precious ewe-lamb that he protects is the Virgin Mary; the furious wolf is Satan, whose bite will infect with the taint of Original Sin; and Mary's defence, like the impregnable wall of a sheepfold, is her own Immaculate (that is, sinless) Conception, which allowed Christ to be born fully human but untainted by Adam's fall. (The odd image of Mary as a lamb is an oblique reference to this doctrine.)

PERFORMANCE Refrain, four voices (there is no evidence of instrumental doubling in this repertory); verse, solo voice.

23

Verbum caro factum est: Y la Virgen le dezia

(Christmas)

Sixteenth-century
(Villancicos de diversos autores, 1556)

TRANSLATION The Word is made flesh for the salvation of you all.

1 And the Virgin said unto him: 'Life of my life, what would I [not] do for you, my Son? Yet I have nothing on which to lay you down.'

2 Oh, worldly riches! will you not give some swaddling clothes to Jesus, who is born among the animals, as you can see?

From the same source as 'Riu, riu, chiu' (22). The refrain (both text and music) is closely based on the short responsory *Verbum caro* sung at terce on Christmas Day.

PERFORMANCE Refrain, four voices or choir; verse, four voices.

See *NOBC* for *E la don, don Verges Maria* (no. 50).

24

Gaudete!

(*Christmas*)

(*Piae Cantiones, 1582;
Jistebnice Cantional, 1420*)

Fourteenth-century (Piae Cantiones, 1582)

TRANSLATION Rejoice! rejoice! Christ is born of the Virgin Mary; rejoice!

1 The time of grace has come for which we have prayed; let us devoutly sing songs of joy.

2 God is made man, while nature wonders; the world is renewed by Christ the King.

3 The closed gate of Ezekiel has been passed through; from where the Light has risen [the East] salvation is found.

4 Therefore let our assembly sing praises now at this time of purification; let it bless the Lord: greetings to our King.

No music is given for the verses in *Piae Cantiones*. They derive from the medieval Bohemian song 'Ezechielis porta', which Finnish clerical students would have encountered in Prague and which shared a tune with a Czech vernacular Christmas song that still survives. Finno, the editor of *Piae*

Cantiones, was probably responsible for the refrain. It adapts the words of one of the medieval verses to the music which, in various forms, was sung throughout Lutheran Germany to Luther's single-stanza grace before meat, 'Danket dem Herren'.

Verse 3 refers to the eastern gate of the city in Ezekiel's vision (Ezekiel 44:2). The gate is a traditional symbol of Mary as perpetual virgin.

PERFORMANCE Refrain, choir or four voices, with instruments *ad lib.*; verse, solo voice(s). Earlier settings lack accidentals; this need not imply uninflected performance, but the careful keyboard intabulations of 'Danket dem Herren' by Ammerbach (1571 and 1583) sharpen only the final leading note.

See *NOBC* for *Psallite Unigenito* (no. 52).

25

En! natus est Emanuel
Lo! born is our Emmanuel

(*Christmas*)   *Michael Praetorius (1571–1621)*

1. En! na - tus est E - ma - nu - el, _____ Do - mi - nus,
1. Lo! born is our Em - ma - nu - el, _____ Christ the Lord,

Quem prae - dix - it Ga - bri - el, Do - mi - nus. _____
As fore - told by Ga - bri - el, Christ _____ the Lord. _____

REFRAIN

Sal - va - tor nos - ter est.
the Sa - viour of man - kind.

Sal - va - tor nos - ter est.
the Sa - viour of _____ man - kind.

Do - mi - nus _____ Sal - va - tor nos - ter _____ est, _____ Sal - va - tor nos - ter est.
Christ the Lord, _____ the Sa - viour of man - kind, _____ the Sa - viour of _____ man - kind.

Sal - va - tor nos - ter est.
the Sa - viour of man - kind.

(*continued overleaf*)

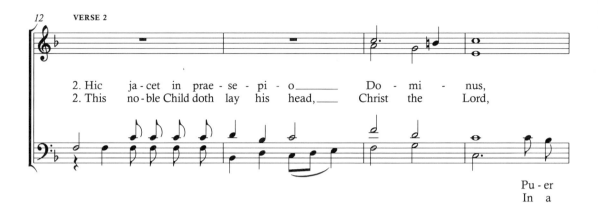

VERSE 2

2. Hic ja - cet in prae - se - pi - o_____ Do - mi - nus,
2. This no - ble Child doth lay his head,_____ Christ the Lord,

Pu - er
In a

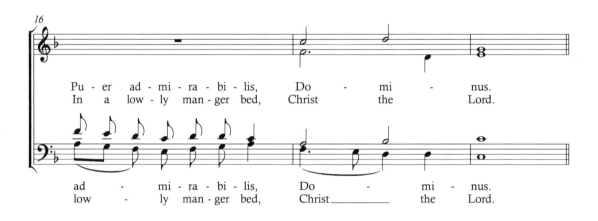

Pu - er ad - mi - ra - bi - lis, Do - mi - nus.
In a low - ly man - ger bed, Christ the Lord.

ad - mi - ra - bi - lis, Do - mi - nus.
low - ly man - ger bed, Christ_____ the Lord.

REFRAIN

Sal - va - tor nos - ter est.
the Sa - viour of man - kind.

Sal - va - tor nos - ter est.
the Sa - viour of_____ man - kind.

Do - mi - nus_____ Sal - va - tor nos - ter__ est,_____ Sal - va - tor nos - ter est.
Christ the Lord,__ the Sa - viour of man - kind,_____ the Sa - viour of_____ man - kind.

Sal - va - tor nos - ter est.
the Sa - viour of man - kind.

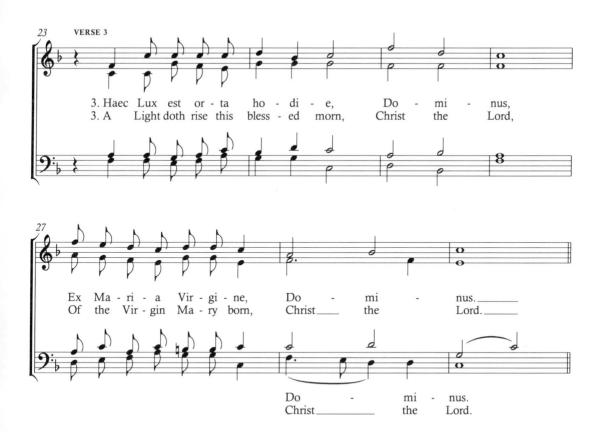

Traditional (tr. editors)

All Praetorius's harmonizations in *NOBC* are from parts V and VI of the largest of his publications, the *Musae Sioniae* ('The Muses of Sion'), 1605–10, its nine volumes corresponding to the number of the choirs of angels, or heavenly muses. Parts IV–VI are a comprehensive treatment of liturgical hymnody.

PERFORMANCE Four voices or choir, with instruments *ad lib.*

26

Puer natus in Bethlehem
A Boy is born in Bethlehem
Ein Kind geborn zu Bethlehem

I

(*Christmas*)

Thirteenth-century?
(arr. Michael Praetorius,
1571–1621, adapted)

1. Pu - er na - tus in Beth - le - hem, Beth - le - hem; Un - de gau - det Ie - ru - sa - lem. Al - le - lu - ia! al - le - lu - ia!
1. A Boy is born in Beth - le - hem, Beth - le - hem; Re - joice, there - fore, Je - ru - sa - lem! Al - le - lu - ia! al - le - lu - ia!

Beth - le - hem; al - le - lu - ia!

2 Assumpsit carnem Filii
   Dei Patris altissimi.
   Alleluia!

2 Our human flesh doth he take on,
   High Word of God, the eternal Son.
   Alleluya!

† See performance note.

3   Per Gabrielis nuncium
Virgo concepit Filium.

3   When Mary Gabriel's words received,
Within her was her Son conceived.

*4   De matre natus virgine,
Sine virili semine.

*4   From virgin's womb doth he proceed
No human father doth he need.

*5   Sine serpentis vulnere
De nostro venit sanguine.

*5   From serpent's wound immune was he,
Yet shared he our humanity.

*6   In carne nobis similis,
Peccato sed dissimilis.

*6   'Tis flesh like ours he's clothèd in,
Though free from man's primeval sin.

7   Tanquam sponsus de thalamo,
Processit matris utero.

7   As from his chamber strides the groom,
So comes he from his mother's womb.

8   Hic iacet in praesepio
Qui regnat sine termino.

8   Within the manger doth he lie,
Who reigns eternally on high.

9   Cognovit bos et asinus
Quod puer erat Dominus.

9   The ox and ass that Child adored
And knew him for their heavenly Lord.

*10   Et angelus pastoribus
Revelat quis sit Dominus.

*10   To shepherds did an angel come
To tell them there was born a Son.

11   Magi de longe veniunt;
Aurum, thus, myrrham offerunt.

11   The wise men came from lands afar
To offer incense, gold and myrrh.

12   Intrantes domum invicem,
Natum salutant hominem.

12   They stooped to enter, one by one,
To greet in turn the new-born Son.

13   In hoc natali gaudio,
Benedicamus Domino.

13   At this glad birth, with one accord
Let us rejoice and bless the Lord!

14   Laudetur sancta Trinitas,
Deo dicamus gratias.

14   To Holy Trinity be praise, [be praise,
be praise,]
And thanks be given to God always.

Thirteenth-century?
(*vv. 1, 3–14 Piae Cantiones, 1582*
v. 2 Hereford Breviary, 1505)

tr. editors

III

Thirteenth-century?
(Piae Cantiones, 1582, arr. editors)

(*Christmas*)

1. Pu - er na - tus in Beth - le - hem,
1. Ein Kind ge - born zu Beth - le - hem,
1. A Boy is born in Beth - le - hem,

1. Pu - er na - tus in Beth - le - hem,
1. Ein Kind ge - born zu Beth - le - hem,
1. A Boy is born in Beth - le - hem,

Beth - le - hem;___ Un - de gau - det Ie - ru - sa - lem.
des freu - et sich Je - ru - sa - lem. (H)al -
Re - joice, there-fore, Je - ru - sa - lem!

Beth - le - hem;___ Un - de___ gau - det Ie - ru - sa - lem.
des freu - et sich Je - ru - sa - lem. (H)al -
Re - joice,___ there-fore, Je - ru - sa - lem!

- le - lu - ia! (H)al - le - lu - ia!___
- le - lu - ia! (H)al - le - lu - ia!___
- le - lu - ia! (H)al - le - lu - ia!___

72

2 Hic iacet in praesepio
  Qui regnat sine termino.

3 Magi de longe veniunt;
  Aurum, thus, myrrham offerunt.

4 Intrantes domum invicem,
  Natum salutant hominem.

5 Adorant eum humiles,
  Dicentes: 'Homo Deus es.'

6 In hoc natali gaudio,
  Benedicamus Domino.

Thirteenth-century?

2 Hier liegt es in dem Krippelein;
  ohn' Ende ist die Herrschaft sein.
  Halleluja!

3 Die König' aus Saba kamen her;
  Gold, Weihrauch, Myrrhe brachten sie dar.

4 Sie gingen in das Haus herein, [ins
    Haus herein]
  und grüssten das Kind und die Mutter sein.

5 Sie fielen nieder auf ihre Knie
  und sprachen: 'Gott und Mensch ist hie.'

6 Für solche gnadenreiche Zeit,
  sei Gott gelobt in Ewigkeit.
  Fifteenth-century
  (Praetorius, 1609, modernized)

2 Within a manger doth he lie,
  Who reigns eternally on high.
  Alleluya!

3 From distant Saba came three Kings,
  Gold, incense, myrrh their offerings.

4 They stooped to enter, one by one,
  To greet the Mother and the Son.

5 Then to the Child they bowed the knee,
  Declaring: 'God and Man is he!'

6 For this most joyful time give praise,
    [give praise, give praise,]
  And glory give to God always.
  tr. editors

One of the most venerable of all Christmas *cantiones* (songs). Setting III, like many from the sixteenth century, combines the original tenor tune (tune 2) and the counter-melody that was generated above it (tune 1). Verses 4, 5, 6, and 10 of the Latin text of setting I are the result of 'improvements' by Hermann Bonn (*c.*1504–48), a pupil of Luther and an industrious translator of hymns.

NOBC setting II (not included here) is J. S. Bach's chorale from the cantata 'Sie werden aus Saba alle kommen' (BWV 65).

PERFORMANCE I, voices, with organ and/or other instruments *ad lib.*

III. Each verse may be sung twice, first in Latin and then in English/German:

Latin: sopranos sing tune 2, (*i*) unaccompanied, (*ii*) with organ continuo, or (*iii*) with other voices or instruments; in this last case the small-note alto part should be sung or played and tune 1 sung as the tenor.

English/German: voices and organ (other instruments *ad lib.*). The audience/congregation sings tune 1.

In some sources only one tune (2) is to be sung, with alternating Latin (lines 1, 3) and vernacular (lines 2, 4) texts.

To form a high choir of instruments and voices for the Latin verses, the parts (in descending order) are as follows:

alto (small notes), instruments, up an octave with voice(s) *ad lib.*;
tune 2, voice(s), at treble pitch;
tune 1, instruments, at notated (treble) pitch with voice(s) *ad lib.*;
bass, instruments, up an octave with voice(s) *ad lib.*

Superscript repeat signs in the text indicate which portions should be repeated at the end of the first phrase. Initial small-note crotchets within these repeat signs indicate that an extra upbeat should be sung for this repeat (bar 4 in setting I; bar 2 in setting III).

27

Resonet in laudibus
Let the voice of praise resound
Joseph, lieber Joseph mein
Joseph, dearest Joseph mine

I

(*Christmas*)

Fourteenth-century?
(*Aosta MS 9–E–19*)

1. Re - so - ne - mus lau - di - bus_ Cum jo-cun - di - ta - ti - bus_ Ec - cle - si - am fi -

- de - li - bus. Ap - pa - ru - it___ quem ge - nu - it___ Ma - ri - a.

2 Deus fecit hominem
Ad suam imaginém
Et similitudinem.

3 Deus fecit omnia,
Celum, terram, maria,
Cunctaque nascentia.

4 Ergo nostro concio
In chordis et organó
Benedicat Domino,

5 Et Deo qui venias
Donat et leticiäs
Nos eidem gracias.

Fourteenth-century
(*Aosta MS 9–E–19*)

TRANSLATION 1 Let us make the church resound with the merry praises of the faithful. He whom Mary bore hath appeared.

2 God made man in his own image and likeness.

3 God made all things, the heavens, the earth, the seas, and whatever has been born.

4 Therefore let our company bless the Lord with strings and instrument,

5 and let it give thanks to the same God, who gives us pardon and joys.

This has long been one of the most popular of all Christmas songs in Germany, where it is sung to two quite distinct texts: 'Resonet in laudibus', which dates probably from the fourteenth century, and 'Joseph, lieber Joseph mein', which may be even older. Both were associated with the medieval custom of cradle-rocking during the Christmas services.

NOBC setting III (not included here) is an arrangement of the longer version of the tune and text of 'Resonet in laudibus' from the Mainz Cantual, 1605.

PERFORMANCE I, verses 1–4, soli; verse 5, full; refrains, full.

II, verse, soli; refrain, full.

IV (without refrains): (*i*) choir, with instruments and/or organ *ad lib.*; (*ii*) unison voices and organ.

IV (with refrains): verse, choir with instruments and/or organ *ad lib.*; refrain, full, unison voices and organ, or with different groups taking all sections but the last, which may be full. For performance as a *Wechselgesang* (antiphonal song) or as a play, see the notes to this carol and Appendix 2 in *NOBC*.

When a congregation participates, transposition down a tone is advisable.

See *NOBC* for *Magnum Nomen Domini Emanuel* (no. 56).

II

(*Christmas*)

Fifteenth-century
(*S. Gall MS*)

1. Re - so - net in lau - di - bus Cum ju-cun - dis plau - si - bus Si - on cum_ fi -
1. Let the voice of praise re-sound, Signs of joy be all a-round, Heaven and earth with

- de - li - bus: Ap - pa - ru - it quem ge - nu - it Ma - ri - a!
songs_ a-bound: A Child is born, the Christ, the Son of Ma - ry!

2 Christus natus hodie
   Ex Maria Virgine
   Sine virili semine:

2 Our salvation is begun;
   Mary now doth bear a Son;
   Earthly father hath he none:

3 Pueri, concinite,
   Nato Regi psallite,
   Voce pia dicite:

3 Come, ye choirs, and reverently
   Praise your King on bended knee;
   Sing in sweetest harmony:

4 Sion, lauda Dominum,
   Salvatorem hominum,
   Purgatorem criminum:

4 Sion, praise your God alway,
   Earth's Redeemer, born today!
   All our sins he'll purge away,
      The Child that's born, . . .

5 Deo laus et gloria,
   Virtus et victoria,
   Perpete memoria:

5 Triumph-songs to God we raise;
   His the glory, his the praise
   Unto all the length of days:

(*Mainz Cantual, 1605*)

tr. editors

IV

JOSEPH:

2 Gerne, liebe Muhme mein,
helf' ich dir wiegen dein Kindelein!
Gott, der wird mein Lohner sein
im Himmelreich, der Jungfrau Kind Maria.

(FIRST) ATTENDANT:

3 Freu' dich nun, du christlich' Schar!
Gott, der Himmelskönig klar,
macht uns Menschen offenbar
der uns gebar die reine Magd Maria.

(SECOND) ATTENDANT:

4 Alle Menschen sollen gar
ganz in Freuden kommen dar,
dass ein jeder recht erfahr',
den uns gebar die reine Magd Maria.

(THIRD) ATTENDANT:

5 Uns erschien Emanuel,
wie uns verkündet Gabriel,
und bezeugt Ezechiel:
Du Mensch ohn' Fehl', dich hat gebor'n
Maria!

(FOURTH) ATTENDANT:

6 Ew'gen Vaters ew'ges Wort,
wahrer Gott, der Tugend Hort,
irdisch hier, im Himmel dort
der Seelen Pfort', die uns gebar Maria.

FULL (or THE FOUR ATTENDANTS):

7 Süsser Jesu, auserkorn,
weisst wohl, dass wir war'n verlorn:
Stille deines Vaters Zorn.
Dich hat geborn die reine Magd Maria.

JOSEPH:

2 Gladly, dear one, lady mine,
I will rock this child of thine;
Heavenly light on us both shall shine
In paradise, as prays the mother Mary.

(FIRST) ATTENDANT:

3 Peace to all that have good will!
God, who heaven and earth doth fill,
Comes to turn us away from ill,
And lies so still within the crib of Mary.

(SECOND) ATTENDANT:

4 All shall come and bow the knee;
Wise and happy they shall be,
Loving such a Divinity,
As all may see in Jesus, Son of Mary.

(THIRD) ATTENDANT:

5 Now is born Emmanuel,
As foretold by Ezekiel,
Promised Mary by Gabriel;
Ah! who can tell thy praises, Son of Mary!

(FOURTH) ATTENDANT:

6 Thou my heart with love hast stirred,
Thou, the Father's eternal Word,
Virtue's shining treasure-hoard,
Who ne'er demurred to be the Son of Mary.

FULL (or THE FOUR ATTENDANTS):

7 Sweet and lovely little one,
Princely, beauteous, God's own Son,
Without thee were we all undone:
Our love is won by thine, O Son of Mary.

8 Himmlisch' Kind, o grosser Gott,
   leidest in der Krippen Not.
   Machst die Sünder frei vom Tod,
   du englisch' Brot, das uns gebar Maria.

   (Leipzig University MS, c.1400, modernized)

8 Heavenly Child, thou Lord of all,
   Meanly housed in ox's stall,
   Free our souls, in Satan's thrall:
   On thee we call, thou blessèd Son of Mary.

   tr. Percy Dearmer (1867–1936), adapted editors

(Christmas)

(Mainz Cantual, 1605, arr. editors)

MARY: 1. Jo - seph, lie - ber Jo - seph mein, hilf mir wie - gen mein
      1. Jo - seph, dear - est Jo - seph mine, Help me rock the

Kin - de - lein! Gott,__ der wird mein Loh - ner sein im
Child di - vine; God__ re - ward thee and all__ that's thine In

[Fine ad lib. or v.s. for optional refrain]

Him - mel - reich, der Jung - frau Sohn__ Ma - ri - a.
pa - ra - dise, so prays__ the mo - ther Ma - ry.

heu - ti - gen Tag, am heu - ti - gen Tag_____ in Is - ra - el:
-ma - nu - el, Em - ma - nu - el_____ in Is - ra - el:

von_____ Ma - ri - a ist Heil er - spros - sen in al - le Welt.
Ma - ry's Babe,___ the Sa - viour, our_____ Em - ma - nu - el.

Mag - num No - men Do - mi - ni E - ma - nu - el,
O pro - claim the might - y name: Em - ma - nu - el!

quod___ an - nun - ci - a - tus est per Ga - bri - el.
Ga - bri - el from hea - ven came that Name to tell.

28

Quem pastores laudavere
Shepherds sang their praises o'er him

(Christmas)

Fourteenth-century
(arr. Michael Praetorius, 1571–1621, adapted)

1. Quem pas - to - res   lau - da - ve - re,   Qui - bus an - ge - li   dix - e - re:
1. Shep-herds sang their   prai - ses o'er him,   Called by an - gels to   a - dore him:

'Ab - sit vo - bis   jam__ ti - me - re: Na - tus est__ Rex   Glo - ri - ae!'
'Have no fear, but   come be-fore him: Born__ is now__ your   glo - rious King!'

2   Ad quem magi ambulabant,
    Aurum, thus, myrrham portabant;
    Immolabant haec sincere
    Leoni victoriae;

2   Eastern sages came to view him,
    Judah's conquering Lion knew him,
    Gold, and myrrh, and incense to him
    As their tribute offering.

*3 Exsultemus cum Maria
In coelesti hierarchia:
Natum promant voce pia
Dulci cum melodia;

4 Christo Regi, Deo nato,
Per Mariam nobis dato,
Merito resonet vere:
'Laus, honor, et gloria!'

Fourteenth-century
(Praetorius, 1607, adapted)

*3 On this Child, rejoicing, gaze we;
Led by Mary, anthems raise we;
Reverently, with angels, praise we
With the sweetest melody.

4 Christ our King, from Mary springing,
God made man, salvation bringing,
Thee we worship, ever singing:
'Honour, praise, and glory be!'

Free tr., editors

TRANSLATION Even in its original three-verse form (verses 1, 2, and 4) the literal sense of this text is difficult to tease out, mainly because the principal verb ('resonet') is in the penultimate line: '[v. 1] Unto him whom the shepherds praised, told by the angels "Be not afraid: the King of Glory is born!"; [v. 2] unto him to whom the magi journeyed, to whom they brought gold, frankincense and myrrh, to whom, the victorious Lion [of Judah; see Revelation 5:5], they offered these things with sincerity; [v. 4] unto [him,] Christ the King, the Son of God, given to us through Mary, let "Praise, honour and glory!" right worthily resound!'

Verse 3 was a later addition to this elegant grammatical construction, and takes no account of its single-sentence context. Best seen as a free-standing interpolation, it reads: 'Let us rejoice with Mary in the heavenly hierarchy [of angels]: they praise the Infant in reverent tones [and] with sweet melody.'

The original verses emphasize the kingship of the new-born Christ. This theme is underlined by the reference in verse 4 to the Palm Sunday processional hymn 'Laus, honor et gloria', which was sung at town gates, the west doors of cathedrals, etc., in symbolic re-enactment of Christ's quasi-royal entry into Jerusalem shortly before his death; compare also the acclamations in Revelation 5:12–13.

'Quem pastores' has two distinct manners of performance in both the Catholic and Lutheran liturgies: as a conventional hymn, and (until the eighteenth century in most places) as part of one of the distinctive *Wechselgesänge* ('antiphonal songs'—see notes to *NOBC* no. 55) of Germanic Christmas hymnody. When performed *in Wechsel* it is sung by four boys (or groups of boys in unison, or even small consorts or choirs) who stand holding candles, ideally in high galleries on four sides of the church. Each sings one line of each four-line stanza, so that the tune seems to revolve in the air, as if sung by circling angels, and each 'angelic' verse evokes the 'pastoral' response of the equivalent verse of the hymn 'Nunc angelorum gloria' from the main choir below.

PERFORMANCE (*i*) Choir, with instruments *ad lib.* (see Introduction); (*ii*) voices and organ; (*iii*) four choirs (see above) or, as J. H. Schein (1586–1630) suggests, three choirs, each singing a line and joining together for the fourth line of each verse.

See *NOBC* for *Nun komm, der Heiden Heiland* (no. 58).

29

In dulci jubilo
Good Christian men, rejoice!

I

(*Christmas*)

Thirteenth-century?
(arr. Michael Praetorius, 1571–1621)

1. *In dul - ci ju - bi - lo,*[1]___ nun sing - et und seid
   Let songs___ and glad - ness

froh!___ Un - sers Her - zen Won - ne leit *in prae - se - pi -*
flow!___ All our joy re - cli - neth___

- o,[2]___ und leuch - tet als die Son - ne *ma - tris in gre - mi -*
And like the sun he shi - neth

- o.[3]___ *Al - pha es et O!*[4] *Al - pha es___ et O!___*

[1] with sweet jubilation [2] in a manger [3] in [your] mother's lap [4] You are Alpha and Omega.

2   *O Jesu parvule,*
　　nach dir ist mir so weh.
　　　Tröst mir mein Gemüte,
　o Puer optime;
　　　durch alle deine Güte,
　o Princeps Gloriae,
　trahe me post te!

2   *O Jesu parvule,*[5]
　　I yearn for thee alway!
　　　Comfort me and stay me,
　O Puer optime;[6]
　　　By thy great love I pray thee,
　O Princeps Gloriae,
　Trahe me post te![7]

3   *O Patris caritas!*
　O Nati lenitas!
　　　Wir wärn all' verloren
　per nostra crimina;
　　　so hat er uns erworben
　coelorum gaudia;
　eia, wärn wir da!

3   *O Patris caritas!*
　O Nati lenitas![8]
　　　Condemned we had remainèd
　Per nostra crimina;[9]
　　　But he for us hath gainèd
　Coelorum gaudia:[10]
　In paradise afar,
　Where joys unending are.

4   *Ubi sunt gaudia?*
　Nirgends mehr denn da,
　　　da die Engel singen
　nova cantica,
　　　und die Schellen klingen
　in Regis curia;
　Eia, wärn wir da!

4   *Ubi sunt gaudia*[11]
　More deep than heaven's are?
　　　In heaven are angels singing
　Nova cantica,[12]
　　　In heaven the bells are ringing
　In Regis curia.[13]
　O that we were there!

vv. 1, 2, 4 fourteenth-century
v. 3 Valentin Triller (d.1573)
(Praetorius, 1607)

tr. editors

[5] O infant Jesus　[6] O best of boys　[7] O Prince of Glory, draw me after you [to heaven]　[8] O love of the Father! O mercy of the Son!　[9] through our sins　[10] the joys of heaven　[11] Where are joys(?)　[12] new songs　[13] in the courts of the King

II

(Christmas)

Thirteenth-century?
(arr. J. S. Bach, 1685–1750)

1. *In dul - ci ju - bi - lo,*[1] nun sing - et und_ seid froh!
   Let songs and glad - ness flow!

in prae-se - pi - o,[2]

Un - sers Her - zen Won - ne leit   in prae-se - pi - o,[2]   und
All our joy_ re - cli - neth_   in_ prae-se - pi - o,[2]   And

in_ prae-se - pi - o,[2]

ma - tris   in gre - mi - o.[3]

leuch - tet als_ die Son - ne   ma - tris_ in gre - mi - o.[3]
like_ the sun_ he shi - neth   ma - tris_ in gre - mi - o.[3]

ma - tris_ in gre - mi - o.[3]

[1] with sweet jubilation   [2] in a manger   [3] in [your] mother's lap

2 *O Jesu parvule,*

   nach dir ist mir so weh.

      Tröst mir mein Gemüte,

   o Puer optime;

      durch alle deine Güte,

   o Princeps Gloriae,

   trahe me post te!

3 *O Patris caritas!*

   O Nati lenitas!

      Wir wärn all' verloren

   per nostra crimina;

      so hat er uns erworben

   coelorum gaudia;

   eia, wärn wir da!

4 *Ubi sunt gaudia?*

      Nirgends mehr denn da,

      da die Engel singen

   nova cantica,

      und die Schellen klingen

   in Regis curia;

   Eia, wärn wir da!

2 *O Jesu parvule,*[5]

   I yearn for thee alway!

      Comfort me and stay me,

   O Puer optime;[6]

      By thy great love I pray thee,

   O Princeps Gloriae,

   Trahe me post te![7]

3 *O Patris caritas!*

   O Nati lenitas![8]

      Condemnèd we had remainèd

   Per nostra crimina;[9]

      But he for us hath gainèd

   Coelorum gaudia:[10]

   In paradise afar,

   Where joys unending are.

4 *Ubi sunt gaudia*[11]

   More deep than heaven's are?

      In heaven are angels singing

   Nova cantica,[12]

      In heaven the bells are ringing

   In Regis curia.[13]

   O that we were there!

vv. 1, 2, 4 fourteenth-century
v. 3 Valentin Triller (d.1573)
(Praetorius, 1607)

tr. editors

[4] You are Alpha and Omega.   [5] O infant Jesus   [6] O best of boys   [7] O Prince of Glory, draw me after you [to heaven]
[8] O love of the Father! O mercy of the Son!   [9] through our sins   [10] the joys of heaven   [11] Where are joys(?)
[12] new songs   [13] in the courts of the King

III

2 Good Christian men, rejoice
With heart and soul, and voice!
Now ye hear of endless bliss:
Joy! joy!
Jesus Christ was born for this!
He hath oped the heavenly door,
And man is blessèd evermore:
Christ was born for this!

3 Good Christian men, rejoice
With heart and soul, and voice!
Now ye need not fear the grave:
Peace! peace!
Jesus Christ was born to save!
Calls you one and calls you all,
To gain his everlasting hall:
Christ was born to save!

English version by J. M. Neale (1818–66)

In 1328 the German Dominican monk Heinrich Seuse (Suso) described how one night he had a vision in which he joined angels singing and dancing this carol. He does not suggest that the song was unknown to him, and this account follows others in which heavenly musicians perform known plainchant antiphons, responsories, etc. Though the earliest manuscript source of the carol is from the end of that century, Suso's autobiography tells us that some version must have existed by then. Bach's setting (originally in F) is probably from a lost cantata.

PERFORMANCE I (*i*) voices, with instruments *ad lib*; (*ii*) voices and organ. II, choir and organ. III, choir. II may be sung a little higher: Bach set it in A, with a sounding pitch about a semitone lower than modern pitch. In setting III, the fourth line of each stanza (bar 7) was written to fit a mistranscription from *Piae Cantiones*.

30

Vom Himmel hoch, da komm' ich her
From highest heaven I come to tell

(*Christmas*)

I

Martin Luther (*1483–1546*)
(*arr. Michael Praetorius, 1571–1621*)

1. 'Vom Him-mel hoch, da komm' ich her, ich bring' euch gu-e neu-e Mär,
1. 'From high-est heaven I come to tell The glad-dest news that e'er be-fell;

der gu-ten Mär bring' ich so viel, da-von ich sing'n und sa-gen will.
These ti-dings true to you I bring, And glad-ly of them say and sing.

II

Martin Luther (*1483–1546*)
(*arr. J. S. Bach, 1685–1750*)

1. 'Vom Him-mel hoch, da komm' ich her, ich bring' euch gu-te neu-e Mär, der
1. 'From high-est heaven I come to tell The glad-dest news that e'er be-fell; These

gu-ten Mär bring' ich so viel, da-von ich sing'n und sa-gen will.
ti-dings true to you I bring, And glad-ly of them say and sing.

2 'Euch ist ein Kindlein heut' gebor'n
   von einer Jungfrau, auserkor'n;
   ein Kindelein so zart und fein,
   das soll eu'r Freud' und Wonne sein.

3 'Es ist der Herr Christ unser Gott,
   der will euch führ'n aus aller Not,
   er will eu'r Heiland selber sein,
   von allen Sünden machen rein.

4 'Er bringt euch alle Seligkeit,
   die Gott, der Vater, hat bereit',
   dass ihr mit uns im Himmelreich
   sollt leben nun und ewiglich.

5 'So merket nun das Zeichen recht,
   die Krippen, Windelein so schlecht:
   Da findet ihr das Kind gelegt,
   das alle Welt erhält und trägt.'

6 Des lasst uns alle fröhlich sein
   und mit den Hirten geh'n hinein,
   zu seh'n, was Gott uns hat beschert,
   mit seinem lieben Sohn verehrt.

7 Merk auf, mein Herz, und sieh dort hin:
   Was liegt doch in dem Krippelein?
   Was ist das schöne Kindelein?
   Es ist das liebe Jesulein.

8 Sei uns willkomm'n, du edler Gast!
   Den Sünder nicht verschmähet hast
   und kommst ins Elend her zu mir,
   wie soll ich immer danken dir?

2 'To you today is given a Child,
   Born of a chosen virgin mild;
   That blessèd Child, so sweet and kind,
   Shall give you joy and peace of mind.

3 ''Tis Christ, our Lord and God indeed,
   Your help and stay in every need;
   Your Saviour he is come to be,
   From every sin to set you free.

4 'All blessèdness to you he bears
   Which God the Father's love prepares;
   The heavenly kingdom ye shall gain,
   And now and ever with us reign.

5 'Now hear the sign, and mark with care
   The swaddling clothes and crib so bare;
   There shall ye find this Infant laid
   Who all the world upholds and made.'

6 Then let us all our gladness show,
   And with the joyful shepherds go
   To see what God for us hath done,
   In sending us his glorious Son.

7 Awake, my soul! my heart, behold
   Who lieth in that manger cold!
   Who is this lovely baby boy?
   'Tis Jesus Christ, our only joy.

8 Now welcome, ever-blessèd guest,
   To sinful souls with guilt oppressed;
   In mercy come to our distress!
   How can we thank thy gentleness?

(continued overleaf)

(I)

9. Ach Herr, du Schö-pfer al - ler Ding', wie bist du 'wor-den so ge - ring,
9. Ah, Lord, who all things didst cre - ate, How cam'st thou to this poor es - tate,

dass du da liegst auf dür - rem Gras, da - von ein Rind und E - sel ass.
To make the hay and straw thy bed, Where-on the ox and ass— are fed?

(II)

9. Ach Herr, du Schö-pfer al - ler Ding', wie bist du 'wor-den so— ge - ring, dass
9. Ah, Lord, who all— things didst cre - ate, How cam'st thou to this poor es - tate, To—

du da— liegst auf— dür - rem— Gras, da - von ein— Rind und E - sel— ass.
make the— hay— and— straw thy— bed, Where - on— the— ox— and— ass— are— fed?

10 Und wär' die Welt vielmal so weit,
von Edelstein und Gold bereit',
so wär' sie doch dir viel zu klein,
zu sein ein enges Wiegelein.

11 Der Sammet und die Seiden dein,
das ist grob' Heu und Windelein,
darauf du Kön'g, so gross und reich,
her prangst als wär's dein Himmelreich.

12 Das hat also gefallen dir,
die Wahrheit anzuzeigen mir:
Wie aller Welt Macht, Ehr' und Gut
vor dir nichts gilt, nichts hilft noch tut.

13 Ach, mein herzliebes Jesulein,
mach dir ein rein sanft' Bettelein,
zu ruh'n in meines Herzens Schrein,
dass ich nimmer vergesse dein'!

14 Davon ich all'zeit fröhlich sei,
zu springen, singen immer frei
das rechte Susaninne schon,
mit Herzen Lust den süssen Ton.

15 Lob, Ehr' sei Gott im höchsten Thron,
der uns schenkt' seinen ein'gen Sohn;
des freuen sich der Engel Schar'
und singen uns solch's neues Jahr.

Martin Luther (1483–1546),
modernized

10 Nay, were the world ten times so wide,
With gold and gems on every side,
Yet were it all too small to be
A narrow cradle, Lord, for thee.

11 Thy samite and thy silk array
Are swathing-bands and coarsest hay
Which thou, O King, dost bathe with light
As though enthroned in heaven bright.

12 And all this woe hath come to thee
That thou might'st show the truth to me;
For all the power and wealth of earth
To thee are vile and nothing worth.

13 Ah, Jesu, my heart's treasure blest,
Make thee a clean, soft cradle-nest
And rest enshrined within my heart,
That I from thee may never part.

14 So shall I ever more rejoice,
And dance and sing with heart and voice
The truest lullaby e'er known,
A song of love, of sweetest tone.

15 To God on high all praise be done
Who gave for us his only Son
Whose birth the angels carol clear
And sing us all a glad New Year.

vv. 1–2, 4–13 tr. H. R. Bramley (1833–1917), adapted
vv. 3, 14–15 tr. editors

Luther wrote this hymn for his own family celebration of Christmas Eve, to be sung to the folk-song 'Ich komm aus fremden Landen her' (setting III in *NOBC*). The grander tune given here was probably composed by Luther himself.

PERFORMANCE I, voices and organ with instruments *ad lib.*
    II, choir and organ; or as in the *Christmas Oratorio* (with instrumental interludes between each line).

See *NOBC* for *Christum wir sollen loben schon* (no. 61).

31

Als ich bei meinen Schafen wacht'
While by my sheep I watched at night

I

(*Auserlesene catholische geistliche Kirchengesänge*, 1623, *arr. editors*)

(*Christmas*)

1. Als ich bei mei - nen Scha - fen wacht', ein En - gel mir die
1. While by my sheep I watched at night, Glad ti - dings brought an

Bot - schaft bracht'. *Des bin ich froh, bin ich froh, froh, froh,*
an - gel bright. *†Then all be - low, all be - low, Sing i -*

froh!
- o! *o, o, o! Be-ne-di - ca-mus Do - mi - no, be-ne-di - ca-mus Do - mi - no.*

† See notes

2 Er sagt', es soll geboren sein
zu Bethlehem ein Kindelein.
Des bin ich froh, (etc.)

2 'For you,' he said, 'this blessèd morn
In Bethlehem a Child is born.'
Then all below / How great my joy! (etc.)

3 Er sagt', das Kind liegt dort im Stall
und soll die Welt erlösen all'.

3 'Go where he lies within a stall,
The infant Redeemer of us all.'

4 Als ich das Kind im Stall geseh'n,
nicht wohl konnt' ich von dannen geh'n.

4 There in the stall he sleeping lay;
There by his side I longed to stay.

5 Das Kind zu mir sein' Äuglein wandt',
mein Herz gab ich in seine Hand.

5 Sweetly he gazed into my face:
I in his hands my heart did place.

6 Demütig küsst' ich seine Füss',
davon mein Mund ward zuckersüss.

6 Gently I kissed his tiny feet,
Which to my lips were honey-sweet.

7 Als ich heimging, das Kind wollt' mit
und wollt' von mir abweichen nit.

7 Then to my home I made my way:
Yet still that Child with me did stay.

8 Das Kind legt' sich an meine Brust
und macht' mir da all' Herzenslust.

8 Within my arms that Child did rest:
Oh! how my heart with love was blest.

9 Den Schatz muss ich bewahren wohl,
so bleibt mein Herz der Freuden voll.

9 Close shall I guard this darling Boy,
Thus shall my heart be filled with joy.

c.1500?
(*Auserlesene catholische geistliche
Kirchengesänge, 1623, modernized*)

v. 1 tr. Theodore Baker (1848–1934)
vv. 2–9 tr. editors

II

(*Christmas*)

Seventeenth-century
(Trier Gesangbuch, 1871, arr. editors)

VERSE

1. Als ich bei mei - nen Scha - fen wacht', ein En - gel mir_____ die
1. While by my sheep_____ I watched at night, Glad ti - dings brought_____ an

REFRAIN

FULL ECHO FULL ECHO

Bot-schaft bracht'. *Des bin ich froh, bin ich froh, froh, froh, froh! o, o,*
an - gel bright. †*How great my joy, great my joy! Joy, joy, joy! joy, joy,*

FULL ECHO

o! Be - ne - di - ca - mus Do - mi - no, be - ne - di - ca - mus Do - mi - no.
joy! *Praise to the Lord in heaven on high! Praise to the Lord in heaven on high!*

† See notes

2 Er sagt', es soll geboren sein
zu Bethlehem ein Kindelein.
Des bin ich froh, (etc.)

3 Er sagt', das Kind liegt dort im Stall
und soll die Welt erlösen all'.

4 Als ich das Kind im Stall geseh'n,
nicht wohl konnt' ich von dannen geh'n.

5 Das Kind zu mir sein' Äuglein wandt',
mein Herz gab ich in seine Hand.

6 Demütig küsst' ich seine Füss',
davon mein Mund ward zuckersüss.

7 Als ich heimging, das Kind wollt' mit
und wollt' von mir abweichen nit.

8 Das Kind legt' sich an meine Brust
und macht' mir da all' Herzenslust.

9 Den Schatz muss ich bewahren wohl,
so bleibt mein Herz der Freuden voll.

c.1500?
(*Auserlesene catholische geistliche
Kirchengesänge, 1623, modernized*)

2 'For you,' he said, 'this blessèd morn
In Bethlehem a Child is born.'
Then all below / How great my joy! (etc.)

3 'Go where he lies within a stall,
The infant Redeemer of us all.'

4 There in the stall he sleeping lay;
There by his side I longed to stay.

5 Sweetly he gazed into my face:
I in his hands my heart did place.

6 Gently I kissed his tiny feet,
Which to my lips were honey-sweet.

7 Then to my home I made my way:
Yet still that Child with me did stay.

8 Within my arms that Child did rest:
Oh! how my heart with love was blest.

9 Close shall I guard this darling Boy,
Thus shall my heart be filled with joy.

*v. 1 tr. Theodore Baker (1848–1934)
vv. 2–9 tr. editors*

Setting I replaced the undistinguished chorale tune to which this text was sung in the sixteenth century; it may have originated in a shepherd play, perhaps with an off-stage echo. Though the 1623 source gives no accidentals in bars 1 and 3, they are found in subsequent seventeenth-century books, and were almost certainly always sung.

Setting II presents a later version of the tune, which is the basis of the carol as sung in the US.

We provide two different English refrains (one underlaid in each setting), both free imitations of the German.

PERFORMANCE I (*i*) two solo voices, with or without organ or other instruments; (*ii*) choir(s). Ideally there should be two separated groups.

II, voices and organ.

See *NOBC* for *Es steht ein' Lind' im Himmelreich* (no. 63).

32

Vom Himmel hoch, o Engel, kommt!
Come, angels, come! from heaven, appear!

(*Christmas*)

(*Auserlesene catholische geistliche Kirchengesänge, 1623, arr. editors*)

1. Vom Him - mel hoch, o En - gel, kommt! E - ia!
1. Come, an - gels, come! from heaven, ap - pear!

e - ia! Su - sa - ni, su - sa - ni, su - sa - ni! Kommt
Come

singt und klingt, kommt pfeift und trombt! Hal - le - lu - ja, hal -
sing, come pipe, come trum - pet here! Al - le - lu - ia, al -

-le - lu - ja! Von Je - sus singt und Ma - ri - a.
-le - lu - ia! Et in ex - cel - sis glo - ri - a!

2 Kommt ohne Instrumenten nit,
   Eia, (etc.)
bringt Lauten, Harfen, Geigen mit!
   Halleluja, (etc.)

3 Lasst hören euer Stimmen viel
mit Orgel und mit Saitenspiel!

4 Hier muss die Musik himmlisch sein,
weil dies ein himmlisch' Kindelein.

5 Die Stimmen müssen lieblich gehn
und Tag und Nacht nicht stille stehn.

6 Sehr süss muss sein der Orgel Klang,
süss über allen Vögelsang.

7 Das Lautenspiel muss lauten süss,
davon das Kindlein schlafen müss'.

8 Sing Fried' den Menschen weit und breit,
Gott Preis und Ehr' in Ewigkeit.

    (*Auserlesene catholische geistliche
    Kirchengesänge, 1623, modernized*)

2 Your instruments of music bring:
   Eia, (etc.)
The lute and harp, and bowèd string!
   Alleluia, (etc.)

3 Let strings and organ all agree
To weave a solemn harmony.

4 Celestial music sound on high,
For here a heavenly Child doth lie!

5 Your angel voices gently blend
In psalms and songs that have no end.

6 Let sweetest organ-tones be heard,
More sweet than any singing-bird!

7 With softest touch let lutes reply,
To soothe the Child with lullaby.

8 Sing peace to men, where'er they be:
Sing praise to God eternally!

    tr. editors

The custom of cradle-rocking was particularly popular in Germany (see Introduction). The cradle would stand before the altar, and at Christmas vespers and matins the priest would rock it to a triple-time *Wiegenlied* (cradle-song). 'Eia' (in this context meaning 'hush') and 'susani' (from the Low German 'Suse, Ninne!'—'Sleep, child!') would be devoutly addressed to the Christ-child.

PERFORMANCE (*i*) Choir, with instruments and/or organ *ad lib.*; (*ii*) solo voice with instruments and/or organ; (*iii*) voices and organ.

33

Ein Kindlein in der Wiegen
He smiles within his cradle

(Christmas)

Traditional?
(Corner, 1649, arr. editors)

1. Ein Kind - lein in der Wie - gen, ein klei - nes Kin - de -
1. He smiles with - in his cra - dle, A babe with face__ so

-lein;____ das glei - sset wie ein Spie - gel nach a - de -
bright;____ It beams most like a mir - ror A - gainst a

-li - chem Schein,____ das klei - ne Kin - de - lein.
blaze__ of light:____ This babe__ so burn - ing bright.

2 Das Kindlein, das wir meinen,
   das heisst: Herr Jesu Christ,
   das verleih' uns Fried' und Einigkeit
   wohl hie zu dieser Frist,
   das geb' uns Jesu Christ!

3 Und wer das Kindlein will wiegen,
   das kleine Kindelein,
   der muss das nicht betrüben,
   er muss demüthig sein
   mit Maria der Jungfrau rein!

4 O Jesu, liebstes Kindelein,
   du kleines Kindelein,
   wie gross ist es, die Liebe dein!
   Schleuss' in das Herze mein
   die grosse Liebe dein!

Fourteenth-century?
(Corner, 1649)

2 This babe we now declare to you
   Is Jesus Christ our Lord;
   He brings both peace and heartiness:
   Haste, haste with one accord
   To feast with Christ our Lord.

3 And who would rock the cradle
   Wherein this Infant lies,
   Must rock with easy motion
   And watch with humble eyes,
   Like Mary pure and wise.

4 O Jesus, dearest Babe of all
   And dearest Babe of mine,
   Thy love is great, thy limbs are small.
   O, flood this heart of mine
   With overflow from thine!

tr. Robert Graves (1895–1985)

Both words and tune come from the *Geistliche Nachtigall der Catholischen Teutschen* ('Spiritual Nightingale of the Catholic Germans') of David Gregor Corner (1585–1648), published in Vienna in 1649. The melody may well be a folk tune and the text is thought to date from the fourteenth century. The references to rocking the cradle may mean that the carol was specifically connected with the cradle-rocking custom that played a prominent part in German Christmas services (see previous item).

PERFORMANCE (*i*) Solo voice and continuo; (*ii*) choir, with organ *ad lib.*

34

Es ist ein Roess entsprungen
Of Jesse's line descended
Es ist ein Reis entsprungen
A great and mighty wonder

I

(Christmas)

Sixteenth-century?
(Praetorius, 1609)

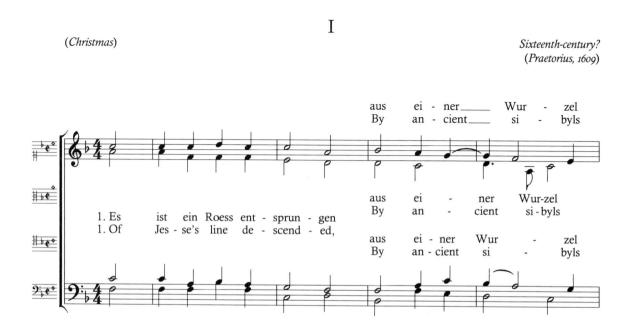

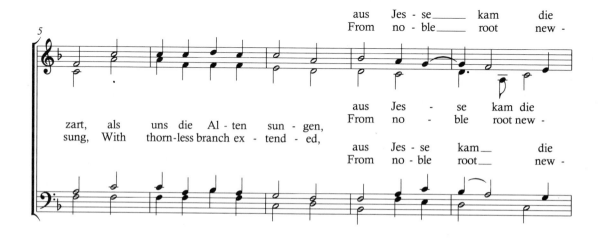

2 Das Roesslein, das ich meine,
    darvon Esaias sagt,
  hat uns gebracht alleine
    Mary die reine Magd
  aus Gottes ewgem Raht
  hat sie ein Kind gebohren
  bleibend ein reine Magd.

3 Das Blümelein so kleine,
    das duftet uns so süss;
  mit seinem hellen Scheine
    vertreibts die Finsternis:
  wahr Mensch und wahrer Gott,
  hilft uns aus allem Leide,
  rettet von Sünd und Tod.

2 That Flower of ancient splendour,
    Of which Isaiah spake,
  Mary, the Rose-branch tender,
    Puts forth for mankind's sake;
  Obedient to God's will,
  A little Child she bears us,
  Yet is a maiden still.

3 The frozen air perfuming,
    That tiny Bloom doth swell;
  Its rays, the night illuming,
    The darkness quite dispel.
  O Flower beyond compare,
  Bloom in our hearts' midwinter:
  Restore the springtime there!

vv. 1, 2 fifteenth-century? (Praetorius, 1609)
v. 3 Friedrich Layritz (1808–59)

Free tr., editors

Alternative translation

1 Lo! how a Rose, e'er blooming,
   From tender stem hath sprung,
Of Jesse's lineage coming
   As seers of old have sung;
It came, a blossom bright,
Amid the cold of winter
When half-spent was the night.

2 Isaiah 'twas foretold it,
   The Rose I have in mind;
With Mary we behold it,
   The Virgin Mother kind:
To show God's love aright
She bore to us a Saviour
When half-spent was the night.

3 O Flower, whose fragrance tender
   With sweetness fills the air,
Dispel in glorious splendour
   The darkness everywhere;
True man, yet very God,
From sin and death now save us
And share our every load.

vv. 1, 2 tr. Theodore Baker (1851–1934)
v. 3 tr. Harriet R. K. Spaeth (1845–1925)

II

(Annunciation; Christmas)

1 Es ist ein Reis entsprungen
   aus einer Wurzel zart,
wie uns die Alten sungen;
   von Jesse kam die Art
und hat ein Blümlein bracht
mitten im kalten Winter
wohl zu der halben Nacht.

2 Das Reislein, das ich meine,
   so uns das Blümlein bringt,
Maria ists, die Reine,
   von der Jesaias singt;
nach Gottes ewgem Rath
hat sie ein Kind geboren
und bleibt doch reine Magd.

TRANSLATION 1 A branch has sprung up from a tender root, as the ancients sang to us [foretold]. The plant rises from Jesse and has produced a flower in the cold midwinter and in the dead of night.
2 The dear branch of which I tell, which brings forth the beloved flower, is the Virgin Mary, of whom Isaiah sings; complying with God's eternal will, she has given birth to a child and yet remains a pure maiden.

3 It was truly described for us by the trusty hand of Luke how the angel Gabriel was sent from heaven to a pure virgin whom God chose for himself to be his mother.
4 The willing angel came into the land of Jewry, to Nazareth; there, unconcealed, he found Mary in her chamber. He cheerfully addressed her thus: 'Hail, pure virgin!

3　Das schrieb uns ohne Mängel
　　　Lucas mit treuer Hand,
　　wie Gabriel der Engel
　　　vom Himmel ward gesandt
　　zu einer Jungfrau rein,
　　die Gott sich auserwählte,
　　sie sollt ihm Mutter sein.

4　Der Engel unverdrossen
　　　fuhr in der Juden Land
　　gen Nazareth; verschlossen
　　　Marien er da fand
　　in ihrem Kämmerlein.
　　Er sprach sie an so freundlich:
　　'Gegrüsst sei, Jungfrau rein,

5　'du bist voll aller Gnaden,
　　　der Herr will mit dir sein,
　　hoch über aller Frauen
　　　will er dich benedein.'
　　Die edle Jungfrau zart,
　　von dieses Engels Grüssen
　　wie sie erschrocken ward!

6　'Du sollst dich nicht entsetzen,'
　　　sprach er, 'o Jungfrau schon!
　　Mein Wort lass dich ergetzen,
　　　ich komm aus Himmels Thron,
　　bring frohe Botschaft dir.
　　Du hast bei Gott Genade
　　gefunden, glaube mir.'

7　'Ein Kindlein wirst du tragen
　　　in deinem keuschen Leib,
　　davon die Schriften sagen,
　　　du überselig Weib!
　　sein Nam ist Jesus Christ:
　　der Herr will ihm verleihen
　　seines Vaters David Sitz.'

8　Da sprach die Jungfrau reine
　　　gar züchtig mit Verstand:
　　'Wie soll mir das geschehen,
　　　die keinen Mann erkannt?'
　　Der Engel sprach zu ihr:
　　'Diess Wunder wird verschaffen
　　der heilge Geist an dir.

9　'Es wird dich überschatten
　　　des Allerhöchsten Kraft
　　und unverletzt bewahren
　　　deine reine Jungfrauschaft,
　　denn dieses Kindlein schon,
　　das von dir wird geboren,
　　ist Gottes ewger Sohn.'

10　Da sprach mit Freud und Wonne
　　　die edle Jungfrau rein,
　　als sie vernahm, sie solle
　　　des Herren Mutter sein,
　　gar willig, unverzagt:
　　'Ich bin des Herren Dienerin,
　　mir gescheh wie du gesagt.'

5 'Thou art full of all grace; the Lord wishes to be with you. High above all women he wishes to glorify you.' The noble, tender virgin, by this angelic greeting how startled she was!

6 'Be not afraid,' he said, 'fair virgin! Rejoice at my words! I come from the throne of heaven to bring you good tidings. You have found favour with God, believe me.

7 'You shall bear a child within your chaste body, as the scriptures foretold, you highly favoured maiden! His name is Jesus Christ: the Lord will grant him the seat of his father, David.'

8 Then spoke the pure virgin, most modestly and with understanding: 'How may this happen to me who have known no man?' The angel replied: 'This wonder will the Holy Spirit accomplish upon you.

9 'The power of the Most High will overshadow you, and preserve intact your pure virginity, for this wondrous Child which shall be born of you is God's eternal Son.'

10 Then, with joy and rapture, the noble virgin spoke, perceiving that she was truly to be the mother of the Lord, utterly meek and undismayed: 'I am the handmaid of the Lord: as you have spoken, so may it happen to me.'

11 Aus heilgen Geistes Kräften
   Maria bald empfieng
den ewgen Himmelsfürsten:
   schau an das Wunderding!
Neun Mond er bei ihr war;
sie wurde Gottes Mutter,
blieb Jungfrau immerdar.

12 Wohl zu denselben Zeiten
   der starke Fürst und Held
Augustus, Römscher Kaiser,
   beschrieb die ganze Welt,
den Zins von Allem nahm,
da Joseph mit Maria
auch hin gen Bethlem kam.

13 Herbergen waren theuer,
   sich fand kein Aufenhalt
als eine alte Scheuer;
   da war die Luft gar kalt.
Wohl in derselben Nacht
Marie gebar den Fürsten,
der Frieden hat gebracht.

14 Lob, Ehr sei Gott dem Vater,
   dem Sohn und heilgen Geist;
Maria, Gottes Mutter,
   auch deine Hülfe leist
und bitt dein Kindelein,
dass Gott durch seine Güte
uns gnädig will verzeihn.

15 Wir bitten dich von Herzen,
   du edle Königin,
bei deines Sohnes Schmerzen,
   wenn wir einst fahren hin
aus diesem Jammerthal;
du wollest uns geleiten
bis in der Engel Saal.

16 So singen wir all' 'Amen!'
   das heisst: 'Nun werd' es wahr,
dass wir begehrn allsammen:'
   O Jesu, hilf uns dar
in deines Vaters Reich!
Darin wolln wir dich loben:
O Gott, uns das verleih!

Fifteenth-century?
(vv. 1–15 Simrock, 1865,
v. 16 Alte catholische
geistliche Kirchengesänge, 1599)

11 By the power of the Holy Spirit Mary directly received the eternal Prince of Heaven: behold a wonder! Nine months did he remain within her; she was made the Mother of God, yet remained eternally a virgin.

12 At this same time the powerful prince and hero Augustus, Emperor of Rome, made a census of the whole world, that everyone might be taxed; and so Joseph, with Mary, made his way towards Bethlehem.

13 Inns were costly; no lodging was to be found except an old stable, where the air was very cold. In that selfsame night Mary bore the Prince who has brought peace.

14 Praise and glory be to the Father, the Son, and the Holy Spirit. Mary, God's mother, lend your aid, too, and beg of your dear Child that God through his goodness may mercifully pardon us.

15 From the heart we beg you, O noble Queen, through the sufferings of your Son, that when we at last depart from this vale of tears you will conduct us into the angelic mansions.

16 So sing we all 'Amen!' That is: 'Would that it were so, what we beg of you altogether.' O Jesu, assist us unto your Father's kingdom! There will we praise you: O God, grant us this!

III

(Christmas)

1 A great and mighty wonder,
   A full and holy cure!
   The Virgin bears the Infant
   With virgin-honour pure.
   Repeat the hymn again:
   'To God on high be glory,
   And peace on earth to men!'

2 The Word becomes incarnate
   And yet remains on high!
   And cherubim sing anthems
   To shepherds, from the sky.

4 Since all he comes to ransom,
   By all is he adored,
   The Infant born in Bethlehem,
   The Saviour and the Lord.

3 While thus they sing your Monarch,
   Those bright angelic bands,
   Rejoice, ye vales and mountains,
   Ye oceans, clap your hands!

5 And idol forms shall perish,
   And error shall decay,
   And Christ shall wield his sceptre,
   Our Lord and God, for ay.

St Germanus (634–c.733)
tr. J. M. Neale (1818–66)

Both words and melody are believed to have originated in the diocese of Trier in the fifteenth or early sixteenth century as a Christmas or Twelfth Night folk carol. The text is found in many different forms, with as many as twenty-three verses. The structure suggests that, like so many folk-songs and carols, it may have grown through a succession of accretions.

In medieval iconography, the tree of Jesse is often depicted as a rose plant. The messianic prophecy of Isaiah 12 declares that 'There shall come forth a rod out of the stem of Jesse, and a branch shall grow out of his roots.' A rod/branch (the Virgin Mary) will grow from the stem/root of Jesse (father of King David and patriarch of Christ's genealogy in popular medieval forms) and will bear a 'little flower' (the Christ-child). It is not clear whether *Ros'* (rose) or *Reis* (branch) was the original reading of line 1.

Text I is the shorter version, as found in many German hymn-books. We have given a free translation of the last three lines that is more in the spirit of the other verses; Layritz's text may be translated thus: 'True man, true God, we crave / That thou from ills defend us, / From sin and death us save!'

Text III has no connection with the German, but is an adaptation of Neale's translation of a hymn from the Greek liturgy for Christmas Day.

PERFORMANCE *(i)* Choir; *(ii)* voices, with organ and/or instruments *ad lib.* Various shortened versions of text II are possible: verses 1, 2, 14–16; 1–11, 14–16; 1–5, 7, 8, 10, 11, 14; 1–3, 11–14 or 11–16.

35

O Jesulein süss! o Jesulein mild!
O Little One sweet! O Little One mild!

I

(Christmas)

Seventeenth-century
(arr. Samuel Scheidt, 1587–1654)

1. O Je - su-lein süss! o Je - su-lein mild! Deines Va - ters Willen hast
1. O Lit - tle One sweet! O Lit - tle One mild! Thy Fa - ther's will thou

du___ er - füllt; bist kom - men aus dem Him - mel - reich, uns
hast___ ful - filled; Thou hast come down from heaven's bright sphere To

ar - men Men-schen wor - den gleich, o Je - su-lein süss! o Je - su-lein mild!
be like us poor mor - tals here. O Lit - tle One sweet! O Lit - tle One mild!

2 O Jesulein süss! o Jesulein mild!
   Deins Vaters Zorn hast du gestillt,
   du zahlst für uns all unser Schuld,
   und bringst uns hin deins Vaters Huld,
   o Jesulein süss! o Jesulein mild!

2 O Little One sweet! O Little One mild!
   Thy Father's anger hast thou stilled;
   Our guilt thou bearest in our place,
   To win for us thy Father's grace.
   O Little One sweet! O Little One mild!

3 O Jesulein süss! o Jesulein mild!
   Mit Freuden hast du die Welt erfüllt,
   du kommst herab vom Himmelssaal,
   und trostst uns in dem Jammerthal,
   o Jesulein süss! o Jesulein mild!

3 O Little One sweet! O Little One mild!
   With joy thy birth the world has filled;
   From heaven thou comest to men below
   To comfort us in all our woe.
   O Little One sweet! O Little One mild!

4 O Jesulein süss! o Jesulein mild!
   Sei unser Schirm und unser Schild,
   wir bitten durch dein Geburt im Stall,
   beschütz uns all vor Sündenfall,
   o Jesulein süss! o Jesulein mild!

4 O Little One sweet! O Little One mild!
   Be thou our guard, be thou our shield;
   By this thy birth we humbly pray:
   O keep us free from sin this day.
   O Little One sweet! O Little One mild!

5 O Jesulein süss! o Jesulein mild!
   Du bist der Lieb ein Ebenbild,
   zünd an in uns der Liebe Flamm,
   dass wir dich lieben allzusamm,
   o Jesulein süss! o Jesulein mild!

5 O Little One sweet! O Little One mild!
   In thee love's beauties are all distilled;
   O light in us love's ardent flame,
   That we may give thee back the same.
   O Little One sweet! O Little One mild!

6 O Jesulein süss, o Jesulein mild!
   Hilf, dass wir thun alls, was du willt,
   was unser ist, ist Alles dein,
   ach lass uns dir befohlen seyn,
   o Jesulein süss! o Jesulein mild!

6 O Little One sweet! O Little One mild!
   Help us to do as thou hast willed.
   Lo! all we have belongs to thee;
   Ah, keep us in our fealty!
   O Little One sweet! O Little One mild!

(Schemelli, 1736)

vv. 1–4 tr. editors
vv. 5, 6 tr. Percy Dearmer (1867–1936), adapted

II

(Christmas)

1. O__ Je - su - lein__ süss!__ o__ Je - su - lein__ mild! Deines Va - ters__
1. O__ Lit - tle One sweet!__ O__ Lit - tle One mild! Thy Fa - ther's

Willen_____ hast du__ er - füllt; bist__ kom - men aus__ dem
will_____ thou hast__ ful - filled; Thou hast__ come down__ from

Him - mel - reich, uns__ ar - men Men - schen wor - den
heaven's__ bright sphere To__ be__ like us__ poor mor - tals

gleich, o Je - su - lein__ süss! o Je - su - lein mild!
here. O Lit - tle__ One__ sweet! O Lit - tle__ One mild!

o_____ Je - su - lein mild!
O_____ Lit - tle One mild!

2   O Jesulein süss! o Jesulein mild!
Deins Vaters Zorn hast du gestillt,
du zahlst für uns all unser Schuld,
und bringst uns hin deins Vaters Huld,
o Jesulein süss! o Jesulein mild!

2   O Little One sweet! O Little One mild!
Thy Father's anger hast thou stilled;
Our guilt thou bearest in our place,
To win for us thy Father's grace.
O Little One sweet! O Little One mild!

3   O Jesulein süss! o Jesulein mild!
Mit Freuden hast du die Welt erfüllt,
du kommst herab vom Himmelssaal,
und trostst uns in dem Jammerthal,
o Jesulein süss! o Jesulein mild!

3   O Little One sweet! O Little One mild!
With joy thy birth the world has filled;
From heaven thou comest to men below
To comfort us in all our woe.
O Little One sweet! O Little One mild!

4   O Jesulein süss! o Jesulein mild!
Sei unser Schirm und unser Schild,
wir bitten durch dein Geburt im Stall,
beschütz uns all vor Sündenfall,
o Jesulein süss! o Jesulein mild!

4   O Little One sweet! O Little One mild!
Be thou our guard, be thou our shield;
By this thy birth we humbly pray:
O keep us free from sin this day.
O Little One sweet! O Little One mild!

5   O Jesulein süss! o Jesulein mild!
Du bist der Lieb ein Ebenbild,
zünd an in uns der Liebe Flamm,
dass wir dich lieben allzusamm,
o Jesulein süss! o Jesulein mild!

5   O Little One sweet! O Little One mild!
In thee love's beauties are all distilled;
O light in us love's ardent flame,
That we may give thee back the same.
O Little One sweet! O Little One mild!

6   O Jesulein süss, o Jesulein mild!
Hilf, dass wir thun alls, was du willt,
was unser ist, ist Alles dein,
ach lass uns dir befohlen seyn,
o Jesulein süss! o Jesulein mild!

6   O Little One sweet! O Little One mild!
Help us to do as thou hast willed.
Lo! all we have belongs to thee;
Ah, keep us in our fealty!
O Little One sweet! O Little One mild!

(Schemelli, 1736)

vv. 1–4 tr. editors
vv. 5, 6 tr. Percy Dearmer (1867–1936), adapted

Scheidt's version of this rocking-carol was intended as a keyboard accompaniment, but is equally suited to choral singing. Bach's setting (II) comes from a hymn-book directed primarily at the domestic market, and was set out for voice with accompanying figured bass. His figuring is so full that the inner parts virtually write themselves.

PERFORMANCE   I (*i*) unison voices and organ; (*ii*) choir and organ.
   II (*i*) solo voice and continuo; (*ii*) choir, with organ *ad lib.*

See *NOBC* for *Wachet auf!* (no. 68) and *Wie schön leuchtet der Morgenstern* (no. 69).

36

Adeste, fideles
O come, all ye faithful

(Latin)

Anon. (*An Essay on the Church Plain Chant, 1782, arr. Thomas Greatorex, 1757–1831, adapted*)

(Christmas)

1. A - de - ste, fi - de - les, Lae - ti, tri - um - phan - tes, Ve - ni - te, ve - ni - te in

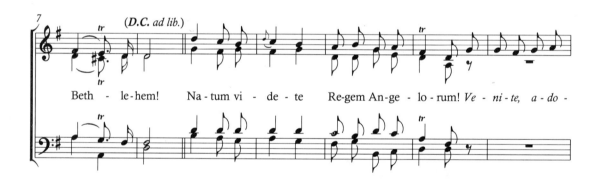

Beth - le-hem! Na - tum vi - de - te Re-gem An-ge - lo - rum! *Ve - ni - te, a - do -*

- re - mus! Ve - ni - te, a - do - re - mus! Ve - ni - te, a - do - re - mus Do - mi - num!

(bb. 21–32 ad lib.;
see performance note)

Na - tum vi - de - te   Re-gem An - ge - lo - rum! Ve - ni - te, a - do - re - mus! Ve -

-ni - te, a - do - re - mus! Ve - ni - te, a - do - re - mus Do - mi - num!

2 ˈDeum de Deo,
  Lumen de Lumine,
  Gestant puellae viscera
  Deum verum, genitum non factum.

  Venite, adoremus! (etc.)

*3 En grege relicto,
    Humiles ad cunas
    Vocati pastores appropriant;
    Et nos ovanti gradu festinemus.

*4 ˈStella duce, Magi,
    Christum adorantes,
    Aurum, thus, et myrrham dant munera;
    Jesu infanti corda praebeamus.

*5 Pro nobis egenum
    Et foeno cubantem,
    Piis foveamus amplexibus;
    Sic nos amantem quis non redamaret?

6 ˈCantet nunc 'Io!'
   Chorus angelorum;
   Cantet nunc aula caelestium:
   † 'Gloria in excelsis Deo!'

7 ˈErgo qui natus
   Die hodierna,
   Jesu, tibi sit gloria,
   Patris aeterni Verbum caro factum.

vv. 1, 2, 6, 7 anon. (eighteenth-century)
vv. 3, 5 Abbé E. J. F. (de) Borderies (1764–1832)
v. 4 anon. (nineteenth-century)

† See performance note.

(English)

Anon. (*An Essay on the
Church Plain Chant, 1782, arr.
Thomas Greatorex, 1757–1831, adapted*)

(*Christmas*)

(*v.1 only*)

1. O come, all ye faith-ful, Joy-ful and tri - um - phant, O come ye, O come ye to

(**D.C.** *ad lib.*)

Beth - le-hem! Come and be - hold him, Born the King of An-gels! *O come, let us a -*

(**Fine** *ad lib.*)

- dore him! O come, let us a - dore him! O come, let us a - dore____ him, Christ__ the Lord!

(*bb. 21–32 ad lib.;
see performance note*)

FULL   SOLI

Come and be - hold him, Born the King of An - gels! O come, let us a - dore him! O

SOLI

come, let us a - dore him! O come, let us a - dore_____ him, Christ_ the Lord!

2 ⁷⟋God of God,
   Light of Light,
   Lo! he abhors not the Virgin's womb;
   Very God,
   Begotten, not created.
      O come, let us adore him! (etc.)

*3 ⁷⟋See how the shepherds
   Summoned to his cradle,
   Leaving their flocks, draw nigh to gaze!
   We, too, will thither
   Bend our hearts' oblations.

*4 ⁷⟋Lo, star-led chieftains,
   Magi, Christ adoring,
   Offer him incense, gold and myrrh;
   We to the Christ-child
   Bring our hearts' oblations.

*5 ⁷⟋Child, for us sinners,
   Poor and in the manger,
   Fain we embrace thee with love and awe;
   Who would not love thee,
   Loving us so dearly?

6 ⁷⟋Sing, choirs of angels!
   Sing in exultation!
   Sing, all ye citizens of heaven above:
   'Glory to God
   In the highest.'

7 ⁷⟋Yea, Lord, we greet thee,
   Born this happy morning;
   Jesu, to thee be glory given,
   Word of the Father
   Now in flesh appearing.

vv. 1, 2, 6, 7 tr. F. Oakeley (1802–80), adapted
vv. 3, 4, 5 tr. W. T. Brooke (1848–1917), adapted

The complex origins of both the words and tune of this universally loved hymn for Christmas Day lie in English Catholic circles of the 1740s. It survives in different versions (in duple and in triple time) in several manuscripts copied by John Francis Wade, and was published in an anonymous *Essay on the Church Plain Chant* in 1782 (see *NOBC*, setting II, not included here). Wider popularity came from a performance at an 'Antient Concert' in 1795: we have adapted the arrangement for soloists and orchestra which Greatorex made for that occasion. Verses 3–5 are later additions and may be omitted.

PERFORMANCE (*i*) SATB soloists, choir, and organ (orchestra in the original). Bars 1–8 are sung first by one soloist (the other soloists taking subsequent verses in turn) and then repeated by all four; the four soloists sing bars 9–20, the written-out repeat (bars 21–32) being sung by full choir and organ (a congregation or concert audience could join in the full section); (*ii*) choir or four soloists, with congregation taking the repeats; (*iii*) voices and organ, without repeats. *NOBC* includes an editorial organ ritornello which may be used with any of these schemes. Ornaments should be sung by soloists or small groups only.

   In verse 4 Greatorex has a fermata at bar 19, perhaps implying a short cadenza by (some of) the soloists; and in the same verse, in the repeat (bar 31) he writes *Adagio*—doubled note lengths might be best (*a tempo* at the editorial ritornello). In verse 6 Greatorex sets the last line as 'Gloria in excelsis, in excelsis Deo', with ♪ ♪♪ on 'Gloria'.

37

Christians, awake!

(Christmas)

John Wainwright *(c.1723–68)*
(arr. editors)

1. Christ - ians, a - wake! Sa - lute the hap - py morn Where - on the Sa - viour of the World was born! Rise to a - dore the my - ste - ry of__ love Which hosts of an - gels chant - ed from a - bove; With them the joy - ful ti - dings first be - gun Of

God in - car - nate and the Vir - gin's Son.

2 Unto the watchful shepherds it was told,
Who heard the angelic herald's voice: 'Behold!
I bring good tidings of a Saviour's birth
To you and all the nations of the earth:
This day hath God fulfilled his promised word,
This day is born a Saviour, Christ the Lord!

*3 'In David's city, shepherds, ye shall find
The long-foretold Redeemer of mankind;
Joseph and Mary, in a stable there,
Guard the sole object of the Almighty's care;
Wrapped up in swaddling-clothes, the Babe divine
Lies in a manger: this shall be your sign.'

*4 He spake, and straightway the celestial choir
In hymns of joy, unknown before, conspire.
The praises of redeeming love they sung,
And heaven's whole orb with Hallelujahs rung;
God's highest glory was their anthem still,
Peace on the earth, and mutual good will.

5 To Bethlehem straight the enlightened shepherds ran
To see the wonder God had wrought for man,
And found, with Joseph and the blessèd Maid,
Her Son, the Saviour, in a manger laid:
To human eyes none present but they two,
Where heaven was pointing its concentred view.

(continued overleaf)

their   glad   hearts with - in   their   bo - soms   burn.

7   Let us, like these good shepherds, then, employ
   Our grateful voices to proclaim the joy;
   Like Mary, let us ponder in our mind
   God's wondrous love in saving lost mankind:
   Artless and watchful as these favoured swains,
   While virgin meekness in our heart remains.

*8   Trace we the Babe, who has retrieved our loss,
   From his poor manger to his bitter Cross,
   Treading his steps, assisted by his grace,
   Till man's first heavenly state again takes place,
   And, in fulfilment of the Father's will,
   The place of Satan's fallen host we fill.

9   Then may we hope, the angelic thrones among,
   To sing, redeemed, a glad triumphal song.
   He that was born upon this joyful day
   Around us all his glory shall display;
   Saved by his love, incessant we shall sing
   Of angels and of angel-men the King.

John Byrom (1692–1763), adapted

Neither Byrom's manuscript nor early editions set out the poem in stanzas, though Wainwright must have addressed the problem when he brought a choir along to sing the hymn to his setting outside Byrom's house on Christmas Night, 1750. Our version is based on the text printed in a Manchester newspaper in 1751, transposing one couplet and adding another of our own (which concludes verse 8) to permit a meaningful stanzaic division of the complete poem. The inner parts in bars 1–20 are editorial.

PERFORMANCE (*i*) Four-part choir and organ, with unison congregation *ad lib.*; (*ii*) unison voices and organ, the choir in four-part harmony in the final strain. If the treble and tenor parts are reversed to restore Wainwright's original setting, some sopranos should continue to sing the melody here. Editorial inter-verse organ interludes are given in *NOBC*.

38

Lo! he comes, with clouds descending
Lo! he comes, an infant stranger

I

(Advent)

Martin Madan (1726–90)
(arr. editors)

1. Lo! he comes, with clouds de - scend - ing,
Thou - sand, thou - sand saints, at - tend - ing,

Once for fa - voured sin - ners slain;
Swell the tri - umph of his train.

[SOLI] [FULL] [SOLI]

Hal - le - lu - jah! hal - le - lu - jah! hal - le -

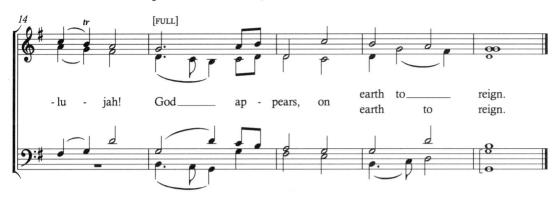

-lu - jah! God_____ ap - pears, on earth to_____ reign.
earth to reign.

2 Every eye shall now behold him
    Robed in dreadful majesty;
  Those who set at nought and sold him,
    Pierced, and nailed him to the tree,
      Deeply wailing
    Shall the true Messiah see.

*3 Every island, sea, and mountain,
    Heaven, and earth, shall flee away;
  All who hate him must, confounded,
    Hear the trump proclaim the Day:
      Come to judgement!
    Come to judgement! Come away!

*4 Now Redemption, long expected,
    See in solemn pomp appear!
  All his saints, by man rejected,
    Now shall meet him in the air!
      Hallelujah!
    See the Day of God appear!

*5 Answer thine own Bride and Spirit,
    Hasten, Lord, the general doom!
  The new heaven and earth to inherit,
    Take thy pining exiles home!
      All creation
    Travails, groans, and bids thee come!

6 The dear tokens of his Passion
    Still his dazzling body bears,
  Cause of endless exultation
    To his ransomed worshippers:
      With what rapture
    Gaze we on those glorious scars!

7 Yea, amen! let all adore thee,
    High on thy eternal throne!
  Saviour, take the power and glory:
    Claim the kingdom for thine own!
      O come quickly!
    Hallelujah! come, Lord, come!

vv. 1, 2, 5–7 Charles Wesley (1707–88)
vv. 3, 4 John Cennick (1718–55)

Wesley's incomparable Advent hymn (text I, verses 1, 2, 6, and 7) was inspired by a hymn by John Cennick. Our version (following that of Wesley's *Hymns of Intercession for all Mankind*, 1758) includes two verses from Cennick's hymn and a verse from another by Wesley. The further imitation by Bishop Richard Mant, entitled 'The Infant Stranger', assigns alternate verses to 'first company' and 'second company', which may refer to twin galleries of charity children in a large London parish church and/or the practice of seating men and women to left and right of the central aisle. Thomas Olivers based the tune (known as 'Olivers') on a country dance, perhaps by Thomas Arne, which he heard whistled in the street. Madan, whose *A*

Collection of Psalm and Hymn Tunes (1769) 'To be used at the Lock Hospital' contains setting II, named his revision 'Helmsley'. (The hospital was a charitable institution for women with venereal infection.)

PERFORMANCE I, voices and organ; II, sopranos (soli or full) and organ continuo. (Text II may be sung to setting I, with or without Mant's division into 'companies'.)

See *NOBC* for *Lift up your heads in joyful hope* (no. 73), *Hark! hear you not a chearful noise* (no. 74), and *Hark! hark what news the angels bring* (no. 75).

II

(*Christmas*)

Martin Madan (1726–90)
after Thomas Olivers (1725–99)

1. Lo! he comes, an infant stranger, Of a lowly
2. Lo! he comes, the great Creator, Calling all the

[CONTINUO]

mother born, *p* Swathed and cradled in a manger,
world to own Him, the Judge and Lord of nature,

Of his pristine glory shorn! *f* Hallelujah!
Seated on his Father's throne.

hallelujah! hallelujah! Praise ye God's incarnate Word!
Praise ye him, the living Lord!

3 Lo! he comes, by man unfriended,
    Fain[1] with stabled beast to rest;
  Shepherds, who their night-fold tended,
    Hailed alone the new-born guest!
      Hallelujah! hallelujah! hallelujah!
    Praise ye Jesse's tender rod!

4 Lo! he comes, around him pouring
    All the armies of the sky;
  Cherub-, seraph-host, adoring,
    Swell his state and loudly cry:
      'Hallelujah! hallelujah! hallelujah!
    Praise ye Christ, the Son of God!'

5 Lo! he comes, constrained to borrow
    Shelter from yon stabled shed,
  He who shall, through years of sorrow,
    Have not where to lay his head.
      Hallelujah! hallelujah! hallelujah!
    Praise him, slighted by his own!

6 Lo! he comes, all grief expelling
    From the hearts that him receive;
  He to each with him a dwelling
    In his Father's house will give.
      Hallelujah! hallelujah! hallelujah!
    Praise him on his glory's throne!

7 Lo! he comes, to slaughter fated
    By a tyrant's stern decree:
  From the sword, with blood unsated,
    Forced in midnight haste to flee.
      Hallelujah! hallelujah! hallelujah!
    Praise him in affliction's hour!

8 Lo! he comes: at his appearing
    All his foes before him fall;
  Proudest kings, his summons hearing,
    On the rocks for shelter call.
      Hallelujah! hallelujah! hallelujah!
    Praise him, girded round with power!

9 Lo! he comes; but who the weakness
    Of his coming may declare,
  When, with more than human meekness,
    More than human woes he bare?
      Hallelujah! hallelujah! hallelujah!
    Praise him, emptied of his might!

10 Lo! he comes; what eye may bear him,
    In his unveiled glory shown?
  Mightiest angels, marshalled near him,
    Serve, and him their mightier own.
      Hallelujah! hallelujah! hallelujah!
    Praise him, with his crown of light!

11 Man, of human flesh partaking,
    Offspring of the Virgin's womb,
  Who, the hopeless wanderer seeking,
    Deigned in lowly guise to come:
      Hallelujah! hallelujah! hallelujah!
    Praise ye the incarnate Word!

12 Son of the eternal Father,
    Who again in power shall come,
  Round him all mankind to gather,
    And pronounce unerring doom:
      Hallelujah! hallelujah! hallelujah!
    Praise ye him, the living Lord!

Richard Mant (1776–1848)

[1] obliged

39

Joy to the world!

(Christmas)

Pre-1833
(rev. William Holford, c.1834,
arr. editors)

And heav'n and na-ture sing,

2 Joy to the earth! the Saviour reigns:
    Let men their songs employ,
  While fields and floods, rocks, hills and
      plains
    Repeat the sounding joy.

*3 No more let sins and sorrows grow,
    Nor thorns infest the ground:
  He comes to make his blessings flow
    Far as the curse is found.

4 He rules the world with truth and grace,
    And makes the nations prove
  The glories of his righteousness
    And wonders of his love.

Isaac Watts (1674–1748)

The origins of this tune have yet to be completely uncovered (the attribution to Handel probably results solely from the resemblance of the opening to 'Lift up your heads' in *Messiah*). It first appears as an English psalm tune in the 1830s, and was set to Watts's text, a paraphrase of Psalm 98, by the American Presbyterian Lowell Mason in 1836.

NOBC setting II (not included here) is an arrangement by Thomas Clark of the English version of the melody.

PERFORMANCE Choir and/or congregation with organ, and instruments *ad lib*.

40

Come, let us all with heart and voice

(Christmas)

c.1780?
(Herman French Collection)

1. Come, let us all____ with heart and voice Join with the an-gels, and re-joice! Join with the an-gels, and re-joice! Join with the an-gels, join with the an-gels in their songs; Join with our hearts as well as tongues! Join with our hearts as_ well as tongues! 'Glo-ry to God!' we

2 Then let us all in praise unite
   To him who left yon world of light;
   He left his Father's glorious throne
   For us a Saviour to be born.

3 'All glory,' then again begin,
   'To him who thus was sent from heaven!
   For ever be his Name adored,
   Of Christ, our Saviour and our Lord!'

c.1780?
(Herman French Collection)

This fine setting, undated and unsigned, is found in three related scores from the Devon village of Widecombe, where the local Methodists and Baptists used to combine their singers and instruments to form the Christmas Night carol party.

PERFORMANCE Choir and instruments. In the vocal sections the instruments double the voices, ornamenting the lines as appropriate (see *NOBC* Appendix 3, and *NOBC*

carols 89 and 96:III for examples). Instrumental parts from the Widecombe band have violins doubling the treble part at pitch and the tenor an octave higher, a flute playing the alto part an octave higher, and a cello doubling the bass, mostly at pitch but with some notes at the lower octave.

See *NOBC* for Billings: *As shepherds in Jewry* (no. 78) and *Shepherds, rejoice!* (no. 79).

41

A virgin unspotted

(Christmas)

William Billings (1746–1800)

1. A virgin unspotted, the prophet[1] foretold, Should bring forth a Saviour, which now we behold, To be our Redeemer from death, hell and sin, Which Adam's transgression involved us in.

2. Through Bethlehem city, in Jury,[2] it was That Joseph and Mary together did pass, And for to be taxed when thither they came, Since Caesar Augustus commanded the same.

Then let us be merry, put sorrow away: Our

[1] Isaiah   [2] Jewry

Sa - viour, Christ Je - sus, was born on this day.

3 But Mary's full time being come, as we
    find,[3]
  She brought forth her first-born to save all
    mankind;
  The inn being full, for this heavenly guest
  No place there was found where to lay him
    to rest.

4 But Mary, blest Mary, so meek and so
    mild,
  Soon wrapped up in swaddlings this
    heavenly Child:
  Contented, she laid him where oxen do
    feed;
  The great God of nature approved of the
    deed.

5 To teach us humility all this was done;
  Then learn we from hence haughty pride
    for to shun;
  A manger's his cradle who came from
    above,
  The great God of mercy, of peace and of
    love.

6 Then presently[4] after, the shepherds did
    spy
  Vast numbers of angels to stand in the
    sky;
  So merrily talking, so sweet they did
    sing:
  'All glory and praise to our heavenly
    King!'

Traditional
(v. 1 Billings, 1778
vv. 2–6 Arnold, 1756)

---

[3] in the gospels   [4] immediately

From *The Singing Master's Assistant* (1778), the second of
Billings's six publications (see notes, *NOBC* no. 78). Billings
prints only verse 1; the others are from John Arnold, *The
Compleat Psalmist* (fourth edn., London, 1756).
  Billings's melody seems to be original, despite echoes of
the folk melody in the refrain. No exact proportion between
the notation of verse and refrain seems intended: the

quavers of the refrain should perhaps be a little faster than
the crotchets of the verse.

PERFORMANCE Choir, with octave doubling of the tenor
(see Introduction).

See *NOBC* for Belcher: *The Lord descended from above* (no.
81).

42

Ye nations all, on you I call

(*Christmas*)

arr. *William Walker* (1809–75)

1. Ye na-tions all,＿ on you I call: come, hear this de - cla - ra - tion, And don't re-fuse this glo-rious news of Je-sus and sal - va - tion! To roy-al Jews came first the news of Christ the great Mes - si - ah, As was fore-told by pro-phets old: I - sai-ah, Je - re - mi - ah.

2 To Abraham the promise came, and to his seed for ever,
A light to shine in Isaac's line, by Scripture we discover.
Hail, promised morn! the Saviour's born, the glorious Mediator—
God's blessèd Word, made flesh and blood, assumed the human nature.

3 His parents, poor in earthly store to entertain the stranger,
   They found no bed to lay his head but in the ox's manger;
   No royal things, as used by kings, were seen by those that found him,
   But in the hay the stranger lay, with swaddling bands around him.

4 On the same night a glorious light to shepherds there appearèd;
   Bright angels came in shining flame: they saw and greatly fearèd.
   The angels said: 'Be not afraid! although we much alarm you,
   We do appear good news to bear, as now we will inform you.

5 'The city's name is Bethlehem, the which God hath appointed;
   This glorious morn a Saviour's born, for him God hath anointed.
   By this you'll know, if you will go to see this little stranger:
   His lovely charms in Mary's arms, both lying in a manger.'

6 When this was said, straightway was made a glorious sound from heaven;
   Each flaming tongue an anthem sung: 'To men a Saviour's given!
   In Jesus' name, the glorious theme, we elevate our voices;
   At Jesus' birth be peace on earth; meanwhile all heav'n rejoices.'

7 Then with delight they took their flight, and wing'd their way to glory;
   The shepherds gazed, and were amazed to hear the pleasing story.
   To Bethlehem they quickly came, the glorious news to carry,
   And in the stall they found them all, Joseph, the Babe, and Mary.

8 The shepherds then return'd again to their own habitation;
   With joy of heart they did depart, now they have found salvation.
   'Glory,' they cry, 'to God on high, who sent his Son to save us!
   This glorious morn the Saviour's born: his name it is Christ Jesus.'

William Walker? (1809–75)

'Singin' Billy' Walker's *The Southern Harmony*, from which 'Ye nations all' is taken, was one of the early shape-note collections, first published in New Haven in 1835. Walker probably notated the tune (which is found in many variants in this repertory) from oral tradition, and added other parts in the manner of the extemporary harmonization of the European-derived Calvinist sects.

Lines 3 and 4 of verse 5 seem to mean: 'You will recognize him by this, if you go to see the little stranger: he is lying in all his beauty in the arms of Mary, and they both [rather than both of Mary's arms] are lying in a manger.'

PERFORMANCE Choir, with the usual shape-note octave doublings (see Introduction). The rests in bar 9 should perhaps be ignored. George Pullen Jackson, the pioneering shape-note scholar, says that shape-note singers have a common custom of 'not tolerating any dead spaces or long rests . . . which are felt as needed to make the rhythmic form mathematically correct or quadratic . . . the leaders and singers deliberately disregard the rest-beat and proceed as though it did not exist.'

43

Glory to God on high

(Christmas)

Jeremiah Ingalls (1764–1838)

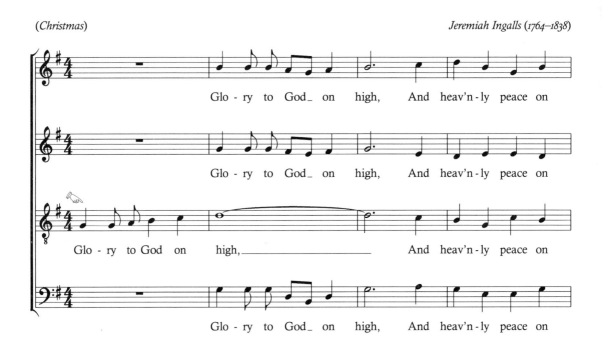

Glo - ry to God_ on high, And heav'n - ly peace on

Glo - ry to God_ on high, And heav'n - ly peace on

Glo - ry to God on high,_____ And heav'n - ly peace on

Glo - ry to God_ on high, And heav'n - ly peace on

earth! Good will to men, to an - gels joy,_____

earth! Good will to men, to an - gels joy,_____

earth! Good will to

earth! Good will to

Isaac Watts (1674–1748)

A singing-school master in New England all his life, Ingalls played both sacred and secular music on his 'bass viol' (cello or double bass, as in English gallery bands), the use of which he introduced to both Newbury and Rochester churches. 'Glory to God on high' comes from his only publication, *The Christian Harmony* (1805).

PERFORMANCE   Voices, with octave doubling of the tenor (see Introduction); cello or double bass *ad lib*.

The generally high tessitura in Ingalls's book suggests a low pitch standard. Performance in G is more exciting, but F may be closer to what was intended.

44

Hail the blest morn!

I

(Christmas)

arr. William Walker (1809–75)

VERSE

1. Hail the blest morn! See the great Me-di-a-tor Down from the re-gions of
Shep-herds, go wor-ship the Babe in the man-ger! Lo! for his guard the bright

REFRAIN

glo-ry de-scend!
an-gels at-tend. *Bright-est and best of the sons of the morn-ing, Dawn on our dark-ness and lend us thine*

aid; *Star in the East, the ho-ri-zon a-dorn-ing, Guide where our in-fant Re-deem-er was laid!*

II

(Christmas)   *(Songs for All Time)*

1. Hail the blest morn! See the great Me-di-a - tor Down from the re - gions of
   Shep-herds, go wor - ship the Babe in the man - ger! Lo! for his guard the bright

glo - ry de-scend!
an - gels at-tend.

Bright - est and best of the sons of the morn - ing,

Dawn on our dark - ness and lend us thine aid; *Star in the East,__ the ho -*

- ri - zon a - dorn - ing, *Guide where our in - fant Re - deem - er was laid!*

2 Cold on his cradle the dewdrops are shining,
    Low lies his bed with the beasts of the stall;
  Angels adore him, in slumber reclining,
    Wise men and shepherds before him do fall.

3 Say, shall we yield him, in costly devotion,
    Odours of Edom and off'rings divine,
  Gems from the mountain and pearls from the ocean,
    Myrrh from the forest and gold from the mine?

4 Vainly we offer each ample oblation,
    Vainly with gold would his favour secure;
  Richer by far is the heart's adoration,
    Dearer to God are the prayers of the poor.

v. 1 anon.
Refrain and vv. 2–4 after Reginald Heber (1783–1826)

Like 42, the tune of setting I is probably an example of the unwritten music of the American Methodists, Baptists, and Presbyterians, and is set by Walker in a style that reflects the kind of harmonies that singers would improvise. Setting II is a major-mode variant transcribed from the singing of Mrs Rachel Ritchie, of Kentucky.

PERFORMANCE I, voices, with the usual shape-note octave doublings (see Introduction).

II, solo, or unison voices; perhaps solo verses, unison refrains.

See *NOBC* for *Hark! hark! glad tidings charm our ears* (no. 85).

45

Stille Nacht! heilige Nacht!
Silent night! holy night!

I

(Christmas Night)

Franz Xaver Gruber (1787–1863)
(reconstructed by the editors)

1. Stil - le Nacht! hei - li - ge Nacht! Al - les schläft;
1. Si - lent night! ho - ly night! Sleeps the earth,

ein - sam wacht nur das trau - te hei - li - ge Paar.
calm and quiet; Love - ly Child, now take thy rest:

Hol - der Knab im lock - ig - ten Haar, schla - fe in himm - lisch - er
On thy mo - ther's gen - tle breast Sleep in hea - ven - ly

(continued overleaf)

Ruh! _____ schla - fe in _ himm - lisch - er Ruh!
peace! _____ Sleep _ in _ hea - ven - ly peace!

2 Stille Nacht! heilige Nacht!
Gottes Sohn, o wie lacht
Lieb' aus deinem göttlichen Mund
da uns schlägt die rettende Stund,
Jesus, in deiner Geburt!
Jesus, in deiner Geburt!

2 Silent night! holy night!
When thou smil'st, love-beams bright
Pierce the darkness all around;
Son of God, thy birth doth sound
Our salvation's hour!
Our salvation's hour!

3 Stille Nacht! heilige Nacht!
die der Welt Heil gebracht
aus des Himmels goldenen Höhn.
Uns der Gnaden Fülle läßt sehn
Jesum in Menschengestalt,
Jesum in Menschengestalt.

3 Silent night! holy night!
From the heaven's golden height
Christ descends, the earth to free;
Grace divine! by thee we see
God in human form!
God in human form!

4 Stille Nacht! heilige Nacht!
wo sich heut alle Macht
väterlicher Liebe ergoß,
und als Bruder huldvoll umschloß
Jesus die Völker der Welt,
Jesus die Völker der Welt.

4 Silent night! holy night!
God above at that sight
Doth with fatherly love rejoice,
While earth's peoples, with one voice,
Jesus their brother proclaim!
Jesus their brother proclaim!

(continued overleaf)

5 Stille Nacht! heilige Nacht!
   lange schon uns bedacht,
   als der Herr vom Grimme befreit
   in der Väter urgrauer Zeit
   aller Welt Schonung verhieß,
   aller Welt Schonung verhieß.

6 Stille Nacht! heilige Nacht!
   Hirten erst kundgemacht
   durch der Engel Alleluja;
   tönt es laut bei Ferne und Nah:
   'Jesus der Retter ist da!
   Jesus der Retter ist da!'

Joseph Mohr (1792–1849)

5 Silent night! holy night!
   Adam's sin damned us quite,
   But the Son, to set us free
   From the Father's stern decree,
   Now in his mercy is born!
   Now in his mercy is born!

6 Silent night! holy night!
   Shepherds first with delight
   Heard the angelic 'Alleluia!'
   Echoing loud, both near and far:
   'Jesus, the Saviour, is here!
   Jesus, the Saviour, is here!'

Free tr., editors

This carol was written and first performed by the curate and assistant organist of the Lower Austrian (now Bavarian) town of Oberndorf, at the Christmas Night mass in 1818. Gruber played the guitar, but the idea that this was because the organ had suddenly broken down seems to be a later accretion to the story. What Mohr and Gruber did was in no way out of the ordinary—except that they produced a carol of Schubertian charm which has captivated listeners from that first performance on.

The original manuscript score has been lost, if it ever existed. The vocal and 'organ' staves of setting I are from an autograph manuscript (dated 1818, but probably from 1856) for voices and 'quiet organ accompaniment'. It lacks tenor and bass parts in the refrain, and we have taken these from another autograph. The organ part is patently a direct transcription from the original guitar part, which we have reconstructed on the bottom staff. The manuscripts vary between the simple and ornamented versions of bars 11 and 15. Gruber also made two arrangements for orchestra.

The melody of setting II (little known in Austria and Germany, and sadly inferior to the original) was the result of the early dissemination of a mistranscription by a family group of Austrian 'folk singers', who passed the carol off as traditional.

PERFORMANCE I (*i*) The original version (SATB and guitar): TB soli to bar 12 and SATB chorus thereafter, using the unornamented versions of bars 11 and 15 shown small above the staff. (*ii*) A 'standard' Gruber parish-choir setting (SATB and organ): SA chorus to bar 12 and SATB chorus thereafter. Organ plays the SA staff as right hand and the bass-clef staff as left hand. (*iii*) The '1818' autograph (SA and organ): SA soli to bar 12 and SA chorus thereafter. The 'quiet [8'] organ' as (*ii*).

II, choir, with organ *ad lib.*

See *NOBC* for Gifford: *Arise, and hail the sacred day!* (no. 87).

II

Modern version
after Franz Xaver Gruber (1787–1863)
(arr. editors)

(*Christmas Night*)

1. Si - lent night! ho - ly night! All is calm, all is bright
2. Si - lent night! ho - ly night! Shep - herds quake at the sight;
3. Si - lent night! ho - ly night! Son of God, love's pure light,

Round yon Vir - gin Mo - ther and Child; Ho - ly In - fant so ten - der and mild,
Glo - ries stream_ from hea - ven a - far, Heaven - ly hosts_ sing: 'Al - le - lu - ia!
Ra - diant, beams from thy ho - ly face With the dawn of re - deem - ing grace,

Sleep in hea - ven - ly peace!___ Sleep_ in hea - ven - ly peace!
Christ the Sa - viour is born!___ Christ_ the Sa - viour is born!'
Je - sus, Lord, at thy birth!___ Je - sus, Lord, at thy birth!

(tr. John F. Young, 1820–85)

46

Rejoice, ye tenants of the earth

(Christmas)

William Gifford (fl. c.1805)

(Verses overleaf)

The carol that the Mellstock choir performed for Fancy Day, the newly arrived village schoolmistress, in Thomas Hardy's *Under the Greenwood Tree* (1872). *NOBC* nos. 46:IV and 47:II feature in the same novel, and in real life all three were performed by Hardy's father's carol party.

We have printed the setting in C, following some of the manuscript sources, but it is in D in Gifford's *Twelve New Psalm Tunes* (London, 1805), and that is a better key for instruments.

PERFORMANCE Choir and instruments—two flutes or violins, cello (or bassoon), and organ. The organ could be omitted if the cello plays throughout.

The instruments play at pitch in the symphonies, and double the voices as follows: flute/violin 1 doubles the soprano and might ornament the line as appropriate (see *NOBC* nos. 89 and 96:III for examples); flute/violin 2 doubles the alto at the higher octave in the full sections; the cello/ bassoon should double the bass at the lower octave whenever possible in the full sections, with ornamentation as flute/violin 1. (See also Introduction.)

See *NOBC* for *Rouse, rouse from your slumbers* (no. 89) and *Awake, and join the cheerful choir* (no. 90).

Your Sa-viour, Christ, is born!_____ Your Sa-viour, Christ, is
born!_____

Your Sa-viour, Christ, your Sa-viour, Christ, is born!   is

(INSTRUMENTS)   tr   SYMPHONY

born!   Your Sa - viour, Christ, is___ born!

born!

tr   D.S.

2 Behold! a meteor, shining bright,
    Conducts the eastern sages right
      To Judah's distant land,
    And guides to Bethlehem their road,
    Then fixes o'er his low abode,
      Directed by his hand;

3 And there they find the new-born King,
   To whom they did their offerings bring
     And worship at his feet,
  While angels, flying from their home,
  Proclaim that he alone is come,
    Salvation to complete.

4 For us these acclamations fly,
  For us he's born, below to die,
    That he may reign above:
  Then let us all our voices raise
  And sound abroad our Saviour's praise
    For his unbounded love.

William Gifford? (*1805*)

47

Sound, sound your instruments of joy!
(Seraphic Minstrels)

(Christmas)

W. B. Ninnis
(fl. c.1810–30?)

u - ni - ver - sal joy Wel-come, wel-come, wel-come a new - born King!

2 See! see the glad'ning dawn appears,
   Bright angels deck the morn;
   Behold! the great I AM is given;
   The King of Glory born.

3 Surprising scene! stupendous love!
   The Lord of Life, descend!
   He left his glorious realms above
   To be the sinner's friend.

4 Let heav'n and earth and sea proclaim
   Thy wondrous love abroad,
   And all the universal frame
   Sing praises to our God.

Eighteenth-century
(vv. 1, 2, 4 Ben Barnicoat, 1927;
v. 3 Ralph Dunstan, 1925)

This carol comes from Ben Barnicoat's *Old Cornish Carols* (1927), where it is reproduced from manuscripts written and collected by his grandfather. It has been transposed down a tone.

PERFORMANCE Choir, with instruments and/or organ *ad lib.* (see Introduction). The bass runs in bars 3–4 and 7 are probably instrumental, but can be taken vocally in purely choral performances. The text repeats in verses 2–4 are indicated above the lines. 'Sing praise, sing praise' should be sung in verse 4.

48

Hark! the herald angels sing

I

(*Christmas*)

Felix Mendelssohn (*1809–47*)
(*arr. editors*)

1. Hark! the he - rald an-gels sing:_ 'Glo-ry to the new-born King! Peace on earth and

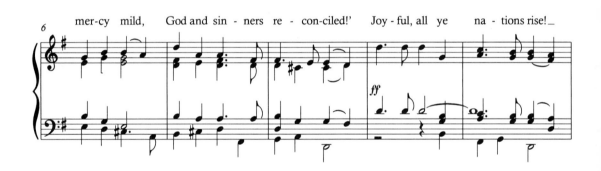

mer-cy mild, God and sin - ners re - con-ciled!' Joy - ful, all ye na - tions rise!_

Join the tri-umph of the skies! U - ni-ver-sal Na-ture say: 'Christ the_ Lord is

born to-day!'   Hark! the he-rald   an-gels sing: 'Glo-ry___ to   the   new-born King!'

2 Christ, by highest heaven adored,
   Christ the everlasting Lord:
   Late in time behold him come,
   Offspring of a Virgin's womb.
   Veiled in flesh the Godhead see!
   Hail the incarnate Deity,
   Pleased as man with man to dwell:
   Jesus, our Emmanuel!

3 Come, Desire of Nations, come:
   Fix in us thy humble home!
   Rise, the Woman's conquering Seed,
   Bruise in us the Serpent's head!
   Adam's likeness, Lord, efface:
   Stamp thy image in its place!
   Second Adam, from above,
   Reinstate us in thy love!

4 Mild, he lays his glory by,
   Born that man no more may die,
   Born to raise the sons of earth,
   Born to give them second birth.
   Hail the heaven-born Prince of Peace!
   Hail the Sun of Righteousness!
   Light and life to all he brings,
   Risen with healing in his wings.

Charles Wesley (1707–88), adapted

This 'Hymn for Christmas-Day' has always been the most popular of Charles Wesley's hymns, appearing in more hymn-books than any other, usually in an adapted form. Mendelssohn's setting (I) is from his *Festgesang* (1840) for male voices and brass, commissioned to celebrate what was believed to be the 400th anniversary of Johann Gutenberg's invention of printing. H. J. Gauntlett united it with Wesley's hymn in a curious monorhythmic arrangement which appeared in 1858, but a slightly earlier version by W. H. Cummings soon became standard. Though much closer to Mendelssohn's setting, Cummings's version (like Gauntlett's) weakens it with apparently arbitrary changes, and we believe that ours is the first to transcribe it directly. Setting II, from Martin Madan's 'Lock Collection' (see note

to no. 38), is one of many other settings of the hymn: it is probably by the music historian Charles Burney.

PERFORMANCE I, voices and organ. It may be performed with Mendelssohn's brass parts (2 trumpets, 4 horns, 3 trombones, ophicleide). There was no organ in the original, but it could effectively double the brass. One performance scheme might be to sing verses 1 and 4 with full forces, verse 2 with organ only, and verse 3 with men's voices and brass. (When organ alone provides the accompaniment it is probably best to substitute Gs for the bass Ds on the first beat in bars 1 and 5.) See *NOBC* for three suggested organ interludes by S. S. Wesley.

II, high voices and organ.

II

(*Christmas*)

'C. B.' (*Madan, 1769*)

Charles Wesley (1707–88) and others

49

Once, in royal David's city

(*Christmas*)

Henry John Gauntlett (1805–76)

1. Once, in roy - al Da - vid's ci - ty, Stood a low - ly cat - tle_ shed
2. He came down to earth from hea - ven Who is God and Lord of_ all,

Where a mo - ther laid_ her_ ba - by In a man - ger for_ his_ bed;
And his shel - ter was_ a_ sta - ble, And his cra - dle was_ a_ stall;

Ma - ry_ was_ that mo - ther mild, Je - sus_ Christ_ her on - ly_ child.
With the_ poor_ and mean and low - ly Lived on_ earth_ our Sa - viour ho - ly.

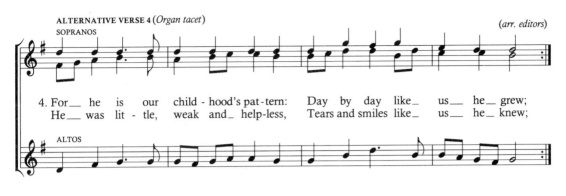

3 And through all his wondrous childhood
    He would honour and obey,
Love and watch the lowly maiden
    In whose gentle arms he lay;
Christian children all must be
    Mild, obedient, good as he.

4 For he is our childhood's pattern:
    Day by day like us he grew;
He was little, weak and helpless,
    Tears and smiles like us he knew;
And he feeleth for our sadness,
    And he shareth in our gladness.

5 And our eyes at last shall see him
    Through his own redeeming love,
For that Child, so dear and gentle,
    Is our Lord in heaven above;
And he leads his children on
    To the place where he is gone.

6 Not in that poor, lowly stable
    With the oxen standing by
We shall see him, but in heaven,
    Set at God's right hand on high,
When, like stars, his children, crowned,
    All in white shall wait around.

Mrs Cecil Frances Alexander (1823–95)

The poem was conceived as one of a sequence of *Hymns for Little Children* (1848), which Mrs Alexander wrote after overhearing a group of her godchildren complaining of the dreariness of the catechism. The original version (1849) of Gauntlett's tune, called 'Irby', was for voice(s) and piano. His four-part arrangement was made for *Hymns Ancient and Modern* (1861); the ascending bass in bars 9 and 11 was added by Henri Friedrich Hémy in his *Crown of Jesus Music* (1864).

PERFORMANCE Voices and organ. The alternative version of verse 4 might also be sung by male voices for verse 2.

See *NOBC* for Berlioz: *The Shepherds' Farewell to the Holy Family* (no. 94).

50

See, amid the winter's snow

(*Christmas*)

John Goss (1800–80)

1. See, a-mid the win-ter's snow, Born for us on earth be-low,

See, the ten - der Lamb ap-pears, Pro-mised from e - ter - nal years!

Hail, thou e - ver - bless - ed morn! Hail, Re-demp - tion's hap - py dawn!

Sing through all Je - ru - sa - lem:___ 'Christ is born in Beth - le - hem!'

2   Lo! within a manger lies
    He who built the starry skies,
    He who, throned in height sublime,
    Sits amid the Cherubim.

3   Say, ye holy shepherds, say:
    What your joyful news today?
    Wherefore have ye left your sheep
    On the lonely mountain steep?

4   'As we watched at dead of night,
    Lo! we saw a wondrous light;
    Angels, singing "Peace on earth",
    Told us of the Saviour's birth.'

5   Sacred Infant, all-divine,
    What a tender love was thine
    Thus to come from highest bliss
    Down to such a world as this!

6   Teach, oh teach us, holy Child,
    By thy face so meek and mild,
    Teach us to resemble thee
    In thy sweet humility!

Edward Caswall (1814–78)

Edward Caswall was one of the many Anglican priests who joined the Roman Church under the influence of John Henry Newman. 'See, amid the winter's snow' was first published in a volume of *Easy Hymn Tunes* in 1851, not long after Caswall's conversion, and the setting by the composer and organist Sir John Goss appeared in Bramley and Stainer's *Christmas Carols New and Old* (second series, *c.*1875).

PERFORMANCE   Voices and organ.

51

Angels, from the realms of glory

I

(*Christmas*)

French traditional
(arr. Martin Shaw 1875–1958)

1. An - gels, from the— realms of glo - ry, Wing your flight o'er— all the earth;

Ye who sang Cre - a - tion's sto - ry Now pro - claim Mes - si - ah's birth!

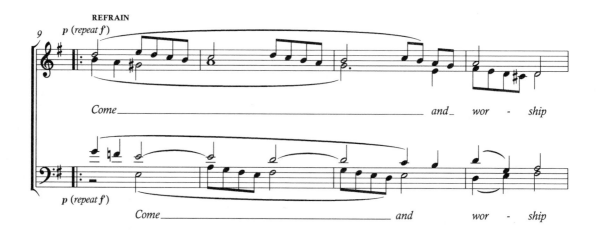

Come_____ and— wor - ship

Come_____ and wor - ship

Christ the new-born King!_____ wor-ship Christ the new-born King!

2 Shepherds, in the field abiding,
    Watching o'er your flocks by night:
God with man is now residing,
    Yonder shines the Infant Light.
    Come and worship Christ the new-born King!

3 Sages, leave your contemplations:
    Brighter visions beam afar.
Seek the Great Desire of Nations:
    Ye have seen his natal star.

4 Saints, before the altar bending,
    Watching long in hope and fear:
Suddenly the Lord, descending,
    In his temple shall appear.

5 Though an infant now we view him,
    He shall fill his Father's throne,
Gather all the nations to him;
    Every knee shall then bow down.

James Montgomery (1771–1854)

II

Henry Smart (1813–79)

VERSE

1. An - gels, from the realms of glo - ry, Wing your flight o'er all the earth;

Ye who sang Cre - a - tion's sto - ry Now pro - claim Mes - si - ah's birth!

REFRAIN

Come and wor - ship, come and wor - ship, wor - ship Christ the___ new - born King!

2 Shepherds, in the field abiding,
   Watching o'er your flocks by night:
God with man is now residing,
   Yonder shines the Infant Light.

3 Sages, leave your contemplations:
   Brighter visions beam afar.
Seek the Great Desire of Nations:
   Ye have seen his natal star.

4 Saints, before the altar bending,
   Watching long in hope and fear:
Suddenly the Lord, descending,
   In his temple shall appear.

5 Though an infant now we view him,
   He shall fill his Father's throne,
Gather all the nations to him;
   Every knee shall then bow down.

James Montgomery (1771–1854)

IV

(Christmas)

Nineteenth-century
(Heath, 1889, arr. editors)

1. An - gels, from the realms of glo - ry, Wing your flight o'er all the earth; Ye who sang Cre -
2. Shep-herds, in the field a - bi - ding, Watch-ing o'er your flocks by night: God with man is
3. Sa - ges, leave your con-tem-pla-tions: Bright - er vis - ions beam a - far.__ Seek the Great De -

- a - tion's sto - ry Now pro-claim Mes - si - ah's birth!
now re - si - ding, Yon-der shines the In - fant Light. *Come and wor - ship, come and wor - ship,*
- sire of Na - tions: Ye have seen his na - tal star.

wor - ship Christ the new - born King! wor - ship Christ the new - born King!

Tune I, from the French noël 'Les anges dans nos campagnes' (116), was chosen for Montgomery's hymn by the editors of *The Oxford Book of Carols* purely on account of the similarity between the opening stanzas of the two texts. In the US the carol is widely sung to tune II.

IV, virtually a little cantata, was published without attribution in William Eade's *Cornish Carols* (pt. I, 1889). Its second part is not a refrain but a common-time reworking

of the entire verse and refrain. *NOBC* setting III (not included here) is an anonymous nineteenth-century church-gallery setting.

PERFORMANCE I, choir; II, voices and organ; IV, soprano and tenor soli, choir, congregation *ad lib.* (bars 19 to end), organ, and instruments *ad lib.*

52

Good King Wenceslas looked out

(*St Stephen's Day*)

Fourteenth-century
Piae Cantiones (1582)
(*arr. John Stainer, 1840–1901*)

1. Good King Wen - ces - las looked out   On the feast of   Ste - phen,
When the snow lay   round a - bout,   Deep and crisp and   e - ven;

Bright - ly shone the   moon that night,   Though the frost was   cru - el,

When a   poor man   came in sight,   Gath-'ring win - ter   fu - el.

2 'Hither, page, and stand by me;
    If thou know'st it, telling—
Yonder peasant, who is he?
    Where and what his dwelling?'
'Sire, he lives a good league hence,
    Underneath the mountain,
Right against the forest fence,
    By Saint Agnes' fountain.'

3 'Bring me flesh, and bring me wine!
    Bring me pine logs hither!
Thou and I will see him dine
    When we bear them thither.'
Page and monarch forth they went,
    Forth they went together,
Through the rude wind's wild lament
    And the bitter weather.

4 'Sire, the night is darker now,
    And the wind blows stronger;
Fails my heart, I know not how,
    I can go no longer.'
'Mark my footsteps, good my page,
    Tread thou in them boldly:
Thou shalt find the winter's rage
    Freeze thy blood less coldly.'

5 In his master's steps he trod,
    Where the snow lay dinted;
Heat was in the very sod
    Which the saint had printed.
Therefore, Christian men, be sure,
    Wealth or rank possessing,
Ye who now will bless the poor
    Shall yourselves find blessing.

J. M. Neale (1818–66)

Wenceslas is the German form of Vaclav. Vaclav the Good reigned in Bohemia from 922 to 929, later becoming the Czech patron saint. Neale's carol is not based on any known incident in the saint's life: it is probably no more than a pious illustration of the virtue of charity—St Stephen's Day (Boxing Day, 26 December) is a traditional day for giving to the poor. The tune is that of a spring song from *Piae Cantiones* (1582).

PERFORMANCE Voices and organ.

53

What child is this

(*Christmas*)

Traditional
(*arr. John Stainer, 1840–1901*)

1. What child is this—who, laid to rest,—On Ma-ry's lap—is sleep-ing, Whom

an-gels greet—with an-thems sweet While shep-herds watch—are keep-ing?

This, this—is Christ the King, Whom shep-herds guard—and an-gels sing:

Haste, haste—to bring him laud,—The Babe,—the Son—of Ma-ry!

2 Why lies he in such mean estate
   Where ox and ass are feeding?
   Good Christians fear: for sinners here
   The silent Word is pleading.
   Nail, spear shall pierce him through,
   The Cross be borne for me, for you;
   Hail! hail the Word Made Flesh,
   The Babe, the Son of Mary!

3 So bring him incense, gold and myrrh;
   Come, peasant, king, to own him!
   The King of Kings salvation brings:
   Let loving hearts enthrone him!
   Raise, raise the song on high!
   The Virgin sings her lullaby.
   Joy! joy! for Christ is born,
   The Babe, the Son of Mary!

William Chatterton Dix (1837–98)

'What child is this' was written for the tune of 'Greensleeves' in about 1865 and appeared with Stainer's setting in *Christmas Carols New and Old* in 1871. See 'The old yeare now away is fled' (*NOBC* no. 135) for a seventeenth-century variant of the 'Greensleeves' tune.

PERFORMANCE (*i*) Choir; (*ii*) voices and organ.

54

Three Kings of Orient

(Epiphany)

John Henry Hopkins (1820–91)

REFRAIN [S.A.T.B. FULL]

O___ Star of Won-der, Star of Night, Star with roy-al beau-ty bright,

West-ward lead-ing, still pro-ceed-ing, Guide us to thy per-fect light.

INTERLUDE

GASPARD:

2 Born a king on Bethlehem plain,
Gold I bring to crown him again,
King for ever, ceasing never
Over us all to reign.
    [CHORUS] *O Star of Wonder,* (etc.)

MELCHIOR:

3 Frankincense to offer have I,
Incense owns a Deity nigh;
Prayer and praising all men raising,
Worship him, God on high.
    [CHORUS] *O Star of Wonder,* (etc.)

BALTHAZAR:

4 Myrrh is mine; its bitter perfume
Breathes a life of gathering gloom;
Sorrowing, sighing, bleeding, dying,
Sealed in the stone-cold tomb.
    [CHORUS] *O Star of Wonder,* (etc.)

GASPARD, MELCHIOR, BALTHAZAR:

5 Glorious now behold him arise,
King, and God, and sacrifice.
Heaven sing: 'Alleluia';
'Alleluia' the earth replies.
    [CHORUS] *O Star of Wonder,* (etc.)

John Henry Hopkins (1820–91)

Hopkins was rector of Christ's Church, Williamsport, Pennsylvania, when he published his little collection of *Carols, Hymns, and Songs* in 1865. It is a model of clarity and simplicity, though only this carol has become widely known.

PERFORMANCE Hopkins's performance instructions are as lucid as his verse: 'Each of verses 2, 3, and 4 is sung as a solo, to the music of Gaspard's part in the 1st and 5th verses, the accompaniment and chorus being the same throughout. Only verses 1 and 5 are sung as a trio. Men's voices are best for the parts of the three kings, but the music is set in the G clef for accommodation of children.' We suggest full choir in the refrains. The accompaniment can be either organ or piano (Hopkins does not specify the instrument).

55

Away in a manger

I

(Christmas)

William J. Kirkpatrick (1838–1921)

1. A - way in a__ man - ger, no__ crib for a bed, The__ lit - tle Lord
2. The cat - tle are__ low - ing, the__ Ba - by a - wakes, But__ lit - tle Lord
3. Be near me, Lord Je - sus: I__ ask thee to stay Close by me for -

[T.B. ad lib.]

Je - sus laid__ down his sweet head; The stars in the__ bright sky looked
Je - sus, no__ cry - ing he makes. I love thee, Lord Je - sus! look__
-ev - er, and__ love me, I pray; Bless all the dear__ child - ren in__

down where he lay— The__ lit - tle Lord Je - sus, a - sleep on the hay.
down from the sky, And stay by my cra - dle till__ morn - ing is nigh.
thy ten - der care, And take us to hea - ven to__ live with thee there.

Anon. (vv. 1, 2 Kirkpatrick, 1885;
v. 3 Charles H. Gabriel, 1892)

II

James R. Murray (1841/2–1905)

(*Christmas*)

1. A - way in a man - ger, no crib for a bed, The lit - tle Lord
2. The cat - tle are low - ing, the poor Ba - by wakes, But lit - tle Lord

[T.B. *ad lib.*]

Je - sus laid down his sweet head; The stars in the sky____ looked
Je - sus, no cry - ing he makes. I love thee, Lord Je - sus! look

down where he lay— The lit - tle Lord Je - sus, a - sleep on the hay.
down from the sky, And stay by my cra - dle to watch lul - la - by.

Anon. (Murray, 1887)

Both the words and tune II continue to be erroneously ascribed in the US to Martin Luther, the latter also sometimes to an apparently non-existent 'R. Mueller'. The untraced (and probably untraceable) original hymn perhaps derived from one of the many children's dramatic presentations mounted by American Lutherans in 1883 to mark the 400th anniversary of the birth of their founder. Tune I is standard in England, tune II in the US.

The simple settings for voice(s) and keyboard that both Murray and Kirkpatrick provided are refreshing alternatives to the sophisticated SATB settings sometimes heard in carol services today. For choral performance we have added equally simple tenor and bass parts.

PERFORMANCE I and II (*i*) solo, unison, or two-part voices, with piano, harmonium, guitar, etc. (omitting the middle stave); (*ii*) choir.

56

O little town of Bethlehem

I

(*Christmas*)

Traditional
(arr. Ralph Vaughan Williams, 1872–1958)

1. O lit-tle town of__ Beth-le-hem, How still we see thee lie! A-bove thy deep and dream-less sleep The si-lent stars go__ by. Yet in thy dark streets shi - neth The e-ver-last-ing Light: The__ hopes and fears of__ all__ the years Are met in thee to-night.

II

(*Christmas*)

Lewis H. Redner (1831–1908)

1. O lit-tle town of Beth-le-hem, How still we__ see thee lie! A -

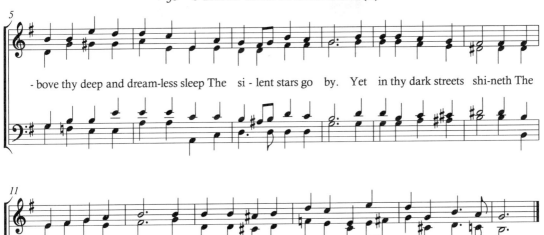

-bove thy deep and dream-less sleep The si - lent stars go by. Yet in thy dark streets shi-neth The e - ver-last-ing Light: The hopes and fears of all the years Are_ met in_ thee to-night.

2 O morning stars, together
    Proclaim the holy Birth!
And praises sing to God the King,
    And peace to men on earth;
For Christ is born of Mary,
    And, gathered all above,
While mortals sleep, the angels keep
    Their watch of wondering love.

3 How silently, how silently
    The wondrous gift is given!
So God imparts to human hearts
    The blessings of his heaven.
No ear may hear his coming,
    But, in this world of sin,
Where meek souls will receive him, still
    The dear Christ enters in.

4 Where children pure and happy
    Pray to the blessèd Child;
Where misery cries out to thee,
    Son of the mother mild;
Where Charity stands watching
    And Faith holds wide the door,
The dark night wakes, the glory breaks,
    And Christmas comes once more.

5 O holy child of Bethlehem,
    Descend to us we pray;
Cast out our sin, and enter in:
    Be born in us today!
We hear the Christmas angels
    The great glad tidings tell;
O come to us, abide with us,
    Our Lord Emmanuel!

Phillips Brooks (1835–93)

III

(*Christmas*)

Henry Walford Davies (1869–1941)

2 O morning stars, together
   Proclaim the holy Birth!
And praises sing to God the King,
   And peace to men on earth;
For Christ is born of Mary,
   And, gathered all above,
While mortals sleep, the angels keep
   Their watch of wondering love.

3 How silently, how silently
   The wondrous gift is given!
So God imparts to human hearts
   The blessings of his heaven.
No ear may hear his coming,
   But, in this world of sin,
Where meek souls will receive him, still
   The dear Christ enters in.

4 Where children pure and happy
   Pray to the blessèd Child;
Where misery cries out to thee,
   Son of the mother mild;
Where Charity stands watching
   And Faith holds wide the door,
The dark night wakes, the glory breaks,
   And Christmas comes once more.

5 O holy child of Bethlehem,
   Descend to us we pray;
Cast out our sin, and enter in:
   Be born in us today!
We hear the Christmas angels
   The great glad tidings tell;
O come to us, abide with us,
   Our Lord Emmanuel!

Phillips Brooks (1835–93)

Brooks, an Episcopalian priest, wrote this hymn for the children of his Sunday School. It was inspired by a visit, on Christmas Eve 1865, to the field outside Bethlehem where the annunciation to the shepherds is said to have taken place.

Tune I, 'Forest Green', is Vaughan Williams's arrangement of the melody of a ballad which he collected in the Surrey village of that name in 1903. The long upbeat to the final strain (bar 12) is not in the melody as he originally transcribed it, but was his preferred version for the hymn-tune.

Redner, Brooks's organist at his church in Philadelphia, conceived what is now the standard US setting (II) during a profound slumber on Christmas Day 1868, committing it to paper immediately on awaking.

Walford Davies' setting originally consisted of two verses for solo piano and one for choir, with an introductory recitative from St Luke. He made the present adaptation (III) himself.

PERFORMANCE I, II, III, voices and organ; III can also be effective with choir alone.

See *NOBC* for Cornelius: *Drei Kön'ge wandern aus Morgenland* (no. 102).

57

It came upon the midnight clear

I

(Christmas)

Richard Storrs Willis (1819–1900)
(arr. Uzziah Christopher Burnap, 1834–1900)

1. It came up-on the mid-night clear, That glo-rious song of old, From an - gels, bend - ing near the earth To touch their harps of gold: 'Peace on the earth, good - will to men From heaven's all - gra - cious King!' The world in so - lemn still - ness lay To hear the an - gels sing.

2 Still through the cloven skies they come,
　　With peaceful wings unfurled,
And still their heavenly music floats
　　O'er all the weary world:
Above its sad and lowly plains
　　They bend on hovering wing,
And ever o'er its Babel sounds
　　The blessèd angels sing.

3 Yet with the woes of sin and strife
　　The world has suffered long:
Beneath the angels' strain have rolled
　　Two thousand years of wrong,
And man, at war with man, hears not
　　The love-song which they bring:
O hush the noise, ye men of strife,
　　And hear the angels sing!

4 And ye, beneath life's crushing load,
　　Whose forms are bending low,
Who toil along the climbing way
　　With painful steps and slow,
Look now! for glad and golden hours
　　Come swiftly on the wing;
O rest beside the weary road,
　　And hear the angels sing!

5 For lo! the days are hastening on,
　　By prophet-bards foretold,
When, with the ever-circling years,
　　Comes round the Age of Gold,
When peace shall over all the earth
　　Its ancient splendours fling,
And the whole world give back the song
　　Which now the angels sing.

Edmund H. Sears (1810–76)

II

(Christmas)

Traditional?
adapted by Arthur Sullivan (1842–1900)

1. It__ came up-on the__ mid-night clear, That glo-rious song__ of old, From an-gels, bend-ing near the earth To__ touch their harps of gold: 'Peace on the earth, good-will to men From heaven's all-gra-cious King!' The world in__ so-lemn still-ness lay To__ hear the__ an-gels sing.

2 Still through the cloven skies they come,
  With peaceful wings unfurled,
And still their heavenly music floats
  O'er all the weary world:
Above its sad and lowly plains
  They bend on hovering wing,
And ever o'er its Babel sounds
  The blessèd angels sing.

3 Yet with the woes of sin and strife
  The world has suffered long:
Beneath the angels' strain have rolled
  Two thousand years of wrong,
And man, at war with man, hears not
  The love-song which they bring:
O hush the noise, ye men of strife,
  And hear the angels sing!

4 And ye, beneath life's crushing load,
  Whose forms are bending low,
Who toil along the climbing way
  With painful steps and slow,
Look now! for glad and golden hours
  Come swiftly on the wing;
O rest beside the weary road,
  And hear the angels sing!

5 For lo! the days are hastening on,
  By prophet-bards foretold,
When, with the ever-circling years,
  Comes round the Age of Gold,
When peace shall over all the earth
  Its ancient splendours fling,
And the whole world give back the song
  Which now the angels sing.

Edmund H. Sears (1810–76)

Sears was a Unitarian clergyman, typical in his social concern, untypical in his belief in the divinity of Christ. Tune I was arranged by Burnap from Willis's Organ Study No. 23. Tune II, which is reminiscent of the Sussex Mummer's Carol (see *The Oxford Book of Carols*, 1928, no. 45), is Sullivan's adaptation of an eight-bar melody that was sent to him by a friend.

PERFORMANCE   I and II, voices and organ.

58

Ding-dong ding!

(Christmas)

(*Piae Cantiones, 1582,*
arr. G. R. Woodward, 1848–1934)

Ding-dong ding!__ Ding-a-dong-a-ding! Ding-dong, ding-dong, ding-a-dong ding!

Up, good Christ-en Folk, and li-sten_ How the mer-ry church__
Tell the sto-ry How from glo-ry__ God came down at Christ -

__ bells ring, And, from stee-ple,__ Bid good peo-ple Come a-dore the
- mas-tide, Bring-ing glad-ness,_ Cha-sing sad-ness, Show'r-ing bless-ings

G. R. Woodward (1848–1934)

¹ of the Virgin Mary   ² Christ is born today

The tune is taken from a secular Latin song in *Piae Cantiones*. Woodward ignored the fact that in the original, bars 1–4 are repeated at the end: it could be effective to repeat from the opening rather than from bar 5, and perhaps also to repeat bars 1–4 at the end, as is sometimes done. PERFORMANCE   Choir.

59

Past three o'clock

(*Christmas*)

Traditional
(*arr. Charles Wood, 1866–1926*)

REFRAIN

Past three o'-clock, And a cold,_ frost-y morn-ing: Past three o'-clock: Good_ mor-row, mas-ters all!

Fine VERSE

1. Born is a Ba - by,
2. Se - raph quire sing - eth,

D.C.

Gen-tle as may be, Son_ of_ th'e - ter - nal Fa - ther su - per-nal.
An - gel bell ring-eth: Hark how they rime_ it, Time it and chime it!

3 Mid earth rejoices
 Hearing such voices
 Ne'ertofore so well
 Carolling 'Nowell'.

4 Hinds o'er the pearly,
 Dewy lawn early
 Seek the high stranger
 Laid in the manger.

5 Cheese from the dairy
 Bring they for Mary,
 And, not for money,
 Butter and honey.

6 Light out of star-land
 Leadeth from far land
 Princes to meet him,
 Worship and greet him.

7 Myrrh from full coffer,
 Incense they offer;
 Nor is the golden
 Nugget withholden.

8 Thus they: I pray you,
 Up, sirs, nor stay you
 Till ye confess him
 Likewise, and bless him.

Refrain traditional
Verses G. R. Woodward (1848–1934)

The tune of this carol (printed by John Playford in *The English Dancing Master*, 3rd. edn., 1665) and the words of the refrain originally constituted the call of the London waits, originally town watchmen but by the seventeenth century a band of civic musicians. This 'signature tune' (like those of their counterparts elsewhere) probably derived from the hourly call of their medieval predecessors. The 'verse' section was probably originally instrumental, but Woodward set words to it in his best antiquarian manner. PERFORMANCE Choir.

60

Blessed be that maid Marie

(*Christmas*)

Traditional
(*arr. Charles Wood, 1866–1926*)

VERSE

1. Bless-ed be that maid Ma - rie;— Born he was of her bo - dy;—
Ve - ry God ere time be - gan,— Born in time the Son of Man.—

REFRAIN

E - ya! Ihe - sus ho - di - e Na - tus est de Vir - gi - ne.[1]

2 In a manger of an ass
   Jesu lay and lullèd[2] was;
   Born to die upon the Tree
   Pro peccante homine.[3]

3 Sweet and blissful was the song
   Chanted of the angel throng:
   'Peace on earth, alleluya!
   In excelsis gloria.'[4]

4 Fare three kings from far-off land,
   Incense, gold and myrrh in hand;
   In Bethlem the Babe they see,
   Stelle ducti lumine.[5]

5 Make we merry on this fest,
   In quo Christus natus est;[6]
   On this Child I pray you call,
   To assoil[7] and save us all.

*Fifteenth-century (Sloane MS,
rev. G. R. Woodward, 1848–1934)*

[1] Rejoice! Jesus is born today of a virgin   [2] soothed [with a lullaby]   [3] for sinful man   [4] glory in the highest   [5] led by the light of a star   [6] on which Christ was born   [7] absolve

The tune, 'Staines Morris', is one of a large and complex family of related morris tunes.
PERFORMANCE Choir.

See *NOBC* for Wood: *Hail, blessed Virgin Mary!* (no. 107).

61

Ding! dong! merrily on high

(*Christmas*)

Thoinot Arbeau (1520–95)
(*arr. editors*)

1. Ding! dong! mer-ri-ly on high___ In___ heav'n the___ bells are ring-ing;
Ding! dong! ve-ri-ly the sky___ Is___ riv'n with an-gel sing-ing.

Glo
Glo - - ria, glo - - - ria,

Glo - - ria,

ri - a! Ho - san - na___ in___ ex - cel - sis!

glo - - ri - a!

2 E'en so here below, below,
　　Let steeple bells be swungen,
　　And 'Io, io, io!'
　　　By priest and people sungen.

3 Pray you, dutifully prime
　　Your matin chime, ye ringers!
　　May you beautifully rime
　　Your evetime song, ye singers!

G. R. Woodward (1848–1934)

'Thoinot Arbeau' is the anagrammatical name of Jehan Tabourot, a French cleric who published a treatise on dancing, *Orchésographie*, in 1588. The tune is that of the 'Branle de l'official', a vigorous and rather saucy dance which involved the men lifting the women into the air, as in Queen Elizabeth's favourite *volta*. 'L'official' probably refers to *l'office*, the servants' hall. (See *NOBC* no. 108 for two instrumental versions).

PERFORMANCE Voices, with instruments *ad lib.*

62

Lullay, my liking
I saw a maiden
Myn Lyking

I

Gustav Holst (1874–1934)

(Christmas)

Lullay, my liking, my dear son, my sweeting;

Lullay, my dear heart, mine own dear darling!

VERSE 1
SOLO
1. I saw a fair maiden sitten and sing: She
lulled a little child, a sweete lording. *(Repeat refrain)*

VERSE 2
SOLO
2. That eternal Lord is he that made alle thing: Of
alle lordes he is Lord, Of alle kinges King. *(Repeat refrain)*

(continued overleaf)

VERSE 3
SOLO
(21)

3. There was mic - kle[1] me - lo - dy at that Child - es birth: Al - though

they were in hea - ven's bliss they ma - de mic - kle mirth.

(Repeat refrain)

VERSE 4
FULL

4. An - gels bright they sang that night, and said - en to that Child: 'Bless - ed be

thou, and so be she that is both meek and mild!'

(Repeat refrain)

VERSE 5
SOLO

5. Pray we now to that Child and to his mo - ther dear; God

grant them all his bless - ing that now ma - ken cheer!

Fifteenth-century
(Sloane MS, adapted)

[1] much

II

(Christmas)

Edgar Pettman (1866–1943)

VERSE

1. I saw a maid-en sit-ting and sing: She lull'd her child, a lit-tle lord-

REFRAIN
Slower
SOPRANO(S) [& ORGAN]

FULL

-ing. Lul - lay,_____ lul - lay,_____ my_ dear_ son, my sweet-ing; Lul -

Faster

- lay,_ lul - lay,_ my_ dear son, my_ own_ dear dear - ing.

2 This very Lord, he made all things,
   And this very God, the King of all kings.

3 There was sweet music at this child's birth,
   And heaven filled with angels, making
   much mirth.

4 Heaven's angels sang to welcome the child
   Now born of a maid, all undefiled.

5 Pray we and sing on this festal day
   That peace may dwell with us alway.

Fifteenth-century
(Sloane MS, adapted)

Music © 1923 B. Feldman and Co. Ltd., trading as H. Freeman and Co., London WC2H 0EA

III

R. R. Terry (1865–1938)

(*Christmas*)

Allegro moderato ♩ = 112

[ORGAN] *f* (*repeat* *mf*)

[Ped.]

VERSE
mf SOPRANOS

1. I saw a fair— may - den— syt - tin and sing: She
2. That same— Lord is he— that— made al - le thing; Of
3. There was mic-kle[1] me - lo - dy at that Chyld-e's birth:—
4. An - gels bright sang— their— song to that Chyld: 'Blyss-

Fine

mf

v. 1: cresc. e rit. / v. 2: rall.
v. 3: cresc. molto rall. / v. 4: cresc. molto rit.

v. 2: cresc.

lull - - ed a lyt - tel childe, a swee - te lord - ing.
al - le lord - is he is Lord, of al - le kyng - es Kyng.
All that were in heav'n - ly bliss, they made— mic - kle mirth.
-id be thou, and so be she, so meek and so— mild!'

v. 2: cresc.

(*see above*)

[1] much

182

Fifteenth-century
(*Sloane MS, adapted*)

The same fifteenth-century carol from the Sloane Manuscript (British Library, MS 2593) is set by each composer, though the degree of updating and rewriting varies significantly. No fifteenth-century setting survives.

PERFORMANCE I, choir; II (*i*) choir, (*ii*) choir and organ; III, choir and organ.

See *NOBC* for R. O. Morris: *Love came down at Christmas* (no. 110).

63

In the bleak mid-winter

I

(Christmas)

Harold Darke (1888–1976)

In the bleak mid - win - ter   A sta - ble - place suf - ficed   The

Lord___ God al - might - y___ Je - - - sus Christ.

D.C. for v. 3

mp [CHOIR *with* ORGAN *ad lib.*]

S. *semplice*

A.

4. What can I give him,   Poor as I   am?   If   I   were a

mp   T.   B.

shep - herd___ I would bring a lamb;_____   If   I   were a

Christina Rossetti (1830–94)

Christina Rossetti did not intend this fine poem as a hymn or carol. The free rhythm does not easily lend itself to a single-verse setting such as Holst's (II, overleaf), but the problem is effortlessly solved in Harold Darke's through-composed setting (I), an object-lesson in *multum in parvo*.

See *NOBC* for Warlock: *Bethlehem Down* (no. 112) and Rubbra & Webern: *Dormi, Jesu!* (no. 113).

PERFORMANCE   I, soprano (verse 1) and tenor (verse 3) soli, choir, and organ. Darke does not specify forces for the other verses, but verse 2 provides an effective contrast if sung unaccompanied; his small notes in bars 37–40 imply optional organ accompaniment in verse 4.

II (*i*) choir with organ *ad lib.*, (*ii*) unison voices and organ.

II

(*Christmas*)   *Gustav Holst (1874–1934)*

1. In the bleak mid - win - ter   Frost - y wind made   moan,___
4. An - gels and arch - an - gels   May have ga - thered   there,___
5. What___ can I give him,   Poor___ as I   am?___

Earth stood hard as ir - on,   Wa - ter like a   stone:
Che - ru - bim and se - ra - phim   Thronged the___ air: But
If I were a shep - herd   I would bring a   lamb;

Snow had fall - en, snow on snow,   Snow___ on___ snow,
on - ly his mo - ther   In her mai - den bliss
If I were a wise___ man   I would do my part;   Yet

In the bleak mid - win - ter,   Long___ a - go.
Wor - shipped the be - lo - ved   With___ a___ kiss.
what I can I give him—   Give___ my___ heart.

(16) VERSES 2, 3

2. Our God, heaven can - not hold___ him   Nor___ earth sus - tain:___
3. E - nough for him, whom Che - ru - bim   Wor - ship night and day,___   A

Heaven and earth shall flee a - way___   When he comes to reign:
breast - ful of milk___ And a man - ger - ful of hay: E -

In the bleak mid - win - ter   A sta - ble - place suf - ficed   The
- nough for him, whom an - gels___   Fall___ down be - fore,   The

Lord___ God al - might - y   Je - sus___ Christ.
ox and ass and ca - mel   Which___ a - dore.

Christina Rossetti (1830–94)

64

Wither's Rocking Hymn

(Christmas)

Ralph Vaughan Williams (1872–1958)

1. Sweet ba - by, sleep! What ailes my dear? What ailes my
2. Thou bless - ed soul, what canst thou fear? What thing to

dar - ling thus to cry? Be still, my childe, and lend thine
thee can mis - chief do? Thy God is now thy Fa - ther

ear To heare— me sing— thy lul - la - by.
dear, His ho - ly spouse[1] thy mo - ther, too.

[1] i.e., the Church

17

pp

My   pret - ty   lambe,   for - bear_____ to   weep;
Sweet   ba - bie,   then,   for - bear_____ to   weep;

CHOIR (UNACCOMPANIED)

pp

Sweet_____   ba   -   bie,

pp

21

Be   still,   my   dear;   sweet   ba - bie,   sleep!
Be   still,   my   babe;   sweet   ba - bie,   sleep!

sleep!_____   sweet   ba - bie,   sleep!

*3   Though thy conception was in sin,
       A sacred bathing² thou hast had;
     And, though thy birth unclean hath bin,³
       A blamelesse babe thou now art made.
     Sweet babie, then, forbear to weep;
     Be still, my dear; sweet babie, sleep!

 4   Whilst thus thy lullabie I sing,
       For thee great blessings ripening be:
     Thine Eldest Brother is a King,
       And hath a kingdome bought for thee.
     Sweet babie, then, forbear to weep;
     Be still, my babe; sweet babie, sleep!

 5   Sweet babie, sleep, and nothing fear;
       For whosoever thee offends
     By thy Protector threatned are,
       And God, and angels, are thy friends.
     Sweet babie, then, forbear to weep;
     Be still, my babe; sweet babie, sleep!

 6   When God-with-us was dwelling here
       In little babes he took delight:
     Such innocents as thou, my dear,
       Are ever precious in his sight.
     Sweet babie, then, forbear to weep;
     Be still, my babe; sweet babie, sleep!

² baptism   ³ [through original sin]

7   A little infant once was hee,
    And strength in weaknesse then was
      laid
  Upon his Virgin Mother's knee,
    That power to thee might be convaied.
  Sweet babie, then, forbear to weep;
  Be still, my babe; sweet babie, sleep!

*8   In this, thy frailty and thy need,
    He friends and helpers doth prepare,
  Which thee shall cherish, clothe and feed,
    For of thy weal they tender are.
  Sweet babie, then, forbear to weep;
  Be still, my babe; sweet babie, sleep!

9   The King of Kings, when he was born,
    Had not so much for outward ease;
  By him such dressings were not worn,
    Nor suchlike swadling-clothes as these.
  Sweet babie, then, forbear to weep;
  Be still, my babe; sweet babie, sleep!

*10   Within a manger lodged thy Lord,
    Where oxen lay and asses fed:
  Warm rooms we do to thee afford,
    An easie cradle, or a bed.
  Sweet babie, then, forbear to weep;
  Be still, my babe; sweet babie, sleep!

11   The wants that he did then sustain
    Have purchased wealth, my babe,
      for thee;
  And, by his torments and his pain,
    Thy rest and ease securèd be.
  My babie, then, forbear to weep;
  Be still, my babe; sweet babie, sleep!

*12   Thou hast (yet more!) to perfect this,
    A promise and an earnest[4] got
  Of gaining everlasting blisse,
    Though thou, my babe, perceiv'st it not.
  Sweet babie, then, forbear to weep;
  Be still, my babe; sweet babie, sleep!

George Wither (1588–1667)

[4] pledge

This poem is from Wither's *Haleluiah* (1641). Unlike his earlier *Hymnes and Songes of the Church* (1623) (see *NOBC* no. 45), *Haleluiah* was published without tunes, though according to its title page the contents would fit 'easie tunes, to be sung in families, &c.' Vaughan Williams's setting, for *The Oxford Book of Carols* (1928), gave only verses 1, 4, 6, 7, 9 and 11, in modern spelling. Like most of the poems in the first volume of *Haleluiah*, 'A Rocking Hymn' was intended for directly practical use, as a cradle song.

PERFORMANCE   (*i*) Solo voice and instrument (presumably keyboard; the instrument could substitute for the choir in the refrains); (*ii*) choir and organ or piano.

65

Torches

(Christmas; New Year)

John Joubert (b. 1927)

Alla marcia

1. Tor-ches, tor-ches, run with tor-ches All the_ way to_ Beth-le-hem! Christ is born and now lies sleep-ing: Come and sing your song to him! Come and sing your song to him!

(unaccompanied ad lib.)

2. Ah, ro - ro, ro - ro,_ my_ ba - by, Ah,_ ro - ro, my_ love, ro - ro;
Ro - ro,____ ro ____ ro,____

Joubert rescued this text from the pages of *The Oxford Book of Carols* (1928), where it was mutely enduring a joyless marriage to a debased and dimly harmonized version of its Galician traditional melody.

PERFORMANCE Choir and organ.

Galician traditional
(tr. J. B. Trend, 1887–1958)

66

Watt's Cradle Hymn

(*Christmas*)

American traditional
(*adapted and arr. editors*)

1. Hush! my dear, lie still and slumber; Holy angels guard thy bed! Heav'n-ly blessings without number Gently falling on thy head. Sleep, my babe; thy food and raiment, House and home thy friends provide: All with-

-out thy care or— pay-ment, All— thy— wants are— well— sup - plied.

2 How much better thou'rt attended
   Than the Son of God could be
 When from heaven he descended
   And became a child like thee!
 Soft and easy is thy cradle,
   Coarse and hard thy Saviour lay
 When his birth-place was a stable
   And his softest bed was hay.

*3 Was there nothing but a manger
   Cursèd sinners could afford
 To receive the heav'nly stranger?
   Did they thus affront their Lord?
 Soft! my child; I did not chide thee,
   Though my song might sound too hard:
 'Tis thy mother sits beside thee,
   And her arms shall be thy guard.

*4 See the kindly shepherds round him,
   Telling wonders from the sky!
 Where they sought him, there they
     found him,
   With his Virgin Mother nigh.
 See the lovely Babe addressing:
   Lovely Infant, how he smiled!
 When he wept, the mother's blessing
   Soothed and hushed the Holy Child.

5 Lo! he slumbers in his manger,
   Where the hornèd oxen fed;
 Peace, my darling, here's no danger,
   Here's no ox a-near thy bed.
 May'st thou live to know and fear him,
   Trust and love him all thy days;
 Then go dwell for ever near him,
   See his face and sing his praise!

Isaac Watts (1674–1748)

Watts's 'Cradle-Hymn' was first published in his *Moral Songs* (1706), at the end of what he called 'these Songs for Children'. In our verse 3 he gives 'nurse that' as an alternative to 'mother', with the note 'Here you may use the words, Brother, Sister, Neighbour, Friend etc.' We include ten of the fourteen four-line stanzas.

Elizabeth Poston, in *The Second Penguin Book of Christmas Carols* (1970), married the text to the tune that forms our bars 1–16. This was one of the most popular shape-note melodies (see Introduction), and may ultimately derive from a European folk tune. We have added a middle eight bars for variety, but those who wish may restore Watts's four-line stanzas and sing them to bars 1–16 only.

PERFORMANCE (*i*) Voice and instrument (guitar, harp, etc.); (*ii*) choir.

See *NOBC* for Britten: *A Boy was born in Bethlehem* (no. 116) and *A Hymn to the Virgin* (no. 117).

67

Make we joy now in this fest

(*Christmas*)

William Walton (*1902–83*)

[1] in which Christ is born   [2] the Only-begotten of the Father   [3] let every age perceive (that)

we— of him— and   say— 'Wel-come! *Ve - ni— Re - demp - tor gen - ci - um.'*[4]
for— to   seek— with their— pre - sents, *Ver - bum— su - per - num pro - di - ens*[5]

3   *A solis ortus cardine*[6]
   So mighty a lord is none as he,
   And to our kind he hath him knit
   Adam parens quod polluit.[7]

4   *Maria ventre concepit,*[8]
   The Holy Ghost was aye her with.
   Of her in Bethlem born he is,
   Consors Paterni luminis.[9]

5   *O Lux beata Trinitas!*[10]
   He lay between an ox and ass,
   Beside his mother-maiden free:
   Gloria tibi Domine![11]

Fifteenth-century
(modernized)

[4] come, Redeemer of the nations   [5] the high Word coming forth   [6] from the rising of the sun   [7] which our father Adam defiled   [8] Mary conceived in her womb   [9] sharing in the light of his Father   [10] O Light of the Holy Trinity   [11] Glory to thee, O Lord!

Walton produced a steady trickle of church music, including several Christmas carols, throughout his life. This 'old English carol for unaccompanied mixed voices' was commissioned by *The Daily Dispatch* and first published in the issue of 24 December 1931.

PERFORMANCE   Choir.

68

There is no rose of such virtue

(*Christmas*)

John Joubert (*b. 1927*)

Andantino semplice

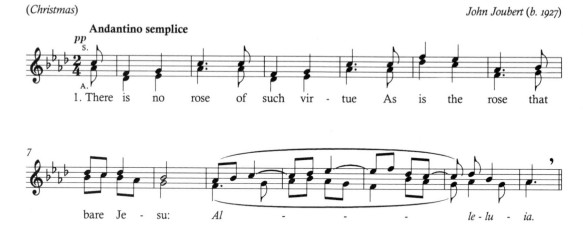

1. There is no rose of such vir - tue As is the rose that

bare Je - su: *Al* - - - *le - lu - ia.*

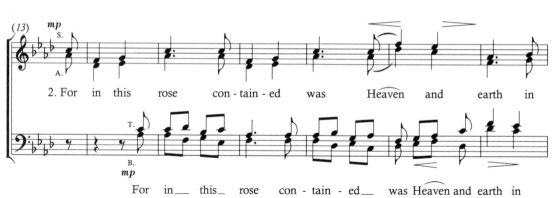

2. For in this rose con - tain - ed was Heaven and earth in

For in__ this__ rose con - tain - ed__ was Heaven and earth in

lit - tle__ space: *Res* _____ *mi - ran - da.*

lit - tle space: *Res* _____ *mi - ran - da.*

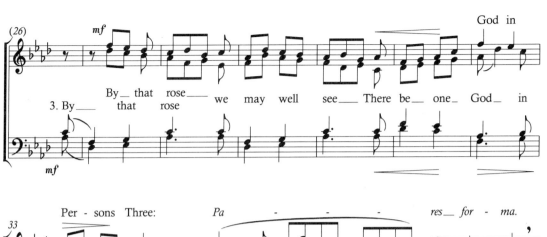

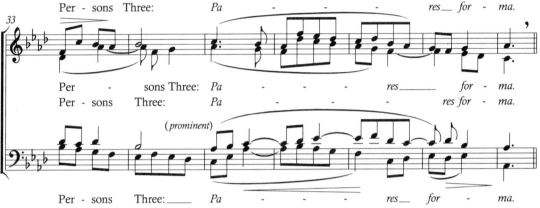

Fifteenth-century (modernized)

For a fifteenth-century setting and notes on the text see   PERFORMANCE   Choir.
'Ther is no rose of swych vertu' (13). Joubert's setting (his
op. 14) dates from 1954.

69

Adam lay ybounden

(*Christmas*)

Boris Ord (1897–1961)

[1] clergy   [2] the Bible

Ne had ne-ver our__ La - dy A - been hea-ve - ne__ queen. Bless - ed be the

time That ap - ple ta - ken was; There - fore we moun[3] sing - en: 'De - o

gra - ci - as! De - o gra - ci - as!'

Fifteenth-century
(Sloane MS, modernized)

[3] must

The text comes from the same fifteenth-century manuscript as 'Lullay, my liking' (62). Boris Ord's beautiful carol was his only published composition. It has long retained its place in the Service of Nine Lessons and Carols at King's College, Cambridge, as a memorial to one of the chapel's most distinguished recent directors of music.

PERFORMANCE Choir.

See *NOBC* for Maxwell Davies: *The Fader of heven* (no. 122) and Gardner: *When Christ was born of Mary free* (no. 123).

70

The Boar's Head Carol

(Christmas)

English traditional
(Fyfe, 1860)

Lively

1. The boar's head in hand bear I, Be-decked with bays and rose - ma-ry; And I

pray you my mas - ters be mer - ry, Quot es - tis in con - vi - vi - o.[1]

Ca - put ap - ri de - fe - ro Red - dens lau - des Do - mi - no,

lau - des Do - mi - no, lau - des Do - mi-no, Do - mi - no.[2]

[1] as many as are at the feast [2] I bring in the boar's head, giving thanks to the Lord

ALTERNATIVE REFRAIN

(Queen's College, 1901)

Ca - put ap - ri   de - fe - ro   Red - dens lau - des Do - mi - no.

2 The boar's head, as I understand,
   Is the bravest dish in all the land
   When thus bedecked with a gay garland;
   Let us *servire cantico.*[3]

3 Our steward hath provided this
   In honour of the King of Bliss,
   Which on this day to be servèd is
   In Reginensi Atrio.[4]

English traditional
(Fyfe, 1860)

[3] serve it with a song   [4] in Queen's Hall

The carol that traditionally accompanies the ceremonial entry of the main dish of the Christmas feast at The Queen's College, Oxford. The tune would appear to derive from a Restoration bass pattern; we give a version of it from Fyfe's *Christmas, its Customs and Carols* (1860) which represents the carol as it was sung at that time. The college has no record of any setting earlier than the one dating from 1901 (and still sung), in which the refrain was rewritten.

So central was the role of the wild boar's head in English feasts that the species was extinct in England by the end of the seventeenth century.

PERFORMANCE Choir.

See *NOBC* for *Come all you faithful Christians* (no. 125).

71

The holly and the ivy

(*Christmas*)

English traditional
(Sharp, 1911, arr. editors)

1. The hol-ly and the i-vy, When they are both full grown, Of all the trees that are in the wood, The hol-ly bears the crown.

The ri-sing of the sun And the run-ning of the deer, The play-ing of the mer-ry or-gan, Sweet sing-ing in the choir.

2 The holly bears a blossom
   As white as the lily flower,
   And Mary bore sweet Jesus Christ
   To be our sweet Saviour.

3 The holly bears a berry
   As red as any blood,
   And Mary bore sweet Jesus Christ
   To do poor sinners good.

4 The holly bears a prickle
   As sharp as any thorn,
   And Mary bore sweet Jesus Christ
   On Christmas Day in the morn.

5 The holly bears a bark
   As bitter as any gall,
   And Mary bore sweet Jesus Christ
   For to redeem us all.

6 The holly and the ivy,
   When they are both full grown,
   Of all the trees that are in the wood,
   The holly bears the crown.

English traditional
(*Sharp, 1911*)

This text and tune are the versions now standard. Cecil Sharp transcribed them from the singing of Mrs Mary Clayton at Chipping Campden, Gloucestershire, supplementing and correcting the text from other sources for publication in 1911. We suspect that the words of the 'refrain' may well have been newly tacked on to the older carol by a Birmingham broadside publisher around 1710. The (ident- ical) text for verses 1 and 6 is probably the original refrain for a four-verse carol comprising the present verses 2–5 and sung in the old pattern of refrain–verse–refrain, etc.; this scheme may easily be restored.

PERFORMANCE Choir.

72

Now the holly bears a berry
(The St Day Carol)

English traditional
(*Oxford Book of Carols, 1928,*
arr. editors)

(*Christmas*)

1. Now the hol - ly bears a ber - ry as white as the milk, And— Ma - ry bore— Je - sus who was wrapped up in silk.
2. Now the hol - ly bears a ber - ry as green as the grass, And— Ma - ry bore— Je - sus who— died on the cross.

And— Ma - ry bore— Je - sus Christ, our Sa - viour for to be, And the

first tree of the green-wood, it was the hol - ly; Hol - ly! hol -

- ly! And the first tree of the green-wood, it was the hol - ly.

3 Now the holly bears a berry as black as a coal,
   And Mary bore Jesus, who died for us all.

*4 Now the holly bears a berry as red as the blood,
   And Mary bore Jesus, who died on the Rood.

*vv. 1–3 English traditional
v. 4 W. D. Watson (Oxford Book of Carols, 1928)*

The melody belongs to the vast family of 'A virgin unspotted' (82) variants and is remarkable for beginning each line with the same figure. The carol is also unusual in equating the holly with the Virgin: more usually holly is a masculine symbol, and it is ivy, its feminine counterpart, that is associated with Mary (see notes, *NOBC* no. 126).

PERFORMANCE   Choir.

73

The Cherry Tree Carol

I
The Cherry Tree [Part I]

(Christmas)

English traditional
(Hutchens MS, arr. editors)

1. Jo - seph was an old man, and an old__ man_ was_ he__ When

he wed - ded__ Ma - ry in the land of Ga - li - lee,__ when

he__ wed - ded Ma - ry in the land of__ Ga - li - lee.

2 When Joseph was married and Mary home had got,
   Mary proved with child, by whom Joseph knew not.

3 Joseph and Mary walked through an orchard good,
   Where was cherries and berries, so red as any blood.

*4 Joseph and Mary walked through an orchard green,
Where was berries and cherries, as thick as might be seen.

5 O then bespoke Mary, so meek and so mild:
'Pluck me a cherry, Joseph; they run so in my mind.'

6 O then bespoke Joseph, with words most reviled:
'Let him pluck thee a cherry that brought thee with child.'

7 O then bespoke Jesus, all in his mother's womb:
'Bow down, then, thou tallest tree, for my mother to have some!

*8 'Go to the tree, Mary, and it shall bow to thee,
And the highest branch of all shall bow to Mary's knee.'

9 Then bowèd down the tallest tree, it bent to Mary's hand;
Then she cried: 'See, Joseph, I have cherries at command.'

10 O then bespoke Joseph: 'I have done Mary wrong.
But cheer up, my dearest, and do not be cast down!

*11 'O eat your cherries, Mary, O eat your cherries now!
O eat your cherries, Mary, that grow upon the bough!'

12 Then Mary plucked a cherry, as red as any blood;
And she did travel onward, all with her heavy load.

English traditional
(*Hone, 1823, adapted*)

This ballad probably had a longer medieval ancestor which was also in three sections and may well have been the work of a cleric. We have freely amended and expanded Hone's text (*Ancient Mysteries Described*, 1823) from other sources to give a balanced structure and (with choral performance in mind) a relatively smooth fit with the music. The three sections evoke the journey to Bethlehem, the moment of the Nativity (Joseph's angelic visitation occurs while he is searching for a midwife), and the sojourn in Bethlehem. (For more on the text of this carol, see notes to *NOBC* no. 128.)

The ballad has been associated with several melodies. The received tradition, from the eighteenth century onward, is of a single tune for however much of the ballad is sung, though earlier practice may have been different; a single tune is perhaps best for solo performance. Our three tunes correspond to those given (as tunes 1, 3, and 4) in the revised edition (1964) of the *Oxford Book of Carols* (1928).

PERFORMANCE I, II, III (*i*) unaccompanied voice, perhaps using the same tune throughout; (*ii*) choir. The ballad can be sung complete or in one of the following forms: part I alone; parts I and II; part II alone; or parts II and III. Starred verses may be omitted without disturbing the narrative.

See *NOBC* for *When righteous Joseph wedded was* (no. 129).

II
Joseph and the Angel
[The Cherry Tree, Part II]

(*Christmas*)

English traditional
(*Terry, 1923, arr. editors*)

1. As Jo - seph was a - walk - ing, he heard an an - gel sing:___ 'This
night___ shall___ be born - ed our hea - ven - ly King.___

2   'He neither shall be bornèd in housen nor in hall,
    Nor in the place of Paradise, but in an ox's stall.

3   'He neither shall be clothèd in purple nor in pall,
    But in the fair white linen, as usen babies all.

4   'He neither shall be rockèd in silver nor in gold,
    But in a wooden cradle that rocks upon the mould.[1]

5   'He neither shall be christenèd in white wine nor red,
    But with the fair spring water with which we were christenèd.'

English traditional
(*Hone, 1823, adapted*)

[1] ground

III
Mary and Jesus
[The Cherry Tree, Part III]

(Christmas)

English traditional
(Sharp MS, arr. editors)

1. Then Ma-ry took her young son and set him on her knee,— Say-ing:

'My dear son,— tell— me how— this world shall— be!',— say-ing:

'My dear son,— tell— me how— this— world shall— be!'

2 'O I shall be as dead, mother, as the stones in the wall,
   And the stones in the streets, mother, shall mourn for me all.

3 'And upon a Wednesday my vow I will make,
   And upon Good Friday my death I will take.

4 'And upon the third day my uprising shall be,
   And the sun and moon together shall rise up with me.

5 'The people shall rejoice, and the birds they shall sing
   To see the uprising of the heavenly King.'

English traditional
(Hone, 1823, adapted)

74

O Joseph, being an old man truly
Joseph, being an aged man truly

I

(*Christmas*)

English traditional
(Vaughan Williams, 1920)

VERSES 1–4

1. O Joseph, being an old man truly, He married a virgin fair and free; A purer virgin could no man see Than he chose for his wife and his dearest dear.

2. They lived both in joy and bliss; But now a strict commandment is: In Jewry land no man should miss To go along with his dearest dear

3. Unto the place where he was born, Unto the emperor to be sworn, To pay a tribute that's duly known, Both for himself and his dearest dear.

4. And when they were to Bethlehem come The inns were filled, both all and some; For Joseph entreated them every one, Both for himself and his dearest dear.

VERSES 5–7

5. Then they were constrained presently Within a stable all night to lie, Where they did oxen and asses tie, With his true love and his dearest dear.

*6. The Virgin pure thought it no scorn To lie in such a place forlorn; But against the next morning our Saviour was born, Even Jesus Christ, our dearest dear.

7. The King of all power was in Bethlehem born, Who wore for our sakes a crown of thorn: Then God preserve us both even and morn, For Jesus' sake, our dearest dear!

English traditional
(Sandys, 1833)

II

English traditional
(arr. Ralph Vaughan Williams, 1872–1958)

Ah,_____ Ah,_____

†1. O Jo - seph, being an old man tru - ly, He__ mar-ried a vir - gin

Ah,_____ Ah,_____

fair and free; A pu - rer vir - gin could no man see Than he

Ah._____

chose for his__ wife and his dear - est__ dear.

Ah._____

† Follow text of I for verses 2–7.

The text is from William Sandys's *Christmas Carols, Ancient and Modern* (1833; see *NOBC* Appendix 4). He gives no melody, and both of the tunes given here were collected with different words. Vaughan Williams married the splendid tune of I/II (which is related to no. 84 setting II and *NOBC* no. 140) with six verses selected from Sandys's sixteen, omitting the story of 'doubting Joseph' which forms the substance of the carol. We give this now familiar selection with tune I/II, adding the starred verse 6 so that the seven comprise Sandys's verses 1 and 11–16. The eleven verses

given with tune III take the alternative route, and comprise Sandys's verses 1–10 and 16. This tune was collected by A. L. Lloyd with a song beginning 'A pretty young girl all in the month of May'.

NOBC setting IV (not included here) is based on a tune and bass in the Cornish Davey MS.

PERFORMANCE I, solo voice, perhaps with a drone on A or A–E, or on a 'rocking' drone alternating between A–E and G–D, one chord per bar (two in bar 2).

II, choir.

III, (*i*) solo voice; (*ii*) choir.

III

(*Annunciation; Christmas*)

English traditional
(*Lloyd, 1967, arr. editors*)

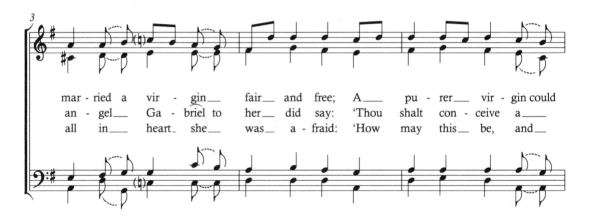

VERSES 1–3

1. Jo - seph, being an a - ged___ man___ tru - ly, He
2. The vir - gin___ pure there___ was___ no nay; The
3. The an - gel no soon - er this mes - sage said But

mar - ried a vir - gin___ fair___ and free; A___ pu - rer___ vir - gin could
an - gel___ Ga - briel to her___ did say: 'Thou shalt con - ceive a___
all in___ heart___ she___ was___ a - fraid: 'How may this___ be, and___

no___ man___ see Than he chose for his wife___ and his dear - est dear.
Child this___ day, The___ which shall___ be___ our___ dear - est dear.'
I a pure___ maid? Say___ then___ to___ me,___ my___ dear - est dear.'

VERSES 4–6

4. 'The Ho - ly Ghost,_ Ma - ry, shall come_ un - to thee; The
 5. Jo - seph,_ being a_____ per - fect mild_ man, Per -
6. Then an - swer-ed Ma - ry,_____ meek_ and_ mild: 'I

power of it shall_ o - ver - sha - dow thee, And_ thou shalt_ bear a_____
-cei - ving that Ma - ry with child_ was gone, Said:_ 'Tell me,_ Ma - ry, and
know no_ fa - ther un - to_ my child But the Ho - ly_ Ghost, and_

(continued overleaf)

Son tru - ly, The_ which shall_ be_____ our_ dear - est dear.'
do not_ frown, Who_ hath_ done_ this,_ my_ dear - est dear?'
I un - de - filed, That_ hath_ done_ this,_ my_ dear - est dear.'

VERSES 7–9

7. But Jo - seph, ___ think - ing her most ___ un - just, Yield -
8. But whilst in ___ heart he ___ thought the same The
9. Who said: 'Fear ___ not to ___ take ___ to thee Thy

- ing her ___ bo - dy to un - law - ful lust, Out ___ of his ___ house he ___
an - gel ___ Ga - briel ___ to ___ him came As ___ he lay sleep - ing ___
true and ___ faith - ful ___ wife, ___ Ma - ry: Most ___ true and ___ faith - ful is

thought for to thrust His ___ own ___ true ___ love, ___ his ___ dear - est dear.
on a ___ frame, Still ___ dream - ing ___ on ___ his ___ dear - est dear;
she to ___ thee; Then ___ turn ___ not a - way ___ thy ___ dear - est dear!'

VERSES 10–11

10. When Jo - seph a - rose from his sleep___ so sound His
11. The King of all power was in Beth - lehem born, Who

love to___ Ma - ry did more___ a - bound; He___ would not___ for ten___
wore for___ our___ sakes a crown of thorn: Then God pre - serve us both

thou - sand___ pound For - sake___ his___ love___ and___ dear - est dear.
even and___ morn, For___ Je - sus'___ sake,___ our___ dear - est dear!

English traditional
(Sandys, 1833)

75

The Seven Joys of Mary
The Seven Rejoices of Mary
The Blessings of Mary

I
The Seven Joys of Mary

(*Christmas*)

English traditional
(arr. R. R. Terry, 1865–1938)

VERSE

1. The first good joy that Ma - ry had, it was the joy of one:___ To

REFRAIN

see her own___ Son, Je - sus, to suck at her___ breast - bone;___ To

suck at her breast - bone, good man,___ and bless - ed may he be:_____ Sing

Fa - ther, Son and Ho - ly Ghost, to all___ e - ter - ni - ty.___

2 The next good joy that Mary had, it was the joy of two:
To see her own Son, Jesus, to make the lame to go;

To make the lame to go, good man, and blessèd may he be,
Sing Father, Son and Holy Ghost, to all eternity.

3 The next good joy that Mary had, it was the joy of three:
To see her own Son, Jesus, to make the blind to see;

To make the blind to see, good man, (etc.)

4 The next good joy that Mary had, it was the joy of four:
To see her own Son, Jesus, to read the Bible o'er;

To read the Bible o'er, good man, (etc.)

5 The next good joy that Mary had, it was the joy of five:
To see her own Son, Jesus, to make the dead alive;

To make the dead alive, good man, (etc.)

6 The next good joy that Mary had, it was the joy of six:
To see her own Son, Jesus, to bear the Crucifix;

To bear the Crucifix, good man, (etc.)

7 The next good joy that Mary had, it was the joy of seven:
To see her own Son, Jesus, to wear the crown of heaven;

To wear the crown of heaven, good man, (etc.)

English traditional
(Brand, 1853–5; Sandys, 1833)

II
The Seven Rejoices of Mary

(Christmas)

Irish traditional
(Journal of the Irish Folk
Song Society, arr. editors)

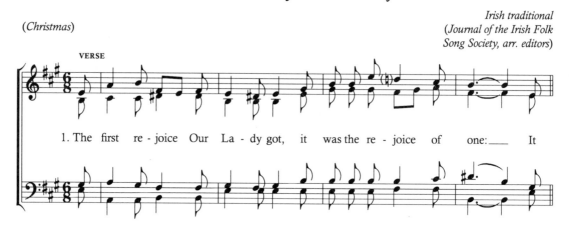

1. The first re-joice Our La-dy got, it was the re-joice of one:___ It

was the re-joice of her___ dear Son___ when he was born___ young,___ it

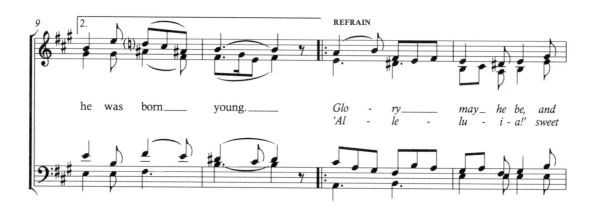

he was born___ young.___   Glo - ry___ may_ he be, and
'Al - le - lu - i - a!' sweet

bless - ed now___ is she,_____ And those___ who sing the
'Al - le - lu - i - a!'_____ Sing 'Al - le - lu - ia! the

se - ven long ver - ses in hon - our of Our La - dy._____ Sing
hea - vens are true!'___ Sing 'Al - le - lu - i- - - - a!'_____

2 The second rejoice Our Lady got, it was the rejoice of two:
   It was the rejoice of her dear Son when he was sent to school.

3 The third rejoice Our Lady got, it was the rejoice of three:
   It was the rejoice of her dear Son when he led the blind to see.

4 The next rejoice Our Lady got, it was the rejoice of four:
   It was the rejoice of her dear Son when he read the Bible o'er.

5 The next rejoice Our Lady got, it was the rejoice of five:
   It was the rejoice of her dear Son when he raised the dead to life.

6 The next rejoice Our Lady got, it was the rejoice of six:
   It was the rejoice of her dear Son when he carried the Crucifix.

7 The next rejoice Our Lady got, it was the rejoice of seven:
   It was the rejoice of her dear Son when he opened the gates of heaven.

Irish traditional
(*Journal of the Irish Folk Song Society*)

III
The Blessings of Mary

(*Christmas*)

US traditional
(Journal of American Folklore, 1935)

1. The ve - ry first bless - ing Ma - ry had, it was the bless-ing of one: To think that her Son, Je - sus, could live a fa - ther's son; *Could live a fa - ther's son, like th'Em - ma - nu - el in glo - ry, Fa - ther, Son and the Ho - ly Ghost, through all e - ter - ni - ty.*

2 The very next blessing Mary had, it was the blessing of two:
To think that her Son, Jesus, could read the Scriptures through;

Could read the Scriptures through, like th'Emmanuel in glory, (etc.)

3 The very next blessing Mary had, it was the blessing of three:
To think that her Son, Jesus, could set the sinner free;

Could set the sinner free, (etc.)

4 The very next blessing Mary had, it was the blessing of four:
To think that her Son, Jesus, could live for evermore;

Could live for evermore, (etc.)

5 The very next blessing Mary had, it was the blessing of five:
To think that her Son, Jesus, could bring the dead to live;

Could bring the dead to live, (etc.)

6 The very next blessing Mary had, it was the blessing of six:
To think that her Son, Jesus, could heal and cure the sick;

Could heal and cure the sick, (etc.)

7 The very next blessing Mary had, it was the blessing of seven:
To think that her Son, Jesus, could conquer hell and heaven;

Could conquer hell and heaven, (etc.)

8 The very next blessing Mary had, it was the blessing of eight:
To think that her Son, Jesus, could make the crooked straight;

Could make the crooked straight, (etc.)

9 The very next blessing Mary had, it was the blessing of nine:
To think that her Son, Jesus, could turn water into wine;

Could turn water into wine, (etc.)

10 The very next blessing Mary had, it was the blessing of ten:
To think that her Son, Jesus, could write without a pen;

Could write without a pen, (etc.)

US traditional
(*Journal of American Folklore, 1935*)

The many variants of this text collected in Britain and the United States, with their differing numbers of Joys, reflect the popularity and diversity of the medieval devotion from which they all derive. It grew from the same roots as the Rosary and did not survive the Reformation, but sets of vernacular devotional verses lived on in folk tradition, increasingly garbled and sometimes associated with Advent luck-visits. The text with tune I approximates to what Bramley and Stainer established as the standard modern 'art' version, in their *Christmas Carols New and Old* (1871), and Terry's setting is from his *Two Hundred Folk Carols*

(1933). Both tune and text of II were transcribed (very ambiguously) by the foundress of the Irish Folk Song Society, from a phonograph recording she had made of a Mrs Lines, of Portlaw, Co. Waterford. Text and tune of III were transcribed from the singing of a Mr Will Brady of Carthage, North Carolina, by Richard Chase. (See notes in *NOBC* for an explanation of all three texts.)

PERFORMANCE I and II, choir; III, one or two voices, with guitar *ad lib.*

76

Tomorrow shall be my dancing day

English traditional
(*Sandys, 1833, arr. editors*)

1. To - mor-row shall be___ my dan - cing day; I would___ my
2. Then was___ I born of a vir - gin pure; Of her___ I
3. In a man - ger laid___ and wrapped I was, So ve - ry

true___ love did___ so chance To___ see the le - gend of___ my
took___ flesh - ly___ sub - stance. Thus was I knit___ to man's na -
poor;___ this was___ my chance, Be - twixt an ox and a sil - ly poor

play, To call my true___ love to___ the dance. *Sing O my___ love,*
- ture, To call my true___ love to___ the dance. *Sing___*
ass, To call my true___ love to___ my dance.

O___ my love, my love, my love, This have I done___ for my___ true love.
O my love,___

ALTERNATIVE REFRAIN

Sing O my love, O my love, my love, my love, This have I done for my true love.

4 Then afterwards baptized I was;
   The Holy Ghost on me did glance,
My Father's voice heard from above
   To call my true love to my dance.

5 Into the desert I was led,
   Where I fasted without substance;
The devil bade me make stones my bread,
   To have me break my true love's dance.

6 The Jews on me they made great suit,
   And with me made great variance,
Because they loved darkness rather than light,
   To call my true love to my dance.

7 For thirty pence Judas me sold,
   His covetousness for to advance:
'Mark whom I kiss, the same do hold!'
   The same is he shall lead the dance.

8 Before Pilate the Jews me brought,
   Where Barabbas had deliverance;
They scourgèd me and set me at nought,
   Judged me to die to lead the dance.

9 Then on the cross hangèd I was,
   Where a spear my heart did glance;
There issued forth both water and blood,
   To call my true love to my dance.

10 Then down to hell I took my way
   For my true love's deliverance,
And rose again on the third day,
   Up to my true love and the dance.

11 Then up to heaven I did ascend,
   Where now I dwell in sure substance
On the right hand of God, that man
   May come unto the general dance.

English traditional
(Sandys, 1833)

One of many songs traditionally sung at Christmas that trace the whole life of Christ (and thus resist truncation for carol services and concerts). The text has not been found elsewhere, and may have originated in the sung and danced conclusion to the first or second day of a three-day Cornish religious drama (see notes, *NOBC*). The tune has close relatives in no. 78 and *NOBC* no. 166.

PERFORMANCE (*i*) Choir, with instruments *ad lib.*; (*ii*) solo voice and a bass instrument; (*iii*) verse, solo; alternative refrain, three voices or choir. Our three-part arrangement of the refrain is modelled on improvisatory three-man performance.

77

The Twelve Days of Christmas

(Christmas; Twelfth Night)

*English traditional
(arr. editors)*

(15)

5. On the fifth day of Christ-mas my true love sent to me   five__ gold__ rings,

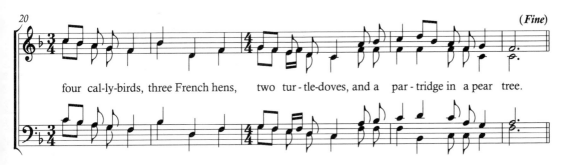

20   *(Fine)*

four cal-ly-birds, three French hens,   two tur-tle-doves, and a par-tridge in a pear tree.

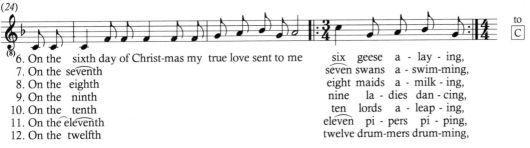

(24)

6. On the sixth day of Christ-mas my true love sent to me   six geese a - lay - ing,
7. On the seventh   seven swans a - swim-ming,
8. On the eighth   eight maids a - milk - ing,
9. On the ninth   nine la - dies dan - cing,
10. On the tenth   ten lords a - leap - ing,
11. On the eleventh   eleven pi - pers pi - ping,
12. On the twelfth   twelve drum-mers drum-ming,

to C

English traditional
(Husk, 1864)

The song is found in different forms in broadsides from the eighteenth century onward, and derives from a traditional Twelfth-Night forfeits game in which each person was required to recite a list of objects named by the previous player and add one more. The tune (one of many) reached its modern standard form only in 1909, with the inspired (and copyrighted) addition of the phrase to which 'five gold rings' is sung. (It has infiltrated *NOBC* setting II not included here, a version sung by the men of the Copper family from Sussex, who preserve an oral part-singing tradition.) The pear tree is probably from the French *perdrix* (partridge); the cally- (or colly-) birds are blackbirds, the gold rings possibly a corruption of 'goldspinks' (Scottish dialect for goldfinches) or 'gulderer' (a gulder-cock is a turkey).

PERFORMANCE   Choir.

See *NOBC* for *In those twelve days* (no. 134) and *The old yeare now away is fled* (no. 135).

78

Rejoice and be merry

(*Christmas*)

English traditional
(*Oxford Book of Carols, 1928,
arr. editors*)

1. Re - joice and be mer - ry in songs and in mirth; O praise our Re - deem - er, all mor - tals on earth! For this is the birth - day of Je - sus our King, Who brought us sal - va - tion: his prai - ses we'll sing.

2   A heavenly vision appeared in the sky;
    Vast numbers of angels the shepherds did spy,
    Proclaiming the birthday of Jesus our King,
    Who brought us salvation: his praises we'll sing.

3   Likewise a bright star in the sky did appear,
    Which led the wise men from the East to draw near;
    They found the Messiah, sweet Jesus our King,
    Who brought us salvation: his praises we'll sing.

4   And when they were come, they their treasures unfold,
    And unto him offered myrrh, incense and gold.
    So blessèd for ever be Jesus our King,
    Who brought us salvation: his praises we'll sing.

English traditional
(*Oxford Book of Carols, 1928*)

The words and tune are from an old Dorset church-gallery tune-book and were communicated to the editors of *The English Carol Book* (second series, 1919) by the Revd L. J. T. Darwall. The present whereabouts of the gallery book are not known.

The tune is closely related to those of no. 76 and *NOBC* no. 166.

PERFORMANCE   Choir.

79

The first 'Nowell!'
'Nowell and nowell!'

I

(*Epiphany; Christmas*)

English traditional (*Sandys, 1833,*
arr. John Stainer, 1840–1901)

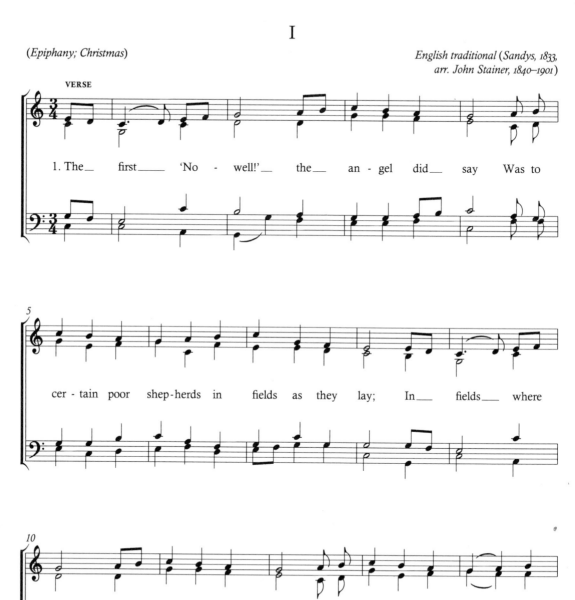

1. The first 'No - well!' the an - gel did say Was to cer - tain poor shep-herds in fields as they lay; In fields where they lay keep-ing their sheep On a cold win - ter's night that

was___ so deep. No - well!___ no - well! no - well!___ no -

- well!___ Born is the King___ of Is - ra - el!

2 They lookèd up and saw a star
   Shining in the east, beyond them far;
   And to the earth it gave great light,
   And so it continuèd both day and night.

3 And by the light of that same star
   Three wise men came from country far;
   To seek for a King was their intent,
   And to follow the star wheresoever it went.

4 This star drew nigh to the north-west:
   O'er Bethlehem it took its rest;
   And there it did both stop and stay,
   Right over the place where Jesus lay.

*5 Then did they know assuredly
   Within that house the King did lie;
   One entered in then for to see,
   And found the Babe in poverty.

6 Then entered in those wise men three,
   Full reverently, upon their knee,
   And offered there, in his presence,
   Both gold and myrrh, and frankincense.

*7 Between an ox-stall and an ass
   This Child there truly bornèd was;
   For want of clothing they did him lay
   All in the manger, among the hay.

8 Then let us all with one accord
   Sing praises to our heavenly Lord
   That hath made heaven and earth of
     nought,
   And with his blood mankind hath bought.

*9 If we in our lifetime shall do well
   We shall be free from death and hell,
   For God hath preparèd for us all
   A resting-place in general.

English traditional
(Sandys, 1833, adapted)

II

(*Christmas; Epiphany*)

English traditional
(recreation by the editors)

1. 'No - well and no-well!' the_ an - gels did say, While shep - herds there in_ the
2. And_ then___ there did ap - pear___ a_ star Whose glo - ry then___ did

fields___ did lay; Late in___ the night_ a - fold - ing_ their sheep, A
shine___ so far; Un - to___ the earth_ it gave a_ great light, And

win - ter's night_ both cold___ and bleak.
there it con - tin - ued a day and a night. *No - well_ and_ no-well! No -*

-well_ and_ no-well! Born is the_ King_____ of Is - ra-el!

3 And by the light of that same star
   Three wise men came from country far;
   To seek a King was their intent:
   They followed the star wherever it went.

4 The star drew near unto the north-west:
   O'er Bethlehem city it took its rest
   And there it did both stand and stay,
   Right over the house where our Lord lay.

5 Then entered in those wise men three,
   With reverence, falling on their knee,
   And offered up, in his presence,
   Both gold and myrrh, and frankincense.

6 Between an ox-manger and an ass,
   Our blest Messiah's place it was;
   To save our souls from sin and thrall,
   He is the Redeemer of us all.

English traditional
(*Journal of the Folk-Song Society, 5, adapted*)

Tune I is the received modern form of the carol, given here in the fine arrangement by Stainer (1871). Like the words, it derives from William Sandys's West Country collection *Christmas Carols Ancient and Modern* (1833). We believe that it evolved in the course of performance of something like our setting II, a conjectural recreation of a gallery setting based on another, and probably older, version of the tune in three different publications. For a more detailed discussion of the process see the note in *NOBC*.

PERFORMANCE I, choir, with organ and congregation *ad lib*.

II (*i*) Solo voice, with unison voices on repeats of the refrain. Some singers might extemporize a little harmony in the refrain, perhaps culling a few figures from our treble, alto, and bass parts at cadences.

(*ii*) Voices, singing one or more parts: melody alone, or melody and bass, or melody, bass, and alto, or all four parts. Congregations could sing the tune in all four cases, either throughout or only in the repeats of the refrain. A more florid version of the tune for the opening of the verse and refrain could be used, as follows:

Whichever version is sung, the tenor should be doubled at the higher octave. Instruments *ad lib*. (see Introduction).

(*iii*) Voice and continuo. The following is a suggested bass and chordal pattern:

The repeat of the refrain is optional in all three schemes.

(bar 2)

80

All hayle to the dayes

(*Christmas*)

English traditional
(*Chappell, 1853–9, arr. editors*)

VERSES 1 & 2

1. All hayle to the dayes[1]___ That me - rite more praise___ Then
2. The Court in all state___ Now o - pens her gate___ And

all___ the rest of the yeare!___ And wel - come the nights___ That
bids a free wel - come to most:___ The Ci - ty, like - wise,___ Though

dou - ble de - lights As well for the poore as the peere![2] Good for - tune at - tend Each
some-what pre - cise,_ Doth will - ing - ly part with her cost;___ And yet, by re - port, From

---

[1] those of the Christmas season [i.e., 25 December to 5 January]   [2] nobleman

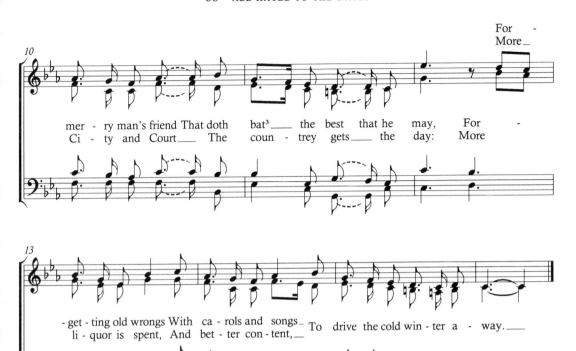

mer - ry man's friend That doth bat³___ the best that he may, For -
Ci - ty and Court___ The coun - trey gets___ the day: More

- get - ting old wrongs With ca - rols and songs_ To drive the cold win - ter a - way.___
li - quor is spent, And bet - ter con - tent,_

3 The gentry there

   For cost do not spare

      (The yeomanry fast in Lent);

   The farmers and such

   Thinke nothing too much

      If they keep but to pay their rent.

   The poorest of all

   Do merrily call

      (Want beares but a little sway)

   For a song, or a tale,

   Ore a pot of good ale,

      To drive the cold winter away.

4 Thus none will allow

   Of solitude now,

      But merrily greete the time,

   To make it appeare

   Of all the whole yeare

      That this is accounted the prime:

   December is seene

   Apparel'd in greene,⁴

      And January, fresh as May,

   Comes dancing along

   With a cup and a song

      To drive the cold winter away.

(continued overleaf)

³ serve, attend   ⁴ houses were decorated with greenery

VERSES 5 & 6

5. This time of the yeare___ Is spent in good cheare;___ Kind
6. To maske and to mum[5]___ Kind neigh - bours will come___ With

neigh - bours to - ge - ther meet___ To sit by the fire___ With
was - sels[6] of not - browne ale,___ To drinke and ca - rouse___ To

friend - ly de - sire___ Each o - ther in love___ to greet;___ Old grud - ges, for - got, Are
all in this house, As mer - ry as bucks in the pale;[7]___ Where cake, bread and cheese Is

The___
At the

put in the pot, All sor - rowes a - side they lay; The___
brought for your fees To make you the lon - ger stay, At the

[5] to act and mime [in plays, games]   [6] wassail-cups
[7] enclosure

old and the yong Doth ca - roll his song— To drive the cold win - ter a - way.—
fire— to warme Will do you no harme

7 When Christmastide
Comes in like a bride,
  With holly and ivy clad,
Twelve dayes in the yeare
Much mirth and good cheare
  In every houshold is had;
The countrey guise[8]
Is then to devise
  Some gambole of Christmas play,
Whereas[9] the yong men
Do best that they can
  To drive the cold winter away.

8 When white-bearded Frost
Hath threatned his worst
  And fallen from branch and brier,
Then time away cals
From husbandry hals[10]
  And from the good countryman's fire,
Together to go
To plow and to sow,
  To get us both food and array;[11]
And thus with content
The time we have spent
  To drive the cold winter away.

English traditional
(Pepys Collection broadside)

[8] custom [9] whereat [10] [farmers'] indoor places of work [11] clothing

We give eight of the twelve verses comprising 'A pleasant Countrey new Ditty: Merrily shewing how To drive the cold Winter away', from a broadside in the Pepys Collection. The broadside was printed in the early seventeenth century, though the ballad may predate it. The tune is as found in Chappell's *The Popular Music of the Olden Time* (1853–9).

PERFORMANCE (*i*) Solo voice; (*ii*) voice with lute, guitar, keyboard, etc. (adapting our bass); (*iii*) choir.

81

On Christmas Night all Christians sing
(The Sussex Carol)

I

(Christmas Night)

English traditional (Journal of the Folk-Song Society, 2, arr. editors)

1. On Christ - mas Night all Christ - ians sing, To

hear the news___ the an - gels bring. an - gels bring:

News of great joy,___ news of___ great mirth,___

News of our___ mer - ci - ful___ King's birth.

2 Then why should men on earth be so sad,
Since our Redeemer made us glad
When from our sin he set us free,
All for to gain our liberty?

3 When sin departs before his grace,
Then life and health come in its place;
Angels and men with joy may sing,
All for to see the new-born King.

4 All out of darkness we have light,
Which made the angels sing this night:
'Glory to God and peace to men,
Now and for evermore. Amen.'

*English traditional
(after Bishop Luke Wadding, d. 1686)*

II

(Christmas Night)

English traditional
(arr. Ralph Vaughan Williams, 1872–1958, adapted)

This very popular carol was sung to many different tunes. The standard one was collected (with this text) by Vaughan Williams from one of his most valued singers, Mrs Verrall, of Monk's Gate, near Horsham, Sussex. Our setting I is modelled on improvisatory three-man performance.

The text derives from a carol in the *Smale Garland of Pious and Godly Songs* (Ghent, 1684) by Luke Wadding, an Irish Franciscan bishop. The posthumous London editions of 1728 and 1731 brought much of the collection's contents—often greatly revised, as · here—into general circulation among English Protestants.

PERFORMANCE I, three men (one tenor could sing bars 1–4, the other the repeat); or men's choir, bars 1–4 perhaps solo, the remainder tutti (unison or harmony). II, unison voices and organ, or unaccompanied choir.

See *NOBC* for *Let all that are to mirth inclined* (no. 140), *The Lord at first did Adam make* (no. 141), and *When God at first created man* (no. 142).

82

A virgin unspotted
A virgin most pure

I

(*Christmas*)

English traditional
(*Chappell, 1853–9, arr. editors*)

1. A__ vir - gin un - spot - ted, the__ pro - phet[1] fore - told, Should bring_ forth a Sa - viour, which_ now we__ be - hold, To__ be__ our Re - deem - er__ from_ death, hell_ and_ sin, Which A - dam's trans - gres - sion in - vol - ved__ us__ in.

[1] Isaiah

2 Through Bethlehem city, in Jewry, it was
   That Joseph and Mary together did pass,
   And for to be taxèd when thither they came,
   Since Caesar Augustus commanded the same.

3 But Mary's full time being come, as we find,[2]
   She brought forth her first-born to save all mankind;
   The inn being full, for this heavenly guest
   No place there was found where to lay him to rest.

4 But Mary, blest Mary, so meek and so mild,
   Soon wrapped up in swaddlings this heavenly Child:
   Contented, she laid him where oxen do feed;
   The great God of nature approved of the deed.

5 To teach us humility all this was done;
   Then learn we from hence haughty pride for to shun.
   A manger his cradle who came from above,
   The great God of mercy, of peace and of love.

6 Then presently[3] after, the shepherds did spy
   Vast numbers of angels to stand in the sky;
   So merrily talking, so sweet they did sing:
   'All glory and praise to our heavenly King!'

English traditional
(Chappell, 1853–9)

[2] in the gospels   [3] immediately

One of the most venerable and widely distributed of all English Christmas carols, found in seemingly endless musical variants. (For an eighteenth-century American setting see 41.) The earliest known version of the text is in a carol publication of 1661, but it probably dates from the previous century. The tune is found for the first time in *The Compleat Psalmodist* (1741) by John Arnold, but was not necessarily the composer's invention. Tune I is a fairly plain version, as sung by carollers at Marsden, near Hereford, in the mid-nineteenth century. II is a very distant variant, collected by Cecil Sharp in Shropshire in 1911. The opening of III probably grew out of an instrumental embellishment of a less extravagant variant (see notes, *NOBC*).

PERFORMANCE I (*i*) solo or unison voices; (*ii*) choir.

II (*i*) solo or unison voices, with accompaniment A *ad lib.* (instrumental or vocal); (*ii*) voices in two parts, with accompaniment B *ad lib.* (instrumental or vocal).

Alternative refrain, choir only.

III, voices, with the tenor doubled at the higher octave, and instruments *ad lib.* (see Introduction).

See *NOBC* for *The angel Gabriel from God was sent* (no. 144), *God's dear Son, without beginning* (no. 145), *A Child this day is born* (no. 146), and *Shepherds, arise* (no. 147).

II

(Christmas)

English traditional (*Journal of the Folk-Song Society, 5, arr. editors*)

VERSE

1. A___ vir - gin un - spot - ted, the___ pro - phet[1] fore - told, Should bring_ forth a___ Sa - viour, which now we be - hold, To___ be___ our Re - deem - er___ from death, hell___ and sin, Which A - dam's trans - gres - sion in - vol - ved___ us in.

REFRAIN

Then let___ us be___ mer - ry,___ cast sor - row___ a - way! Our___ Sa - viour, Christ_ Je - sus, was___ born on___ this day.

OPTIONAL ACCOMPANIMENT A

OPTIONAL ACCOMPANIMENT B

[1] Isaiah

ALTERNATIVE REFRAIN
(16)

Then let us be mer - ry, cast sor - row a - way! Our

Sa - viour, Christ Je - sus, was born on this day.

2   Through Bethlehem city, in Jewry, it was
  That Joseph and Mary together did pass,
  And for to be taxèd when thither they came,
  Since Caesar Augustus commanded the same.

3   But Mary's full time being come, as we find,[2]
  She brought forth her first-born to save all mankind;
  The inn being full, for this heavenly guest
  No place there was found where to lay him to rest.

4   But Mary, blest Mary, so meek and so mild,
  Soon wrapped up in swaddlings this heavenly Child:
  Contented, she laid him where oxen do feed;
  The great God of nature approved of the deed.

5   To teach us humility all this was done;
  Then learn we from hence haughty pride for to shun.
  A manger his cradle who came from above,
  The great God of mercy, of peace and of love.

6   Then presently[3] after, the shepherds did spy
  Vast numbers of angels to stand in the sky;
  So merrily talking, so sweet they did sing:
  'All glory and praise to our heavenly King!'

English traditional
(Chappell, 1853–9)

[2] in the gospels   [3] immediately

III

(Christmas)

English traditional
(Gilbert, 1822, arr. editors)

1. A___ vir - gin_ most_ pure, as the pro - phets do_ tell,
Hath_ brought forth_ a___ ba - by, as it hath be - fell,

To be___ our Re - deem - er from_ death, hell_ and_ sin, Which

A - dam's trans - gres - sion hath_ wrap - ped_ us___ in. *Aye, and*

there - fore_ be you mer - ry, Re - joice and be you mer - ry, Set sor - rows_ a -

-side!   Christ   Je - sus, __ our __   Sa - viour, was __ born   on __ this __ tide.

2 In Bethlehem Jewry a city there was,
   Where Joseph and Mary together did pass,
   And there to be taxèd with many one more,
   For Caesar commanded the same should be so.

3 But when they had entered the city so fair,
   The number of people so mighty was there
   That Joseph and Mary, whose substance was small,
   Could find in the inn there no lodging at all.

4 Then were they constrained in a stable to lie,
   Where horses and asses they used for to tie;
   Their lodging so simple they took it no scorn,
   But against the next morning our Saviour was born.

5 The King of all kings to this world being brought,
   Small store of fine linen to wrap him was sought;
   When Mary had swaddled her young son so sweet,
   Within an ox-manger she laid him to sleep.

6 Then God sent an angel from heaven so high
   To certain poor shepherds in fields where they lie,
   And bade them no longer in sorrow to stay,
   Because that our Saviour was born on this day.

7 Then presently[1] after, the shepherds did spy
   A number of angels that stood in the sky;
   They joyfully talkèd and sweetly did sing:
   'To God be all glory, our heavenly King!'

English traditional
(Gilbert, 1822)

[1] immediately

83

I saw three ships come sailing in

(*Christmas*)

English traditional
(*Bramley and Stainer, c.1878, arr. editors*)

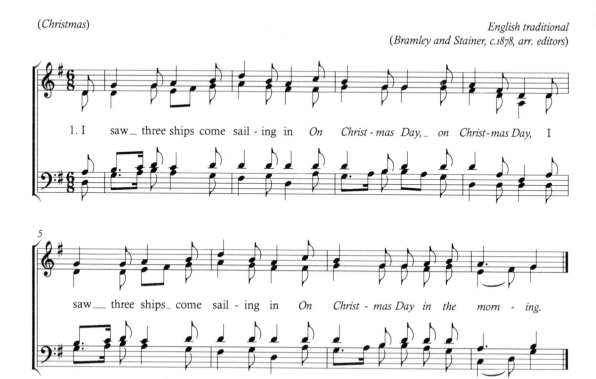

1. I saw— three ships come sail-ing in On Christ-mas Day,— on Christ-mas Day, I

saw— three ships— come sail-ing in On Christ-mas Day in the morn-ing.

2 And what was in those ships all three?

3 Our Saviour Christ and his lady,

4 Pray, whither sailed those ships all three?

5 O they sailed into Bethlehem

6 And all the bells on earth shall ring

7 And all the angels in heaven shall sing

8 And all the souls on earth shall sing

9 Then let us all rejoice amain![1]

English traditional
(*Sandys, 1833*)

[1] greatly

The many variant versions of the text ultimately derive from the story of the Mediterranean journeyings of the supposed relics of the magi, the 'Three Kings of Cologne', the splendour of whose final voyage has remained vivid in European folk memory (see notes in *NOBC*). The earliest printed text dates from 1666.

There are also many variants of the tune, and the one given here is from Bramley and Stainer's *Christmas Carols New and Old* (third series, *c*.1878). *NOBC* setting I (not included here) is a tune and bass printed by Sandys.

PERFORMANCE   Choir.

See *NOBC* for *As I sat on a sunny bank* (no. 149), another variant of this tune.

84

This is the truth sent from above

I

English traditional
(Sharp, 1911)

(Christmas)

1. This is the ___ truth ___ sent ___ from a - bove, The truth of ___ God, the
2. The first thing that ___ I ___ will re - late, That God at ___ first did

God ___ of ___ love; There - fore don't ___ turn me from ___ the door, ___ But
man ___ cre - ate; The next thing ___ which to you ___ I tell— Wo -

Last verse

heark - en all, ___ both ___ rich and ___ poor.
- man ___ was made ___ with ___ him to ___ dwell.

3 Then after that 'twas God's own choice
  To place them both in paradise,
  There to remain from evil free
  Except they ate of such a tree.

4 But they did eat, which was a sin,
  And thus their ruin did begin—
  Ruined themselves, both you and me,
  And all of our posterity.

5 Thus we were heirs to endless woes
  Till God the Lord did interpose;
  And so a promise soon did run:
  That he'd redeem us by his Son.

6 And at this season of the year
  Our blest Redeemer did appear,
  And here did live, and here did preach,
  And many thousands he did teach.

7 Thus he in love to us behaved,
  To show us how we must be saved;
  And if you want to know the way,
  Be pleased to hear what he did say:

*8 'Go preach the Gospel,' now he said,
  'To all the nations that are made!
  And he that does believe on me,
  From all his sins I'll set him free.'

*9 O seek! O seek of God above
  That saving faith that works by love!
  And, if he's pleased to grant thee this,
  Thou'rt sure to have eternal bliss.

*10 God grant to all within this place
  True saving faith, that special grace
  Which to his people doth belong:
  And thus I close my Christmas song.

English traditional
(*A Good Christmas Box, 1847*)

II

(Christmas)

English traditional
(arr. Ralph Vaughan Williams, 1872–1958)

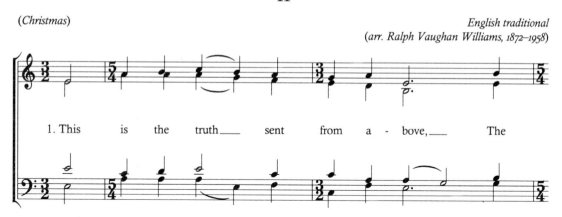

1. This   is   the   truth___   sent   from   a - bove,___   The

truth   of   God,___   the   God   of   love;___   There - fore   don't   turn___   me___

from   the   door,___   But___   heark - en   all,_____   both___   rich___   and___   poor.

2   The first thing that I will relate,
    That God at first did man create;
    The next thing which to you I tell—
    Woman was made with him to dwell.

3   Then after that 'twas God's own choice
    To place them both in paradise,
    There to remain from evil free
    Except they ate of such a tree.

4   But they did eat, which was a sin,
    And thus their ruin did begin—
    Ruined themselves, both you and me,
    And all of our posterity.

5   Thus we were heirs to endless woes
    Till God the Lord did interpose;
    And so a promise soon did run:
    That he'd redeem us by his Son.

6   And at this season of the year
    Our blest Redeemer did appear,
    And here did live, and here did preach,
    And many thousands he did teach.

7   Thus he in love to us behaved,
    To show us how we must be saved;
    And if you want to know the way,
    Be pleased to hear what he did say:

*8 'Go preach the Gospel,' now he said,
    'To all the nations that are made!
    And he that does believe on me,
    From all his sins I'll set him free.'

*9 O seek! O seek of God above
    That saving faith that works by love!
    And, if he's pleased to grant thee this,
    Thou'rt sure to have eternal bliss.

*10   God grant to all within this place
      True saving faith, that special grace
      Which to his people doth belong:
      And thus I close my Christmas song.

English traditional
(*A Good Christmas Box, 1847*)

The text is from the sixteen verses given in *A Good Christmas Box*. Tune I was collected by Cecil Sharp in Shropshire; a choral setting can be found at no. 89. Tune II was collected by Vaughan Williams in Herefordshire. (See no. 74 and *NOBC* no. 140 for variants).

PERFORMANCE   I, voice, perhaps with a one- or two-note drone; II, choir.

85

God rest you merry, gentlemen

I

(*Christmas*)

English traditional
(arr. John Stainer, 1840–1901)

¹ keep

joy, ___ O ___ ti - dings of com - fort and joy!

2 In Bethlehem in Jewry
      This blessèd Babe was born,
   And laid within a manger
      Upon this blessèd morn;
   The which his mother Mary
      Nothing did take in scorn.

3 From God our heavenly Father
      A blessèd angel came,
   And unto certain shepherds
      Brought tidings of the same,
   How that in Bethlehem was born
      The Son of God by name.

4 'Fear not,' then said the angel,
      'Let nothing you affright;
   This day is born a Saviour
      Of virtue, power and might,
   So frequently to vanquish all
      The friends of Satan quite.'

5 The shepherds at those tidings
      Rejoicèd much in mind,
   And left their flocks a-feeding
      In tempest, storm and wind,
   And went to Bethlehem straightway
      This blessèd Babe to find.

6 But when to Bethlehem they came,
      Whereat this Infant lay,
   They found him in a manger
      Where oxen feed on hay;
   His mother Mary, kneeling,
      Unto the Lord did pray.

7 Now to the Lord sing praises,
      All you within this place,
   And with true love and brotherhood
      Each other now embrace.
   The holy tide of Christmas
      All others doth efface.

West Country traditional
(Sandys, 1833)

Tune I is the now standard form of what is by far the most common of English luck-visit tunes, found in endless variants and sung to many different texts. (See *NOBC* nos. 145, 152, 157, 158, 159:I, and no. 131, notes.) It probably came to England from France, and is also found all over Europe. The text, too, exists in many forms, and only in modern times has it come to be sung in church. The tune of setting III is said to have been the most common in the West Country. The melody and bass are patently from a rustic gallery setting, and we have added suitably crude treble and alto parts in the same style. *NOBC* setting II (not included here) is of a Cornish version of the tune from a manuscript of *c.*1845.

PERFORMANCE I (*i*) choir; (*ii*) voices and organ; III, voices, with the tenor doubled at the higher octave (or with soprano and tenor parts swapped), and instruments *ad lib.* (see Introduction).

See *NOBC* for *Come all you worthy gentlemen* (no. 152).

(*Christmas*)

III

West Country traditional
(Sandys, 1833, arr. editors)

VERSE

1. God_ rest[1] you mer - ry, gen - tle - men, Let no-thing you dis - may,
2. From God our heaven-ly Fa - ther A bless-ed an - gel came,

For Je - sus Christ, our Sa - viour, Was born up - on__ this day
And un - to cer - tain shep - herds Brought ti - dings of__ the same,

To__ save us all from Sa - tan's power When we were gone_ a - stray.
How__ that in Beth - le - hem was born The Son of God_ by name.

REFRAIN

O__ ti - dings, O__ ti - dings of com - fort and__ joy!

For__ Je - sus Christ, our_ Sa - viour, Was_ born on__ Christ - mas Day.

[1] keep

3   The shepherds at those tidings
    Rejoicèd much in mind,
And left their flocks a-feeding
    In tempest, storm and wind,
And went to Bethlehem straightway
    This blessèd Babe to find.

4   Now to the Lord sing praises,
    All you within this place,
And with true love and brotherhood
    Each other now embrace.
This holy tide of Christmas
    All others doth efface.

West Country traditional (Sandys, 1833)

86
We wish you a merry Christmas

(*Christmas*)

English traditional (arr. editors)

VERSE

1. We wish you a mer-ry Christ-mas, we wish you a mer-ry Christ-mas, we wish you a mer-ry Christ-mas and a hap-py new year!
2. Now bring us some fig-gy pud-ding, now bring us some fig-gy pud-ding, now bring us some fig-gy pud-ding, and bring it us here!
3. O we won't go un-til we've got some, no, we won't go un-til we've got some, we won't go un-til we've got some, So give it us here!
4. O we all like_ fig-gy pud-ding, yes, we all like_ fig-gy pud-ding, we all like_ fig-gy pud-ding, So bring it out here!

REFRAIN

Glad_ ti-dings we_ bring To you and your kin: We wish you a mer-ry Christ-mas_ And a hap-py_ new year!

The remnant of an *envoie* much used by wassailers and other luck visitors, and still in all too common use by modern doorstep carollers.

PERFORMANCE Voice(s), with refrain in unison or harmony.

See *NOBC* for *Christemas hath made an end* (no. 154).

(*NOBC no. 153*)

87

Wassail! wassail all over the town!
(The Gloucestershire Wassail)

(*Christmas*)

English traditional
(*Oxford Book of Carols, 1928,*
arr. editors)

1. Was - sail!___ was - sail___ all o - ver the town!___ Our toast it is white and our ale_ it_ is brown; Our_ bowl it___ is_ made of the white ma - ple tree: With the was - sail-ing-bowl we'll drink_ to thee!

2. So here is to Cher - ry and to his right cheek!___ Pray God send our mas - ter a good piece of beef, And a good piece of_ beef that_ we all may see; With the was - sail-ing-bowl we'll drink_ to thee!

3 And here is to Dobbin and to his right eye!
Pray God send our master a good Christmas pie,
And a good Christmas pie that we may all see;
With our wassailing-bowl we'll drink to thee!

4 So here is to Broad May and to her broad horn!

May God send our master a good crop of corn,

And a good crop of corn that we may all see;

With the wassailing-bowl we'll drink to thee!

5 And here is to Fillpail and to her left ear!

Pray God send our master a happy new year,

And a happy new year as e'er he did see;

With our wassailing-bowl we'll drink to thee!

*6 And here is to Colly and to her long tail!

Pray God send our master he never may fail[1]

A bowl of strong beer; I pray you draw near,

And our jolly wassail it's then you shall hear.

*7 Come, butler, come fill us a bowl of the best,

Then we hope that your soul in heaven may rest;

But if you do draw us a bowl of the small,

Then down shall go butler, bowl and all!

*8 Then here's to the maid in the lily-white smock

Who tripped to the door and slipped back the lock;

Who tripped to the door and pulled back the pin,

For to let these jolly wassailers in.

English traditional
(*Oxford Book of Carols, 1928*)

---

[1] lack

'Wassail!' means 'Good health!', and wassailers were rural luck visitors who toasted householders from their communal bowl, which was often garlanded and ribboned. The blessings they called down on their hosts and the latter's crops and livestock were highly valued, and the singers would often be fed and given money in addition to having their bowl replenished. The 'Gloucester Wassail' is known from the late eighteenth century, and the version here, now standard, combines transcriptions by Vaughan Williams and Cecil Sharp. Where we give Cherry and Dobbin, the farmer's horses would have been invoked by name; likewise the cows, where we have Broad May, Fillpail, and Colly. Christmas pies were huge, with a game filling, and small beer (verse 7) was a watery second brew.

PERFORMANCE Voices (*i*) in unison; (*ii*) in three parts.

See *NOBC* for *A wassail, a wassail throughout all this town!* (no. 156), *We've been a while a-wandering* (no. 157), and *Wassail, O wassail all over the town!* (no. 158).

88

Here we come a-wassailing
(Wassail Song)

(Christmas; New Year)

English traditional
(Bramley and Stainer, 1871, arr. editors)

3 We are not daily beggars
    That beg from door to door,
  But we are neighbours' children
    Whom you have seen before.

4 Call up the butler of this house,
    Put on his golden ring;
  Let him bring us up a glass of beer,
    And better we shall sing.

5 We have got a little purse
    Of stretching leather skin;
  We want a little of your money
    To line it well within.

6 Bring us out a table,
    And spread it with a cloth;
  Bring us out some mouldy cheese,[1]
    And some of your Christmas loaf.

7 God bless the master of this house,
    Likewise the mistress too,
  And all the little children
    That round the table go.

8 Good master and good mistress,
    While you're sitting by the fire,
  Pray think of us poor children
    Who are wandering in the mire.

English traditional
(Husk, 1864)

[1] blue cheese

The text is from W. H. Husk's *Songs of the Nativity* (1864). His sources included a Manchester chap-book (popular pamphlet) and a Bradford broadside of *c.*1850, and he believed that the carol was a recent conflation by northern wassailers. The tune here (*NOBC* tune II) is as given in Bramley and Stainer's *Christmas Carols, New and Old* (1871), and was from Yorkshire. (So was *NOBC* tune I, not included here, which was sung in Leeds in the 1850s.)

PERFORMANCE   Voice(s), with refrain in unison or harmony.

89

The darkest midnight in December

(*Christmas Night*)

English traditional
(*Sharp, 1911, arr. editors*)

VERSES 1 & 2

1. The dark - est____ mid - night__ in De - cem - ber, No snow nor__ hail nor win - ter's__ storm Shall hin - der__ us__ for to__ re - mem - ber The Babe_ that on__ this__ night was__ born.

2. Four thou - sand__ years__ from__ the Cre - a - tion The world lay__ groan - ing un - der__ sin; No one could_ e - ver ex - pect_ sal - va - tion: No one__ could e - ver__ en - ter__ heaven.

VERSES 3–5

3. A - dam's   fall   had   damned us   all To
4. We   like   beasts   lay   in   a   sta - ble,
5. 'Twas but   pure   love   that   from a - bove Brought

hell, to   end - less   pains   for - lorn; 'Twas so de - creed we'd
Sense - less,   blind, and   dead   by   sin; To help our - selves we
him to   save   us   from   all   harms: Then let us   sing and

(v.4 only)

ne'er   been   freed   Had   not   this   heaven - ly   Babe been   born.
were   not a - ble, But   he   brings   grace   and   life a - gain.
wel - come   him,   The   God   of   Love   in   Ma - ry's   arms!

Irish traditional
(after Fr. William Devereux, fl. 1728)

The text, which is perhaps intended to be sung before the midnight mass, derives from a longer carol by Fr. William Devereux, an Irish poet of great talent. It comes from his collection 'A New Garland', which was never printed and survives only in somewhat debased form in the manuscript word-books of various groups of County Wexford church singers. The poem can be found in its complete eight-line-stanza form with *NOBC* setting I (not included here),

the melody to which it is sung by men of the Devereux family in Kilmore Parish Church, County Wexford. The tune of the present setting was collected by Cecil Sharp with the carol 'This is the truth sent from above' (84:1).

PERFORMANCE   Choir.

See *NOBC* for *Ye sons of men, with me rejoice* (no. 161).

Good people all, this Christmastime

(Christmas)

Irish traditional
(Oxford Book of Carols, 1928,
arr. editors)

we should pray   To____ God,____ with love,____ this Christ-mas Day: In____
come to pass: From____ e - very door____ re - pelled, a - las!   As____

Beth-le - hem____ up - on that morn__ There was a blessed__ Mes - si - ah born.
long fore - told,____ their re-fuge all____ Was but an hum - ble ox - 's stall.

3 Near Bethlehem did shepherds keep
   Their flocks of lambs and feeding sheep;
   To whom God's angels did appear,
   Which put the shepherds in great fear.
   'Prepare and go', the angels said,
   'To Bethlehem; be not afraid,
   For there you'll find, this happy morn,
   A princely Babe, sweet Jesus, born.'

4 With thankful heart and joyful mind
   The shepherds went the Babe to find,
   And, as God's angels had foretold,
   They did our Saviour, Christ, behold.
   Within a manger he was laid,
   And by his side the Virgin Maid
   Attending on the Lord of Life,
   Who came on earth to end all strife.

*5 There were three wise men from afar,
   Directed by a glorious star,
   Came boldly on and made no stay
   Until they came where Jesus lay.
   And when they came unto that place,
   And looked with love on Jesus' face,
   In faith they humbly knelt to greet,
   With gifts of gold and incense sweet.

6 Come, let us then our tribute pay
   To our good God, as well we may,
   For all his grace and mercy shown
   Through his Son to us, till then unknown;
   And when through life we wend our way
   'Mid trials and sufferings, day by day,
   In faith and hope, whate'er befall,
   We'll wait in peace his holy call.

Irish traditional
(Ó Muirithe, *'The Wexford Carols'*, 1982)

The text seems to have been widespread in County Wexford, and has been dubbed both 'The Enniscorthy Christmas Carol' and 'The Wexford Carol'. It is English in origin, however. Verses 1–5 derive from the ballad 'All you that are to mirth inclin'd' (see notes, *NOBC* no. 140); verse 6 may be an Irish addition. The tune was collected with verses 1–5 by Dr W. H. Gratton Flood in Enniscorthy. (See

NOBC notes for an alternative Wexford tune and suggestions for performance in the Wexford manner.)

PERFORMANCE   Choir.

See *NOBC* for *Christmas Day is come!* (no. 163).

91

Oer yw'r gŵr sy'n methu caru
Soon the hoar old year will leave us
Deck the hall with boughs of holly
(Nos Galan)

II

Welsh traditional
(Jones, 1784, arr. editors)

(New Year's Eve)

1. Oer yw'r gŵr sy'n me-thu ca-ru *Fal, la, la, la, la, ___ la, la, la!*
1. Soon the hoar old year will leave us,

Hen fy-ny-ddoedd an-nwyl Cym-ru, *Fal, la, la, la, la, ___ la, la, la!*
But the part-ing must not grieve us:

I-ddo ef a'u câr gyn-hes-af, *Dad-le-a, dad-le-a, ___ la, la, la!*
When the new year comes to-mor-row

13

SOLO ... FULL

Gwyl - iau lla - wen flwy-ddyn nes - af,   *Fal, la, la, la, la,_____ la, la, la!*
Let him find no   trace of sor - row,

2 I'r helbulus oer yw'r biliau,
   Sydd yn dyfod yn y gwyliau,
   Gwrando bregeth mewn un pennill,
   Byth na waria fwy na'th ennill.

3 Oer yw'r eira ar Eryri,
   Er fod gwrthban gwlanen arni,
   Oer yw'r bobol na ofalan',
   Gwrdd a'u gilydd, ar Nos Galan!

                    Welsh traditional

2 He our pleasures may redouble;
   He may bring us store of trouble;
   Hope the best and gaily meet him:
   With a jovial chorus greet him!

3 At his birth he brings us gladness:
   Ponder not on future sadness.
   Anxious care is now but folly:
   Fill the mead-cup, hang the holly!

                    tr. John Oxenford

III

(*New Year*)

1 Deck the hall with boughs of holly:
   'Tis the season to be jolly!
   Fill the mead cup, drain the barrel,
   Troll the ancient Christmas carol.

2 See the flowing bowl before us!
   Strike the harp and join the chorus!
   Follow me in merry measure,
   While I sing of beauty's treasure.

3 Fast away the old year passes,
   Hail the new, ye lads and lasses!
   Laughing, quaffing, all together,
   Heedless of the wind and weather.

                    Anon.

'Nos Galan' ('New Year's Eve') is one of many texts to which this tune was formerly sung. It belongs to the competitive *canu penillion* tradition, in which merrymakers would dance in a ring around a harpist, extemporizing verses in turn and dropping out when invention failed. The harp originally played the 'answering' bars (3–4 etc.), but nonsense syllables came to be substituted as harpers became less common.

This choral setting and *NOBC* setting I for voice and harp (not included here) are adapted respectively from the 1784 and 1794 editions of the harpist Edward Jones's *Musical and Poetical Relics of the Welsh Bards*. Jones gives 'fa, la, la' for lines 1, 2, and 4 in both editions; line 3 is labelled a harp

'Symphony' in 1784 but given the words 'Dadlea . . .' in 1794. Text III, obstinately popular, has minimal connection with the Welsh and dates from an American publication of 1881.

PERFORMANCE Choir. The solo sections should be sung by a succession of voices, as in *canu penillion*.

There is a concise introduction to the pronunciation of Welsh in the appendix to Alan Luff, *Welsh Hymns and their tunes* (London, 1990).

See *NOBC* for *O deued pob Cristion* (no. 165) and *Wel, dyma'r borau gorau i gyd* (no. 166).

92

O Mary and the baby, sweet lamb!

(*Christmas*)

American traditional
(*Poston, 1970, arr. editors*)

The spiritual was transcribed by Elizabeth Poston (*The Second Penguin Book of Christmas Carols*, 1970) from a field recording of the singing of Ella Mitchell and Velma Wright in Texas, January 1937. We have treated the song with some freedom, transposing it down a tone and restoring what we assume was the original verse–refrain form; on the recording there is (in our terms) no refrain after verses 1 and 2.

PERFORMANCE   The song may be sung (at whatever pitch) entirely by two solo voices (I and II), as on the recording (see above), or by a solo voice (I) alternating with three voices (II). In both of these cases the refrain is best omitted after the first verse, since it is identical; alternatively, it may be taken by chorus (also divided into two groups), singing in unison (I) and in three parts (II). In this last case (with the chorus in three parts in both octaves) either or both of our refrain descants may be added. (Descant A is designed for a trio of 'soul sisters' using bold, slow portamenti.) A possible scheme might be:

Verse 1: solo alternating with three voices; refrain: chorus in one or three parts;

Verse 2: as verse 1 (different soloist); refrain as first time, but preceded by, then combined with, descant A;

Verse 3: as verse 1 (different soloist); refrain as first time, but preceded by, then combined with, descant B;

Verse 4: as verse 1 (different soloist); refrain as first time, but preceded by, then combined with, descants A and B together. (This last 'complete' refrain could be repeated at will.)

See *NOBC* for *Mary had a baby* (no. 168).

93

Go tell it on the mountain

(Christmas)

American traditional
(Fenner, 1909, arr. editors)

VERSE
SOLO

1. In the time of Da - vid,_____ Some call him a king, And
2. When I was a seek - er I sought both night and day; I
3. He made me a watch - man Up - on a ci - ty wall, And

if a child is true - born, Lord Je - sus will hear him sing:_____
ask the Lord to help me, And he show_ me the way._____
if I am a Christ - ian I am the_ least of all._____

REFRAIN
FULL

Go tell it on the moun - tain, O - ver the hills and e - ve - ry-where;

Go tell it on the moun - tain That Je - sus Christ_ is born!

Text and tune are from Thomas P. Fenner: *Religious Songs of the Negro as Sung on the Plantations* (Hampton, 1909).

PERFORMANCE Verse, solo voice; refrain, chorus in one, two, or three parts (high or low voices, or both).

94

Rise up, shepherd, and follow!

(Christmas)

American traditional
(*Allen et al., 1867, arr. editors*)

VERSE [SOLO]

1. There's a   star   in the   East   on____   Christ - mas   morn—
2. If   you   take   good____   heed   to the   an - gel's   words—

[FULL]

Rise____ up,   shep-herd, and   fol - low!—

[SOLO]

It - 'll   lead   to the place where the
You'll for - get   your_ flocks, you'll for -

Sa - viour's   born:____
- get   your   herds:____

[FULL]

Rise   up,   shep - herd, and   fol - low!

REFRAIN [FULL]

Leave your sheep and   leave your lambs—   Rise up, shep-herd, and   fol-low!   Leave your ewes and

leave your rams—   Rise up, shep-herd, and   fol-low!   Fol - low,   fol - low,   Rise up, shep-herd, and

fol-low!   Fol-low the Star of   Beth - le - hem—   Rise up, shep-herd, and   fol-low!____

'A Christmas Plantation Song', first published in *Slave Songs of the United States*, ed. W. F. Allen, C. P. Ware, and L. McK. Garrison (1867). The songs were collected during the Civil War, mainly from slaves on the offshore islands of Georgia and South Carolina. The tune is related to various British folk-songs, including a Welsh carol.

PERFORMANCE   Solo voice, alternating with unison chorus (high, low, or at both octaves) or three-part chorus (likewise).

See *NOBC* for *Lullay, thou tiny little child* (no. 171; a version of the Coventry Carol which John Jacob Niles claimed to have heard in Tennessee).

95

Sing we the Virgin Mary

(*Christmas*)

Appalachian traditional?
(*Niles, 1948, arr. editors*)

3 When Jesus was a-borning,

   To earth came heaven down,

   To lie upon a manger,

   Away in Bethlem's town.

4 Ah, blessèd Maiden Mother,

   Beknown to prophecy:

   Now Jesus is a-bornèd,

   And all men knoweth thee.

(*Niles, 1948*)

Melody and words used by permission of G. Schirmer, Inc.

John Jacob Niles (1892–1980) was famous as a collector and performer of folk-songs. Late in life he confessed that his interference with the folk music he had published ranged from alteration to entirely original composition; the three carols by him in *NOBC* are probably among his original works. He claimed to have collected words and tune of this item in Kentucky in 1933. If true, this would appear to be a near-miraculous survival of the fifteenth-century English carol text 'I sing of a maiden that is makeless'.

PERFORMANCE   One or two voices, with optional accompaniment (guitar, etc.). (Niles used to accompany himself on a kind of cello with cross-shaped sound-holes.)

(*NOBC no. 173*)

96

I wonder as I wander

(*Christmas*)

Niles, 1934, arr. editors
(*after a traditional Appalachian original*)

VOICE

INSTRUMENT

1. I won - der as I wan - der, out un - der the sky, How
2. When Ma - ry birthed Je - sus, 'twas in a cow's stall, With
3. If Je - sus had want - ed for a - ny wee thing, A

Je - sus the Sa - viour did come for to die For poor on - 'ry peo - ple like
wise men and farm - ers and shep-herds and all; But high from the hea - vens a
star in the sky or a bird on the wing, Or all of God's an - gels in

you and like I; I won - der as I wan - der out un - der the sky.
star's light did fall, And the pro - mise of a - ges it then did re - call.
heaven for to sing, He sure - ly could have it 'cause he was the King.

Melody and words used by permission of G. Schirmer, Inc.

In the introduction to *The Songs of John Jacob Niles* (1975), Niles reported that he wrote this carol in 1933, basing it on a fragment he had overheard in the courthouse square in Murphy, Cherokee County, North Carolina. He published it in his *Songs of the Hill-Folk* (1934), where verse 1 is repeated after verse 3.

PERFORMANCE Voice; the optional accompaniment may be adapted for any appropriate instrument.

97

The Virgin Mary had a baby boy

(*Christmas*)

Trinidadian traditional
(Connor, 1945, arr. editors)

VERSE [SOLO]

1. The Vir - gin Ma - ry had a ba - by boy, the
2. The an - gels sang___ when the ba - by born, the
3. The wise men went___ where the ba - by born, the

Vir - gin Ma - ry had a ba - by boy, the Vir - gin Ma - ry had a
an - gels sang_ when the ba - by born, the an - gels sang___ when the
wise men went_ where the ba - by born, the wise men went___ where the

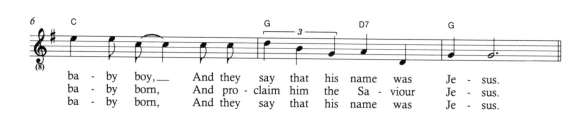

ba - by boy,___ And they say that his name was Je - sus.
ba - by born, And pro - claim him the Sa - viour Je - sus.
ba - by born, And they say that his name was Je - sus.

REFRAIN [FULL]

He come from the glo - ry,   *He come from the glo - rious king - dom:*

O yes, be - liev - er!_____ O yes, be - liev - er!_____

_____ He come from the glo - ry, He come from the glo - rious king - dom!

From *The Edric Connor Collection of West Indian Spirituals and Folk Tunes* . . . (1945). Connor explains: 'This, the only West Indian negro carol I found, was taught me by James Bryce, whose parents and grandparents were in Trinidad before the abolition of slavery in 1834. I met Bryce in 1942, when he was ninety-four years of age, but was still working, in rags, on a grapefruit plantation for 1s. 8d. a day. He died September 13 1943.' The music of the verse is in a calypso idiom, but the refrain, which may predate it, has powerful echoes of Africa and has been harmonized accordingly.

'They say that . . .' (verses 1 and 3) does not imply doubt—compare 'Some call him a king' in 'Go tell it on the mountain' (93).

PERFORMANCE   Verse, solo (perhaps with guitar); refrain, chorus in harmony.

The soloist could improvise further verses *ad lib.*, e.g., 'The shepherds came when the baby born', 'They left their gifts where the baby born', etc. (see 'Mary had a baby', *NOBC* no. 168, for a model).

See *NOBC* for *Es sungen drei Engel* (no. 175).

98

Maria durch ein' Dornwald ging
Blest Mary wanders through the thorn

(*Christmas*)

German traditional
(*arr. editors*)

1. Maria durch ein' Dornwald ging,
1. Blest Mary wanders through the thorn,

Kyrieleison!

Maria durch ein' Dornwald ging, der
Blest Mary wanders through the thorn, That

hatte in sieb'n Jahr'n kein Laub getrag'n!
seven long years no bloom hath borne.

Jesus und Maria!
Jesu et Maria!

2 Was trug Maria unter ihrem Herzen?

Kyrieleison!

Ein kleines Kindlein ohne Schmerzen,
das trug Maria unterm Herzen!

Jesus und Maria!

2 What clasps she to her breast so close?

Kyrieleison!

An innocent child doth there repose,
Which to her breast she claspeth close.

Jesu et Maria!

3 Da hab'n die Dornen Rosen getrag'n,
   Kyrieleison!
   Als das Kindlein durch den Wald getrag'n,
   da haben die Dornen Rosen getrag'n!
   Jesus und Maria!

3 Fair roses bloom on every tree,
   Kyrieleison!
   As through the thorn-wood passeth she
   Fair roses bloom on every tree.
   Jesu et Maria!

4 Wie soll dem Kind sein Name sein?
   Kyrieleison!
   Der Name, der soll Christus sein,
   das war von Anfang der Name sein!
   Jesus und Maria!

4 What shall this Infant callèd be?
   Kyrieleison!
   The Christ, he shall be called truly,
   Which Name he hath borne from eternity.
   Jesu et Maria!

5 Wer soll dem Kind sein Täufer sein?
   Kyrieleison!
   Das soll der Sankt Johannes sein,
   der soll dem Kind sein Täufer sein!
   Jesus und Maria!

5 This holy Name, who shall proclaim?
   Kyrieleison!
   Saint John Baptist shall do the same,
   This holy Name he shall proclaim.
   Jesu et Maria!

6 Was kriegt das Kind zum Patengeld?
   Kyrieleison!
   Den Himmel und die ganze Welt,
   das kriegt das Kind zum Patengeld!
   Jesus und Maria!

6 What christening-gifts to him are given?
   Kyrieleison!
   All things that be, the earth, the heaven,
   As christening-gifts to him are given.
   Jesu et Maria!

7 Wer hat erlöst die Welt allein?
   Kyrieleison!
   Das hat getan das Christkindlein,
   das hat erlöst die Welt allein!
   Jesus und Maria!

7 Who hath the world from sin set free?
   Kyrieleison!
   This Child alone, and only he,
   He hath the world from sin set free.
   Jesu et Maria!

German traditional

tr. editors

This has many of the characteristics of a fifteenth-century German folk carol. The flowering rose is a favourite medieval image and the subject of a multitude of legends (see notes, *NOBC* no. 66). The barren thorn-wood is an image of the fallen world (Genesis 2:9; 3:18), and the birth of Christ, with its promise of Redemption, is symbolized by the return of the thorn trees to their prelapsarian condition.

'Seven long years', like the Hebrew 'forty days', denotes a long passage of time.

PERFORMANCE (*i*) Solo voice, with a unison group singing the refrains; (*ii*) four voices alternating with choir; (*iii*) choir.

99

Kommet, ihr Hirten
Come, all ye shepherds

(German)

(Christmas)

Bohemian traditional
(arr. editors)

[ENGEL:] 1. Kom-met, ihr Hir-ten, ihr Män-ner und Frau'n, kom-met, das lieb-li-che Kind-lein zu schau'n. Chri-stus, der Herr, ist heu-te ge-bo-ren, den Gott zum Hei-land euch hat er-ko-ren. Fürch-tet euch nicht!

[HIRTEN:] 2. Las-set uns seh-en in Beth-le-hems Stall, was uns ver-heis-sen der himm-li-sche Schall. Was wir dort fin-den, las-set uns kün-den, las-set uns prei-sen in from-men Wei-sen: Hal-le-lu-ja!

[ALLE:] 3. Wahr-lich, die En-gel ver-kün-di-ge heut' Beth-le-hems Hir-ten-volk gar gro-sse Freud', nun soll es wer-den Frie-de auf Er-den, den Men-schen al-len ein Wohl-ge-fal-len: Eh-re sei Gott!

(rev.?) Carl Riedel (1827–88)

(English)

(Christmas)

Bohemian traditional
(arr. editors)

[ANGELS:] 1. Come, all ye shep - herds, O come, fol - low me!
[SHEPHERDS:] 2. Let us go see now, in Beth - le - hem's stall,
[ALL:] 3. Tru - ly the an - gels glad ti - dings re - vealed

Fa - thers and mo - thers and chil - dren, come see! Born is the Christ, the
What from the skies was re - vealed to us all; What there we find, a -
Un - to the shep - herds in Beth - le - hem's field: Ti - dings of joy to

Lord of Cre - a - tion, Cho - sen by God to work your sal - va - tion: Be not a - fraid!
- broad we'll be tell-ing: Joy - ful our hearts, with God's prai - ses swell-ing. Hal - le - lu - jah!
all men are gi - ven; Peace on the earth pro-claimed from the hea - ven. Praise be to God!

tr. editors

Both Czech- and German-speaking Bohemians lay claim to this folk melody, though the truth of its origins will probably never be uncovered. The text may well derive from a shepherd drama.

The Czechs sing the tune to a non-pastoral text beginning 'Nesem vám noviny'. They sing it, moreover, immensely slowly, and have been followed in this by the many American college choirs that have enthusiastically adopted the carol: but genre, German text, and tune surely suggest a quick, light style of singing.

PERFORMANCE (*i*) Two soloists (or two-part choir) with two-note drone *ad lib.*; (*ii*) choir. The scoring may be varied for performance within a Nativity play: verse 1 could be taken by two high voices, verse 2 by two men (both verses with instrumental drone), and all four soloists could join with the choir for verse 3.

100

Schlaf wohl, du Himmelsknabe du
O sleep, thou heaven-born Treasure, thou

(German)

(*Christmas*)

Nineteenth-century Bavarian
(Reimann, 1895, arr. editors)

1. Schlaf wohl, du Him - mels - kna - be du, __ schlaf wohl, du sü - sses Kind! ___ Dich fä - cheln En - ge - lein in Ruh' __ mit sanf - tem Him - mels - wind. ___ Wir ar - men Hir - ten

2. Ma - ri - a hat __ mit Mut - ter - blick __ dich lei - se zu - ge - deckt, ___ und Jo - seph hält __ den Hauch zu - rück, __ dass er dich nicht __ er - weckt. ___ Die Schäf - lein, die im

Kind! Dich fä - cheln En - ge - lein in Ruh' __ mit
- deckt, und Jo - seph hält __ den Hauch zu - rück, __ dass

Wir __ ar - men Hir - ten __
Die __ Schäf-lein, die __ im

sin - gen dir___ ein her - zig's Wie - gen - lied - chen für:___

Stal - le sind,___ ver - stum - men vor___ dir, Him - mels - kind.___

___ sin - gen dir___

___ Stal - le sind,___

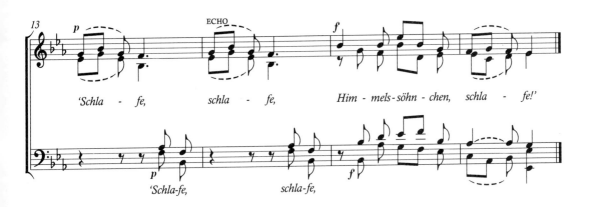

'Schla - fe, schla - fe, Him - mels - söhn - chen, schla - fe!'

'Schla-fe, schla-fe,

3 Bald wirst du gross, dann fliesst dein Blut
    von Golgatha herab,
ans Kreuz schlägt dich der Menschen Wut,
    da legt man dich ins Grab.
Hab immer deine Äuglein zu,
denn du bedarfst der süssen Ruh'.

4 So schlummert in der Mutter Schoss
    noch manches Kindlein ein,
doch wird das arme Kindlein gross,
    so hat es Angst und Pein.
O Jesulein, durch deine Huld
hilf's ihnen tragen mit Geduld.

German traditional
(Simrock, 1865)

This is the early nineteenth-century form of an ancient cradle-rocking carol (see notes, *NOBC* no. 55). A compound misunderstanding by Charles Macpherson has led to the misattribution of the tune to Carl 'Leuner' (in reality Carl Neuner). It is in fact traditional, and the present form is one of several that were evidently reworked by local Bavarian composers (Neuner among them) around 1800.

PERFORMANCE Choir, with organ or piano *ad lib.*

See *NOBC* for *Es kommt ein Schiff geladen / Uns kompt ein Schiff gefahren* (no. 179).

(English)

(*Christmas*)

Nineteenth-century Bavarian
(*Reimann, 1895, arr. editors*)

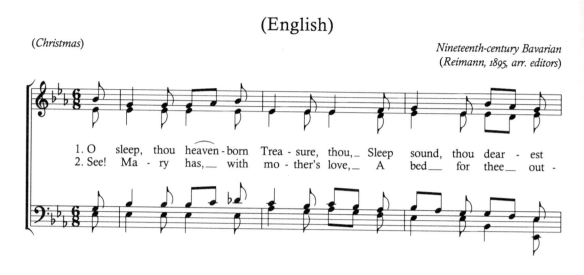

1. O sleep, thou heaven-born Trea - sure, thou,_ Sleep sound, thou dear - est
2. See! Ma - ry has,_ with mo - ther's love,_ A bed_ for thee_ out -

Child;_____ White an - gel - wings_ shall fan thy brow_ With
- spread,_____ While Jo - seph stoops_ him from a - bove_ And

Child; White an - gel - wings_____ shall fan thy brow_ With
- spread, While Jo - seph stoops_____ him from a - bove_ And

breez - es soft_ and mild._____ We shep - herds poor are
watch - es at_ thy head._ The lambs with - in the

We_ shep-herds poor_ are
The_ lambs with - in_ the_

here   to   sing___ A   sim - ple lul - lay to___ our   King:___
stall   so nigh,___ That thou___ mayst sleep,__ have hushed their cry.___

___ here to   sing___
___ stall so   nigh,___

'Lul - la - by,   lul - la - by,   Sleep, sleep soft - ly,   lul - la - by!'

'Lul - la,   lul - la,

3   When man thou art, thy blood will be
        Poured out, mankind to save,
    And men will nail thee to the Tree,
        Men lay thee in the grave.
    So sleep, my Baby, whilst thou may,
    'Twill give thee rest against that day.

4   On mother's knee doth man repose
        While he a child remains:
    But when the child to manhood grows,
        Then knows he woes and pains.
    O holy Child, give grace to all,
    That we endure whate'er befall.

vv. 1, 2, 3 (ll. 5–8)
tr. Charles Macpherson (1870–1927)
v. 3 (ll. 1–4), v. 4 tr. editors

101

O du fröhliche! O du selige!
O most wonderful! O most merciful!

(*Christmas*)

Italian traditional
(arr. Johannes Daniel Falk, 1768–1826)

1. O du fröh - li - che!___ O du se - li - ge!___
1. O most won - der - ful!___ O most mer - ci - ful!___

gna - den - brin - gen - de Weih - nachts - zeit!
Christ, our Sa - viour, is born on earth!

Welt___ ging ver - lo - ren, Christ___ ward ge - bo - ren:
Sin - ners for - gi - ven, Sor - row for - got - ten:

Freu - e,___ freu - e dich, o Chri - sten - heit!
Greet,___ O___ greet we now his glo - rious birth!

2 O du fröhliche!
  O du selige!
    gnadenbringende Weihnachtszeit!
  Christ ist erschienen,
  uns zu versühnen:
    Freue, freue dich, o Christenheit!

2 O most wonderful!
  O most merciful!
    Christ, our Saviour, is born on earth!
  Christ comes among us,
  Christ will redeem us:
    Greet, O greet we now his glorious birth!

3 O du fröhliche!
  O du selige!
    gnadenbringende Weihnachtszeit!
  Himmlische Heere
  jauchzen dir Ehre:
    Freue, freue dich, o Christenheit!

3 O most wonderful!
  O most merciful!
    Christ, our Saviour, is born on earth!
  Armies on high sing
  Praises unending:
    Greet, O greet we now his glorious birth!

v. 1 Johannes Daniel Falk (1768–1826)
vv. 2, 3 Heinrich Holzschuher (fl. 1819)

tr. Anne Ridler

Known as 'The Sicilian Mariners' Hymn' and sung to a purely Marian text beginning 'O sanctissima! O piissima!' or its Italian equivalent, this piece has established itself as a kind of honorary Christmas carol in English-speaking countries. Its origins are mysterious, and quite possibly unconnected with Sicily (see *NOBC* notes). A three-part setting from a London magazine of 1792 is the earliest known source (*NOBC* setting I, not included here), and the song was later published by Gottfried von Herder, who claimed to have collected it during a trip to Italy in 1788. Falk was the warden of a Weimar orphanage, and in 1819 he wrote a drama for his charges to perform (published in 1830). 'O sanctissima!' appears there in versions for Christmas (with two additional verses by a colleague) and other feasts. The Christmas text is now firmly established among Lutherans.

PERFORMANCE Voices, with organ or piano *ad lib.*

102

O Tannenbaum
O Christmas tree

(German)

(Christmas)

German traditional
(arr. editors)

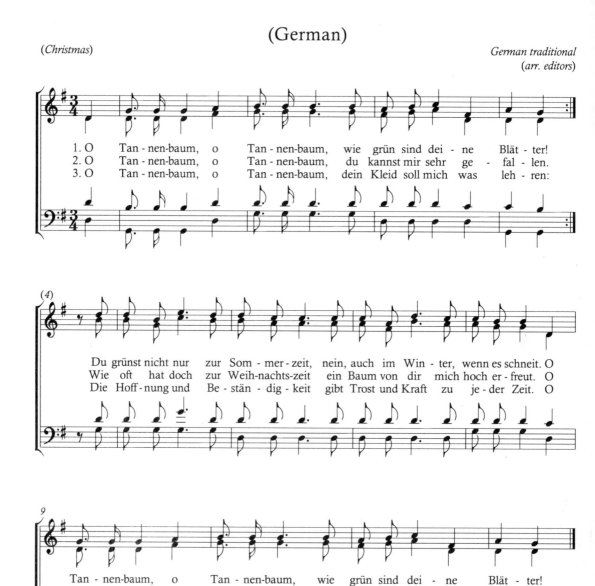

1. O Tan - nen-baum, o Tan - nen-baum, wie grün sind dei - ne Blät - ter!
2. O Tan - nen-baum, o Tan - nen-baum, du kannst mir sehr ge - fal - len.
3. O Tan - nen-baum, o Tan - nen-baum, dein Kleid soll mich was leh - ren:

Du grünst nicht nur zur Som - mer-zeit, nein, auch im Win - ter, wenn es schneit. O
Wie oft hat doch zur Weih-nachts-zeit ein Baum von dir mich hoch er - freut. O
Die Hoff - nung und Be - stän - dig - keit gibt Trost und Kraft zu je - der Zeit. O

Tan - nen-baum, o Tan - nen-baum, wie grün sind dei - ne Blät - ter!
Tan - nen-baum, o Tan - nen-baum, du kannst mir sehr ge - fal - len.
Tan - nen-baum, o Tan - nen-baum, dein Kleid soll mich was leh - ren!

v. 1 German traditional
(August Zarnack, 1820)
vv. 2, 3 Ernst Anschütz (fl. 1824)

(English)

(*Christmas*)

German traditional
(arr. editors)

1. O Christ-mas tree, O Christ-mas tree, With faith - ful leaves un - chan - ging!
2. O Christ-mas tree, O Christ-mas tree, Of all the trees most love - ly!
3. O Christ-mas tree, O Christ-mas tree, Your leaves will sure - ly teach me

Not on - ly green in sum-mer's heat But in the win - ter's snow and sleet: O
Each year you bring re - newed de - light, A - gleam-ing in the Christ-mas night: O
That hope and love and faith - ful - ness Are pre-cious things I can poss - ess: O

Christ - mas tree, O Christ - mas tree, With faith - ful leaves un - chan - ging!
Christ - mas tree, O Christ - mas tree, Of all the trees most love - ly!
Christ - mas tree, O Christ - mas tree, Your leaves will sure - ly teach me.

tr. editors

The symbol of the evergreen was too strongly rooted in the old European religions to be entirely eradicated with the coming of Christianity. The church tolerated these ancient symbols of the continuing life-force at the winter solstice and assimilated them as Christian symbols of the renewal of life at Christ's birth.

Many Germans devoutly believe that Luther invented the Christmas tree. In reality the custom seems to have evolved in late-medieval Rhineland, the Christmas tree being a descendant of the Tree of Life of the mystery plays. By 1850 the Christmas tree was universally popular in Germany, and was seen as a symbol of all that was best in the old Germanic Christmas tradition.

The tune first appeared in print in *Melodien zum Mild-heimischen Liederbuche* (1799), to the words 'Es lebe hoch'.

Verse 1 appeared with the tune in August Zarnack's *Weisenbuch zu den Volksliedern für Volkschulen* (1820) and without it in the companion *Deutsche Volkslieder* of the same year. Zarnack had possibly devised it himself after the ancient and gnomic folk-song 'O Dannebom' (*NOBC* setting II, not included here). Ernst Anschütz, a Leipzig schoolmaster, added verses 2 and 3 in 1824 for his charges to sing, when Christmas trees were beginning to be common in the town.

The familiar translation derives from a later version of the German, with 'wie *treu* sind . . .' in verse 1 giving 'with *faithful* leaves'. 'Tannenbaum' actually means 'fir tree'.

PERFORMANCE   Voices with or without piano.

103

Žežulka z lesa vylítla
Out of the forest a cuckoo flew

(*Christmas*)

Czech traditional
(*arr. editors*)

1. Že - žul - ka z le - sa vy - lí - tla, *ku - ku!* U sa - mých
1. Out of the fo - rest a cuc - koo flew, *cuc - koo!* Seek - ing the

je - sli - ček se - dla, *ku - ku!* Vzdá - vá čest
hea - ven - ly Babe to woo, *cuc - koo!* Near Je - sus'

a pro - zpě___ vu - je, Pá - na své - ho vy -
bed he gave___ in songs The praise that to our

-chva - lu - je, Ku - ku, ku - ku, ku - ku!
God___ be - longs, Cuc - koo, cuc - koo, cuc - koo!

2 Holoubek sedl na báni, *vrku!*
   Dal se silně do houkání *vrku!*
   Jest tomu také povděčen,
   Že jest Ježíšek narozen,
   Vrku, vrku, vrku!

Czech traditional

2 High in the rafters there sat a dove, *cooroo!*
   Cooing to Jesus of his great love, *cooroo!*
   His heart and voice so full of joy
   That heaven sent this lovely Boy!
   Cooroo, cooroo, cooroo!

(*tr. George K. Evans, adapted*)

This is the standard Czech version of the carol, also widely known in America. The variant printed in *The Oxford Book of Carols* (1928) was sent to the editors by a Czech schoolteacher from Polička, in the hills between Bohemia and Moravia.

PERFORMANCE Two solo voices, or two-part choir, at either or both octaves, with instrumental or vocal drone *ad lib.*

104

Hajej, nynej, Ježíšku
Jesu, Jesu, baby dear

(Christmas)

Czech traditional
(arr. editors)

1. Ha-jej, ny-nej, Je-žíš-ku, Je-žíš-ku, Pu-čí-me ti ko-žíš-ku.
2. Ha-jej, ny-nej, mi-láč-ku, mi-láč-ku, Ma-ri-án-ský sy-náč-ku.

1. Je-su, Je-su, ba-by dear, ba-by dear, We will rock your cra-dle here.
2. Je-su, Je-su, dar-ling one, dar-ling one, Gift of hea-ven, Ma-ry's son.

Bu-de-me tě ko-lí-ba-ti, A-bys moh' li-bě po-spa-ti,
Bu-de-me tě ko-lí-ba-ti, A-bys moh' li-bě po-spa-ti,

We will rock you, rock you, rock you; Gent-ly slum-ber as we rock you;
We will rock you, rock you, rock you; Gent-ly slum-ber as we rock you;

Ha-jej, ny-nej, Je-žíš-ku, Pu-čí-me ti ko-žíš-ku.
Ha-jej, ny-nej, mi-láč-ku, Ma-ri-án-ský sy-náč-ku.

Je-su, Je-su, do not fear: We who love you will be near.
Je-su, Je-su, do not fear: We who love you will be near.

Czech traditional
(Free tr., Walter Ehret)

A cradle-song known to all Czechs. A once-popular translation by the editors of *The Oxford Book of Carols* (1928), with lines such as 'Little Jesus . . . do not stir, / We will lend a coat of fur', is far removed from the original Czech.

'Hajej, nynej, Ježíšku' probably accompanied cradle-rocking, a medieval custom which began in Germany and spread through much of Europe (see notes, *NOBC* no. 55).

PERFORMANCE   (*i*) Children's voices with accompaniment; (*ii*) choir.

105

W żłobie leży
Infant holy, Infant lowly

(*Christmas*)

Polish traditional
(arr. editors)

1. W żło-bie le - ży, któż po - bie-ży Ko-lę-do-wać Ma-łe-mu. Je-zu-so-wi,
2. My zaś sa - mi, z pio-sne-czka-mi, Za wa-mi po-śpie-szy-my. A tak te-go
1. In - fant ho-ly, In - fant low-ly, For his bed a cat - tle-stall; Ox-en low-ing,
2. Flocks were sleep-ing, shep-herds keep-ing Vi-gil till the morn-ing new; Saw the glo - ry,

Chrys-tu - so - wi, Dziś nam na - ro - dzo-ne-mu. Pa - stu-szko - wie
Ma - leń-kie - go Niech wszy-scy zo - ba-czy-my. Jak u - bo - go
lit - tle know - ing Christ the Babe is Lord of all. Swift-ly wing - ing
heard the sto - ry, Ti - dings of a gos-pel true. Thus re - joi - cing,

przy-by - waj-cie, Je - mu pięk-nie przy-gry - waj-cie, Ja - ko Pa - nu na-sze-mu.
na - rod-zo - ny, Płacze w staj - ni po - ło - żo - ny Więc go dziś u - cie-szy-my.
an - gels sing-ing, No-wells ring-ing, ti-dings bring-ing: Christ the Babe is Lord of all.
free from sor-row, Prai-ses voi-cing, greet the mor-row: Christ the Babe was born for you.

Polish traditional
tr. Edith M. G. Reed (1885–1933), adapted

This carol is well known in the United States in the form in which it is sung in Poland, but it is still commonly sung in England in a version that misplaces the barlines and perpetuates an obvious misprint in the final cadence (C–B–G for B–A–G).

Edith Reed's telegraphese translation, first published in *Music and Youth* (vol. 1, no. 12, December 1921), a journal she founded and edited, is a clever solution to an almost impossible problem. It was written for the mis-stressed version, but fortunately it works (with a little help from the singers) when the barlines are correctly placed.

PERFORMANCE Choir.

(*NOBC no. 184*)

106

Entre le bœuf et l'âne gris
Oxen and asses stand around

(Christmas)

French traditional
(arr. editors)

VERSE

1. En - tre le bœuf et— l'â - ne gris Dort, dort, dort le pe - tit Fils:
1. Ox - en and ass - es— stand a - round Je - sus, Je - sus sleep-ing sound;

REFRAIN

Mille an - ges di - vins, Mil - le sé - ra-phins, Vo - lent à l'en-tour— De ce Dieu d'a - mour.
From the skies a - bove An-gels ho-ver near, Round the God of Love In the man - ger here.

2 Entre les deux bras de Marie
   Dort, dort le Fruit de la Vie;

3 Entre les roses et les lys
   Dort, dort, dort le petit Fils;

4 Entre les pastoureaux jolis
   Dort, dort, dort le petit Fils;

5 En ce beau jour solennel
   Dort, dort, dort l'Emmanuel;

French traditional

2 Mary's arms are clasped around
   Jesus, Jesus sleeping sound;

3 Rose and lily twine around
   Jesus, Jesus sleeping sound;

4 Shepherds are piping all around
   Jesus, Jesus sleeping sound;

5 Round his cradle now we sing:
   Jesus, born to be our King!

tr. editors

The text was first published in Henri Lemeignen's *Vieux Noëls* (1876) and is thought to have originated in Brittany. The tune is one of many variant versions.

PERFORMANCE (*i*) Solo voice and continuo; (*ii*) choir. Ornaments: see notes, 111.

107

Guillô, pran ton tamborin!

Guillô, come, and Robin too

(Christmas)

Provençal traditional
(Barôzai, 1701, arr. editors)

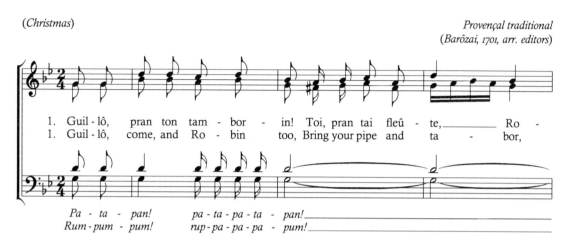

1. Guil - lô, pran ton tam - bor - in! Toi, pran tai fleû - te, _____ Ro -
1. Guil - lô, come, and Ro - bin too, Bring your pipe and ta - bor,

Pa - ta - pan! pa - ta - pa - ta - pan! _____
Rum - pum - pum! rup - pa - pa - pa - pum! _____

- bin! Au son de cés in - stru - man: *Tu - re - lu - re - lu!* pa - ta - pa - ta -
do! Blow the pipe and beat the drum: *Tur - ra - lur - ra - lu!* rup - pa - pa - pa -

— pa - ta - pan! pa - ta - pa - ta - pan! _____
— rum - pum - pum! rup - pa - pa - pa - pum! _____

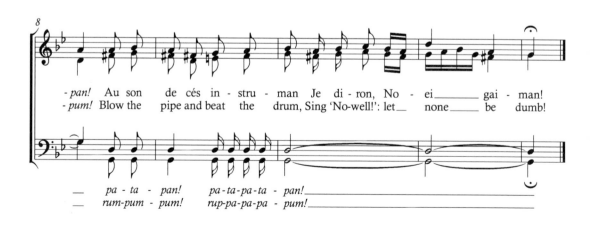

- pan! Au son de cés in - stru - man Je di - ron, No - ei _____ gai - man!
- pum! Blow the pipe and beat the drum, Sing 'No - well!': let _ none _____ be dumb!

— pa - ta - pan! pa - ta - pa - ta - pan! _____
— rum - pum - pum! rup - pa - pa - pa - pum! _____

2   C'étó lai môdȇ autre foi
     De loüé le Roi dé Roi.
    Au son de cés instruman,
     Turelurelu! patapatapan!
    Au son de cés instruman
     Ai nos an fauȇ fairȇ autan.

3   Ce jor le Dialȇ at ai cu,
     Randons an graicȇ ai Jésu
    Au son de cés instruman,
     Turelurelu! patapatapan!
    Au son de cés instruman
     Fezon lai niquȇ ai Satan.

4   L'hommȇ et Dei son pu d'aicor
     Que lai fleûtȇ et le tambor.
    Au son de cés instruman,
     Turelurelu! patapatapan!
    Au son de cés instruman
     Chanton, danson, sautons-an.

Provençal traditional
(Barôzai, 1701)

2   At our Saviour's birth we play:
     This hath ever been our way;
    Blow the pipe and beat the drum:
     Turralurralu! ruppapapapum!
    Blow the pipe and beat the drum,
     For the King of kings is come!

3   'Thanks be unto Christ!' we cry,
     For old Satan's end is nigh!
    Blow the pipe and beat the drum:
     Turralurralu! ruppapapapum!
    Blow the pipe and beat the drum,
     And your nose at Satan thumb!

4   Leap for joy and dance and sing,
     Drum and pipe re-echoing:
    Closer yet than pipe and drum,
     Turralurralu! ruppapapapum!
    Closer yet than pipe and drum
     God and man this day become!

Free tr., editors

A dance-like *noël* that remains popular throughout France as a sung carol. In Provence and Gascony it is also part of the pipe-and-tabor repertory of *noëls* and dances that are played at various points (including the elevation) in the Christmas midnight mass. In some rural churches the place of honour at this service is still given to local shepherds, who bear gifts to the *santon* (crib). Both text and tune are in Gui Barôzai's *Noei borguignon* (1701).

Guillô and Robin are stock characters in Provençal carols: they bring food to the manger in 'Allons, bergers, partons tous', and, like Jeannette and Isabelle in 'Un flambeau' (109), are perhaps being used to suggest the idea of the entire village community.

The Provençal *tambourin* is a large tabor with a long cylindrical body and a snare on the upper head. It is hit with a single drumstick, usually in simple reiterated rhythmic patterns, and has a deep and resonant tone. The 'fleûte' is a fipple flute, the three-holed pipe (*flûte à trois trous*) or *flûtet*, which since the eighteenth century has more generally been known as the *galoubet*. Pipe and tabor were much used for dancing throughout the Middle Ages, and have continued to accompany folk dancing in Provence. The *tambourin* has a wide dynamic range, and the *galoubet* is relatively gentle in its lower register, and shrill in its high, overblown octave. The present carol is perhaps most characteristically performed with loud drum and shrill pipe, and vocal performance might reflect this.

PERFORMANCE (*i*) Voice, with one-note instrumental drone *ad lib.*; (*ii*) two voices with two-note drone; (*iii*) choir; (*iv*) pipe and tabor/*tambourin*, the latter playing a reiterated 𝅘𝅥𝅮𝅘𝅥𝅮𝅘𝅥𝅮|𝅘𝅥 or |𝅘𝅥𝅮𝅘𝅥𝅮𝅘𝅥𝅮𝅘𝅥|rhythm.

'Turelurelu!' is in imitation of the pipe, 'patapatapan!' of the drum.

108

De matin ai rescountra lou trin
Ce matin j'ai rencontré le train
Far away, what splendour comes this way?
(Marcho di Rei)

(Provençal & French)

(*Epiphany*)

Provençal traditional
(arr. Georges Bizet, 1838–75, adapted)

1. De ma - tin ai res-coun-tra lou trin De tres gran rei qu'a-na-voun
2. Dins un char doou-ra de tou - to par Ve - sias lei rei mou-des-te

1. Ce ma - tin j'ai ren-con-tré le train De trois grands rois qui al-laient
2. Dans un char, do - ré de tou - tes parts, On voit les rois, gra-cieux com -

en vou - ya - gi;___ De ma - tin ai res-coun-tra lou trin De
cou - mo d'an - gi;___ Dins un char doou-ra de tou - to par Ve

en voy - a - ge;___ Ce ma - tin j'ai ren-con-tré le train De
- me des an - ges;___ Dans un char, do - ré de tou - tes parts, On

tres gran rei des-su lou gran ca - min. Ai vis d'a - bor___ De
- sias bri - ha de rich-eis e - stan - dar. Oou - sias d'oou - houas,___ De

trois grands rois des-sus le grand che - min. Tout char - gés d'or Les sui -
voit bril - ler de ri-ches é - ten - dards. En - tour les rois,___ De

gar - do cor, De gen ar - ma em' u - no trou-po de pa - gi; Ai
bel - lei vouas, Que de moun Dieou pub - li - a-voun lei lou - an - gi; Oou-
-vants d'a - bord, De grands guer - riers et les gar - des du tré - sor; Tout
bel - les voix Qui du Sei - gneur pro - cla - maient les lou - an - ges; En -

vis d'a - bor__ De gar - do cor, Tou - tei doou - ra des - su sei just' oou cor.
- sias d'oou-houas__ De bel - lei vouas Que di - sien d'er d'un ad - mi - ra - ble chouas.
char - gés d'or Les sui - vants d'a - bord, De grands guer-riers a - vec leurs bou - cli - ers.
- tour les rois,__ De bel - les voix Qui tout en haut chan-taient un air de choix.

3 Tout ravi d'entendre aco d'aqui
Mi sieou rangea per veire l'equipagi;
Tout ravi d'entendre aco d'aqui
De luen en luen leis ai toujour suivi.
L'astre brihan
Qu'ero davan
Servie de guido e menavo les tres magi;
L'astre brihan
Qu'ero davan
S'aresté net quan fougué ver l' Enfan.

J. F. Domergue (fl. 1742)

3 Tout ravi de les entendre ainsi,
Me suis rangé pour voir leur équipage;
Tout ravi de les entendre ainsi,
De loin en loin les ai toujours suivis.
L'astre brillant,
Toujours devant,
Servait de guide et menait les trois mages;
L'astre brillant,
Toujours devant,
S'arrêta net, venu devant l'Enfant.

tr. Stephen Haynes

TRANSLATION (Provençal) 1 One morning I met a procession of three great kings who were travelling on a journey, . . . three great kings on the highway. First I saw their bodyguard of armed men with a group of pages, . . . their tunics all covered with gold.

2 In a carriage, gilded all over, you could see the kings, as comely as angels, . . . rich standards shining. You could hear beautiful voices singing the praises of our Lord, . . . a most choice melody.

3 Ravished by what I heard, I drew near to see the procession; . . . I continued to follow them mile after mile. The blazing star, which went before, guided and led the three magi, . . . stopped when it came before the child.

(tr. Stephen Haynes)

(English)

(*Epiphany*)

Provençal traditional
(arr. Georges Bizet, 1838–75, adapted)

1. Far a - way, what splen-dour comes this way? The wind is wa-ving ma - ny
2. Kings, all three, such splen - did men must be, For each is bril-liant as a
3. Now I hear the sound of mu - sic clear: A page is sing-ing with a

col - oured ban - ners; _ Far a - way, what splen-dour comes this way? I
gold - en sun - rise; _ Kings, all three, such splen - did men must be, Who
voice of sil - ver; _ Now I hear the sound of mu - sic clear; Such

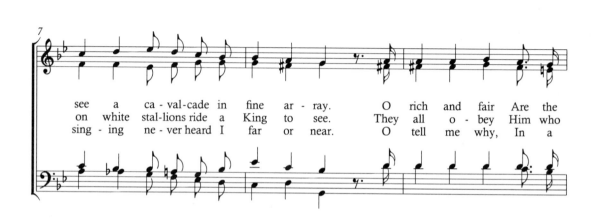

see a ca - val-cade in fine ar - ray. O rich and fair Are the
on white stal-lions ride a King to see. They all o - bey Him who
sing - ing ne - ver heard I far or near. O tell me why, In a

robes they wear,   And bright gold gleams on the   har-ness of the ca - mels;   O
leads by day,   But   e - very night by a   star they have been guid - ed,   They
sta - ble nigh,   They stoop so low to a   ba - by in   a   man - ger?   O

rich and fair Are the robes they wear,   And on their tur-bans glit - ter jew - els rare.
all   o - bey Him who leads by day;   His long white beard is seen from far a - way.
tell me why, In   a   sta - ble nigh,   They wor - ship him who on   a   cross will die?

English version by Mary Barham Johnson

The tune began life as a march, composed (perhaps by Lully) in honour of the celebrated French military hero Henri de la Tour d'Auvergne (1611–75), Vicomte de Turenne. The words were written for the tune in Avignon during the eighteenth century, possibly for use in one of the great processions of the three kings that made their way into Provençal towns on the eve of the Epiphany. Bizet used the carol in his incidental music to Daudet's drama of rustic passion, *L'Arlésienne*, and our arrangement is a stitching together of two different sections from the last act.

PERFORMANCE   (*i*) Solo voice or unison voices (with drone accompaniment); (*ii*) choir. One possible scheme (using Bizet's various treatments of the tune) is: v. 1, unison; v. 2, bars 1–8 unison sopranos and altos followed in canon by unison tenors and basses at a distance of two beats, bars 9–16 in harmony; v. 3, harmony.

109

Un flambeau, Jeannette, Isabelle!
Come with torches, Jeanette, Isabella!

(Christmas)

Provençal traditional
(arr. editors)

1. Un flam - beau,— Jean - nette, I - sa - bel - le! Un flam -
1. Come with torch - es, Jean - ette, I - sa - bel - la! Run un -

-beau,— cou - rons au ber - ceau! C'est Jé - sus, bon - nes gens du ha -
-to— the cra - dle, run! Christ is born: O come— be -

-meau,— Le Christ est né, Ma - rie ap - pel - le,
-fore— him! Ma - ry calls us to a - dore— him;

Ah!　　　ah!　　　ah! que la mère＿ est bel - le,
Oh!　　　oh!　　　oh! such a love - ly mo - ther!

Ah!　　　ah!　　　ah! que l'En - fant＿ est beau!
Oh!　　　oh!　　　oh! such a love - ly Son!

2　C'est un tort quand l'Enfant sommeille,
　　C'est un tort de crier si fort.
　　Taisez-vous, l'un et l'autre, d'abord!
　　Au moindre bruit, Jésus s'éveille,
　　Chut! chut! chut! Il dort à merveille,
　　Chut! chut! chut! voyez comme il dort!

3　Doucement, dans l'étable close,
　　Doucement, venez un moment!
　　Approchez, que Jésus est charmant!
　　Comme il est blanc! Comme il est rose!
　　Do! do! do! que l'Enfant repose!
　　Do! do! do! qu'il rit en dormant!

2　Cease, good neighbours, your noisy prattle!
　　Peace, good neighbours: let him sleep!
　　Shame on him who the silence breaketh
　　And the new-born Babe awaketh:
　　Soft! soft! softly amid the cattle,
　　Soft! soft! softly he slumbers deep.

3　Through the doorway softly filing,
　　To his manger-bed we creep.
　　Torches' glow the Babe discloses,
　　Fair as snow, with cheeks like roses,
　　Hush! hush! hushaby! sweetly smiling,
　　Hush! hush! hushaby! fast asleep!

Provençal traditional
tr. Émile Blémont

Free tr., editors

Torches have always played an important part in Provençal Christmas celebrations. Another tradition is the making of model villages, complete with crib and vividly characterized villagers. Both are reflected in this carol. The French text by Émile Blémont first appeared in 1901, and is a version of the Provençal carol 'Vénès leou vieira la Pieoucelle'. The tune derives from the drinking-song 'Qu'ils sont doux, bouteille jolie', which Charpentier wrote for later performances of Molière's *Le Médecin malgré lui* (1666).

PERFORMANCE (*i*) Solo voice and continuo; (*ii*) choir. Ornaments: see notes, 111.

110

Noël nouvelet!

(French)

(Christmas; New Year)

French traditional
(arr. editors)

1. Noël nouvelet! Noël chantons icy;
2. Quand m'es-veilly et j'eus assez dormy,

Dévotes gens, rendons à Dieu merci;
Ouvris mes yeux, vis un arbre fleury,

Chantons Noël pour le Roi nouvelet:
Dont il issait un bouton vermeillet.

Noël nouvelet! Noël chantons icy!

3   Quand je le vis, mon coeur fut resjouy
    Car grande clarté resplendissait de luy,
    Comme le soleil qui luit au matinet.
    Noël nouvelet! Noël chantons icy!

4   D'un oysillon après le chant j'ouy,
    Qui aux pasteurs disait: 'Partez d'ici!
    En Bethléem trouverez l'Agnelet!'
    Noël nouvelet! Noël chantons icy!

5   En Bethléem, Marie et Joseph vy,
    L'asne et le bœuf, l'Enfant couché parmy;
    La crèche était au lieu d'un bercelet.
    Noël nouvelet! Noël chantons icy!

6   L'estoile vint qui le jour esclaircy,
    Et la vy bien d'où j'estois départy
    En Bethléem les trois roys conduisaient.
    Noël nouvelet! Noël chantons icy!

7   L'un portait l'or, et l'autre myrrhe aussi,
    Et l'autre encens, que faisait bon senty:
    Le paradis semblait le jardinet.
    Noël nouvelet! Noël chantons icy!

8   Quarante jours la nourrice attendy;
    Entre les bras de Siméon rendy
    Deux tourterelles dedans un panneret.
    Noël nouvelet! Noël chantons icy!

9   Quand Siméon le vit, fit un haut cry:
    'Voici mon Dieu, mon Sauveur,
        Jésus-Christ!
    Voicy celui qui joie au peuple met!
    Noël nouvelet! Noël chantons icy!

*10 Un prestre vint, dont je fus esbahy
    Que les paroles hautement entendy,
    Puis les mussa dans un petit livret.
    Noël nouvelet! Noël chantons icy!

*11 Et puis me dit: 'Frère, crois-tu cecy?
    Si tu y crois aux cieux sera ravy:
    Si tu n'y crois, va d'enfer au gibet!
    Noël nouvelet! Noël chantons icy!

12 Et l'autre jour je songeais en mon lict
    Que je voyais ung Enfant si petit
    Qui appelait Jésus de Nazareth.
    Noël nouvelet! Noël chantons icy!

*13 En douze jours fut Noël accomply;
    Par douze vers sera mon chant finy,
    Par chaque jour j'en ai fait un couplet.
    Noël nouvelet! Noël chantons icy!

French traditional
(Grande Bible des noëls, 1721, adapted)

299

(English)

French traditional
(arr. editors)

1. No - ël nou - ve - let! sing___ we this___ new No - ël!
2. Wa - king from sleep, this___ won - der did I see:

Thank we now our God, and___ of his___ good - ness tell;
In a gar - den fair there___ stood a___ beau - teous tree,

Sing we No - ël to greet the new - born King:
Where - on I spied a rose - bud o - pen - ing.

No - ël nou - ve - let! this___ new No - ël we sing!

3 How my heart rejoiced to see that sight divine,
For with rays of glory did the rose-bud shine,
As when the sun doth rise at break of day.
This new Noël sing we: *Noël nouvelet!*

4 Then a tiny bird left off its song, to say
Unto certain shepherds: 'Haste you now away!
In Bethlehem the Lamb of God you'll see.'
Noël nouvelet! this new Noël sing we!

5 Mary and Joseph in Bethlehem
    they found,
Where the ox and ass the Infant
    did surround,
Who in their manger slept upon the hay.
This new Noël sing we: *Noël nouvelet!*

6 Then I saw a star which turned
    the night to day,
Moving ever onward on its shining way,
Leading to Bethlehem the kings all three.
Noël nouvelet! this new Noël sing we!

7 Gold the first did carry;
    myrrh the next did bring;
And the third bore incense,
    the garden perfuming,
So that in paradise I seemed to dwell.
Noël nouvelet! sing we this new Noël!

8 For forty days a nurse the Child sustained,
Mary then a pair of turtle-doves obtained:
In Simeon's hands she placed this offering.
Noël nouvelet! this new Noël we sing!

9 Simeon saw the Child
    and lifted up his voice:
'Lo! my God and Saviour,
    in whom I rejoice;
Jesus, the Christ, the glory of Israël!'
Noël nouvelet! sing we this new Noël!

*10 Greatly did I marvel Simeon's
    words to hear,
Which a priest observed who shortly
    did appear,
Within a book those words to store away.
This new Noël sing we: *Noël nouvelet!*

*11 He of me demanded:
    'Dost thou these words believe?
If thou dost assent, the heavens shall
    thee receive;
If thou dost deny, on hell's great
    gallows swing!'
Noël nouvelet! this new Noël we sing!

12 I beheld these wonders as on my bed I lay,
Dreaming of a Child all at the break of day:
Jesus of Nazareth I saw in my dreaming;
Noël nouvelet! this new Noël we sing!

*13 Twelve are the days that to Noël belong:
Twelve are my verses, so doth end my song;
A day for each verse: a verse for every day;
This new Noël sing we: *Noël nouvelet!*

tr. editors

A mysterious and enchanting *chanson d'aventure* that has been cruelly treated by many English 'translators'. The text is first found in an elegant manuscript of the late fifteenth century. The tune, one of two to which the poem is now sung in France, may be the original. Like *noël*, *nouvelet* had implications of newness and news (*nouvelles* in modern French), and suggests an original association with New Year. The grim priest (verses 10, 11) may represent St Luke, the only Evangelist to describe the Purification. We have substituted 'douze' for the puzzling 'trente jours' ('thirty days') in the final verse, which is found in all French sources of the text. (See *NOBC* notes for other small emendations.)

PERFORMANCE (*i*) Solo voice; (*ii*) choir. Verses 10 and 11 are not entirely suitable for singing in church. Verse 13 will make sense only when the whole *noël* is sung. Possible shortened versions are: verses 1–5, 12; 1–7, 12; 1–5, 8–9, 12; 1–9, 12.

111

Dans cette étable
In this poor stable

(*Christmas*)

French traditional
(arr. editors)

1. Dans cette é - ta - ble Que Jé - sus est char-mant, Qu'il est ai - ma - ble__ Dans
1. In this poor sta - ble, Con - tent - ed, Je - sus lies, As if un - a - ble__ His

son__ a - bais - se - ment! Que d'at-traits à la fois!__ Tous les pa-lais des rois__ N'ont
state to re - al - ize;__ Though dark the night and drear, His beau-ty glow-eth clear: What

rien de com-pa - ra - ble Aux char-mes que je vois Dans cette é - ta - ble!
earth-ly king is a - ble To match the splen-dours here In this poor sta - ble?

OPTIONAL RITORNELLO (*editorial*)

- ble!
- ble!

2 Que sa puissance
    Paraît bien en ce jour,
Malgré l'enfance
    Où l'a réduit l'amour!
Notre ennemi dompté,
L'enfer déconcerté,
    Font voir qu'en sa naissance
Rien n'est si redouté
    Que sa puissance.

3 Sans le connaître,
    Dans sa divinité
Je vois paraître
    Toute sa majesté:
Dans cet Enfant qui naît,
À son aspect qui plaît,
    Je découvre mon maître
Et je sens ce qu'il est
    Sans le connaître.

*4 Plus de misère!
    Un Dieu souffre pour nous
Et de son Père
    Apaise le courroux;
C'est en notre faveur
Qu'il naît dans la douleur;
    Pouvait-il pour nous plaire
Unir à sa grandeur
    Plus de misère?

French traditional
(after Bishop Fléchier, 1632–1710)

2 Bright glory shineth,
    Proclaiming majesty
Where straw enshrineth
    His helpless infancy;
And hell doth quake with dread
To see that homely bed
    Wherein he now reclineth,
For all about his head
    Bright glory shineth!

3 In this poor stranger,
    Who gladly here doth yield
Himself to danger,
    The Godhead lies revealed;
To him each eye doth turn,
For him each heart doth burn,
    For lo! within the manger
Our master we discern
    In this poor stranger!

4 No more of sorrow!
    A God descends
Our mortal form to borrow,
    Though he all men transcends;
To suffer on the tree,
To die on Calvary
    On that yet-distant morrow:
How could Divinity
    Know more of sorrow?

tr. editors

The text was originally published in the 1728 edition of *Cantiques spirituels* by Esprit Fléchier, Bishop of Nîmes. We give the usual modern text, the result of gradually accumulating changes in later editions. *NOBC* contains a different English version, by Henry Farnie.

At the beginning of the eighteenth century the melody was sung to words beginning 'Dans le bel âge / Tout est fait pour aimer'. It is found in both simple and compound time; the latter version has become well known in English-speaking countries through the setting by Gounod.

Ornaments: + most commonly indicates a trill, but other (unspecified) ornaments are sometimes implied; ⌣ indicates a lower appoggiatura, ⌢ an upper.

PERFORMANCE (*i*) Solo voice, or four voices, and continuo; (*ii*) choir and organ.

Possible instrumentations of the ritornello: recorders/flutes/oboes/violins with bass viol/bassoon and/or chordal continuo; alternatively, keyboard solo.

112

Quelle est cette odeur agréable
Shepherds, what fragrance, all-perfuming

(Christmas)

French traditional
(arr. editors)

[1er BERGER:]
1. Quelle est cette o - deur a - gré - a - ble, Ber - gers, qui
[1st SHEPHERD:]
1. Shep - herds, what fra - grance, all - per - fum - ing, Sweet - ly our

Fine
S'ex - ha - le - t'il rien
Did e - ver flowers, at

ra - vit tous nos sens? S'ex - ha - le - t'il rien
sens - es now doth seize? Did e - ver flowers, at

S'ex - ha - le - t'il rien
Did e - ver flowers, at

de sem - bla - ble
spring-tide bloom - ing,

D.C. al Fine

de sem - bla - ble Au mi - lieu des fleurs du prin - temps?
spring - tide bloom - ing, Breathe forth such balm - y scents as these?

de sem - bla - ble
spring - tide bloom - ing,

Seventeenth-century in origin, the text is a little *scena* based on the annunciation to the shepherds in Luke 1, though there is no indication of different characters in the sources. The tune was popular in early eighteenth-century England and France, and was used by D'Urfey, John Gay, and Charles Simon Favart, among others.

PERFORMANCE (*i*) Voice and continuo; (*ii*) vocal consort/ choir and continuo; (*iii*) four tenor/baritone soloists and consort/choir, with continuo *ad lib.* Gabriel could sing verse 4 as well as verse 5 in our English version if preferred, but the French requires the indicated division. Non-dramatic performance is more likely to represent eighteenth-century practice. Ornaments: see notes, 111.

[DEUXIÈME BERGER:]

2 Mais quelle éclatante lumière
  Dans la nuit vient frapper les yeux?
L'astre du jour, dans sa carrière,
  Fût-il jamais si radieux?
Mais quelle éclatante lumière
  Dans la nuit vient frapper les yeux?

[TROISIÈME BERGER:]

3 Voici beaucoup d'autres merveilles!
  Grand Dieu! qu'entends-je dans les airs?
Quelles voix! Jamais nos oreilles
  N'ont entendu pareil concerts.
Voici beaucoup d'autres merveilles!
  Grand Dieu! qu'entends-je dans les airs?

[CHŒUR D'ANGES:]

4 Ne craignez rien, peuple fidèle,
  Écoutez l'Ange du Seigneur;
Il vous annonce une merveille
  Qui va vous combler de bonheur.
Ne craignez rien, peuple fidèle,
  Écoutez l'Ange du Seigneur.

[GABRIEL:]

5 A Bethléem, dans une crèche,
  Il vient de vous naître un Sauveur;
Allons, que rien ne vous empêche
  D'adorer votre Rédempteur!
A Bethléem, dans une crèche,
  Il vient de vous naître un Sauveur.

[CHŒUR D'ANGES ou TOUS:]

6 Dieu tout-puissant, gloire éternelle
  Vous soit renduë jusqu'aux cieux!
Que la paix soit universelle,
  Que la grâce abonde en tous lieux!
Dieu tout-puissant, gloire éternelle
  Vous soit renduë jusqu'aux cieux!

French traditional

[SECOND SHEPHERD:]

2 Whence comes this dazzling radiance, rending
  The gloomy shadows of the night?
Did e'er the morning star, ascending,
  Shed from his car a ray so bright?
Whence comes this dazzling radiance, rending
  The gloomy shadows of the night?

[THIRD SHEPHERD:]

3 Hark! on the trembling air, such singing
  As hath our souls to wonder stirred!
Choirs, in sweet concord, earthwards winging:
  Strains that no mortal ear hath heard!
Hark! on the trembling air, such singing
  As hath our souls to wonder stirred!

[ANGEL CHOIR:]

4 O trusty shepherds, nothing fear ye:
  Hark to the Angel of the Lord!
Tidings from highest heaven hear ye:
  Joys without end shall they afford!
O trusty shepherds, nothing fear ye:
  Hark to the Angel of the Lord!

[GABRIEL:]

5 In Bethlehem, God's will obeying,
  Born is the Saviour of mankind;
Come and adore! make no delaying:
  In yonder stall ye shall him find.
In Bethlehem, God's will obeying,
  Born is the Saviour of mankind.

[ANGEL CHOIR or TUTTI:]

6 Glory to God in highest heaven:
  Let all below his praises sound!
O may such grace to earth be given
  That peace may everywhere abound!
Glory to God in highest heaven:
  Let all below his praises sound!

Free tr., editors

113

Quittez, pasteurs
O leave your sheep

(Christmas)

French traditional
(arr. editors)

1. Quit-tez, pas - teurs, Vos bre - bis, vos hou - let - tes, Vo - tre ha - meau Et
1. O leave your sheep, Your lambs that fol - low af - ter! O leave the brook, The

le soin du trou-peau! Chan - gez__ vos__ pleurs__ En u - ne joie par - fai - te! Al -
pas-ture and the crook! No lon - ger__ weep:__ Turn weep-ing in - to laugh-ter! O

Un Dieu, un Dieu,
The Lord, the Lord,

[SOLI]

- lez tous a - do - rer   Un Dieu,   un Dieu, un   Dieu qui vient vous
shep-herds, seek your goal: The Lord,   the Lord, the   Lord, who co - meth

[SOLI]
Un Dieu, un Dieu,
The Lord, the Lord,

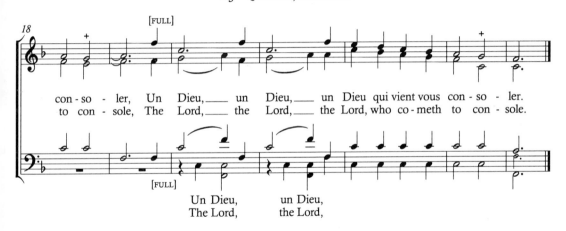

con-so-ler, Un Dieu,— un Dieu,— un Dieu qui vient vous con-so-ler.
to con-sole, The Lord,— the Lord,— the Lord, who co-meth to con-sole.

Un Dieu, un Dieu,
The Lord, the Lord,

2 Vous le verrez
   Couché dans une étable
Comme un enfant
Nu, pauvre, languissant;
Reconnaissez
   Son amour ineffable
Pour nous venir chercher:
Il est le fidèle Berger!

3 Rois d'Orient!
   L'étoile vous éclaire;
A ce grand Roi
Rendez hommage et foi!
L'astre brillant
   Vous mène à la lumière
De ce Soleil naissant;
Offrez l'or, la myrrhe et l'encens.

*4 Esprit Divin,
   A qui tout est possible,
Percez nos cœurs
De vos douces ardeurs!
Notre destin
   Par vous devient paisible;
Dieu prétend nous donner
Le ciel en venant s'incarner.

2 You'll find him laid
   Within a simple stable,
A Babe new-born,
In poverty forlorn;
In love arrayed,
   A love so deep 'tis able
To search the night for you;
'Tis he! 'tis he, the Shepherd true!

3 O kings so great,
   A light is streaming o'er you,
More radiant far
Than diadem or star.
Forgo your state;
   A Baby lies before you
Whose wonder shall be told:
Bring myrrh, bring frankincense and gold!

*4 Come, Holy Ghost,
   Of blessings source eternal!
Our hearts inspire
With thy celestial fire!
The heavenly host
   Praise Christ, the Lord supernal,
And sing the peace on earth
God gives us by his holy birth!

French traditional
(Garnier, 1723)

vv. 1–3 tr. Alice Raleigh
v. 4 tr. John Rutter

The text of this carol is from P. Garnier's *La Grande Bible renouvelée de noëls* (1723). The tune is a Besançon melody, also associated with the song 'Nanon dormait'.

PERFORMANCE (*i*) Choir; (*ii*) voice and harpsichord. Ornaments: see notes, 111.

114

Il est né, le divin Enfant!
Christ is born a Child on earth!

(*Christmas*)

French traditional
(*arr. editors*)

REFRAIN [FULL]

Il est né, le di - vin En - fant! Jou - ez, haut-bois, ré - son - nez, mu - set - tes!
Christ is born a___ Child on earth! Shawm and___ bag - pipe,___ sound his prai - ses!___

Il est né, le di - vin En - fant! Chan - tons tous son a - vè - ne - ment!
Christ is born a___ Child on earth! Sing we all his___ ho - ly___ birth!

Fine

VERSE [SOLI]

1. De - puis plus de qua - tre___ mille ans Nous le pro - met-taient les pro - phè - tes;
1. Twice two thou - sand___ years_ and_ more Pro-phets have fore - told his co - ming;

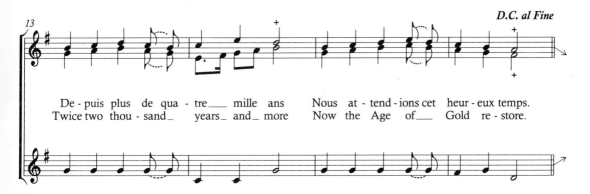

D.C. al Fine

De - puis plus de qua - tre___ mille ans   Nous at - tend - ions cet heur - eux temps.
Twice two thou - sand_   years_ and_ more   Now the Age of___ Gold re - store.

2 Ah! qu'il est beau, qu'il est charmant!
   Ah! que ses grâces sont parfaites!
   Ah! qu'il est beau, qu'il est charmant!
   Qu'il est doux, ce divin Enfant!

3 O Jésus, O Roi tout-puissant,
   Tout petit Enfant que vous êtes,
   O Jésus, O Roi tout-puissant,
   Régnez sur nous entièrement!

French traditional

2 See his grace and beauty mild;
   See his charms in all perfection!
   See his grace and beauty mild;
   Soft he lies, this holy Child!

3 Jesu, man and God in one,
   Helpless babe and King all-powerful;
   Jesu, man and God in one,
   Hail thy rule on earth begun!

tr. editors

The text was first published in Dom G. Legeay's *Noëls anciens* (1875–6). The earliest publication of the tune seems to be R. Grosjean's *Airs des noëls lorrain* (1862), where it is called 'Ancien air de chasse'; the old Normandy hunting tune 'Tête bizarde' is very similar, though in 6/8 time. Perhaps the most likely origin is an eighteenth-century piece in rustic style, and we have harmonized it accordingly.

PERFORMANCE (*i*) Solo voice (or four solo voices) and continuo; (*ii*) soprano and alto duet with bass viol playing the second stave throughout; (*iii*) choir. Ornaments: see notes, 111.

115

Berger, secoue ton sommeil profond!
Shepherd, shake off your drowsy sleep!

(Christmas)

French traditional
(arr. editors)

1. Ber - ger, se - coue ton som - meil pro - fond! Lève - toi et lais - se tes
1. Shep-herd, shake off your drow - sy sleep! Rise and leave__ your

mou - tons jou - er! An - ges du ciel, chan - tant très fort,____
sil - ly sheep! An - gels from heaven a - round are sing - ing,

Ap - por - tez nous la gran - de__ nou - vel - le. *Ber - ger, en chœur chan -*
Ti - dings of__ great joy__ are bring - ing. *Shep-herd, the cho - rus*

- tez   No - ël!   O___ chan - tez,___ chan - tez___ No - ël!
come   and   swell!   Sing___ No - el!___   O   sing___ No - el!

2 Vois comme les fleurs s'ouvrent de nouveau,
    Vois que la neige est rosée d'été,
  Vois les étoiles brillent de nouveau,
    Jetant leurs rayons les plus lumineux.

3 Berger, levez-vous, hâtez-vous!
    Allez chercher l'Enfant avant le jour.
  Il est l'espoir de chaque nation,
    Tous en lui trouveront la rédemption.

French traditional

2 See how the flowers all burst anew,
    Thinking snow is summer dew;
  See how the stars afresh are glowing,
    All their brightest beams bestowing.

3 Shepherd, then up and quick away!
    Seek the Babe ere break of day.
  He is the hope of every nation,
    All in him shall find salvation.

Traditional translation

The text is possibly eighteenth-century; the tune was included in *La Clef des chansonniers* (1717) among the tunes 'more than a century old', and associated with the words 'L'Échelle du temple'.

PERFORMANCE (*i*) Solo voice (or four solo voices) and continuo; (*ii*) choir, with organ *ad lib*. Ornaments: see notes, 111.

116

Les anges dans nos campagnes
Angels we have heard on high
Angels, we have heard your voices

I

(Christmas)

French traditional
(arr. editors)

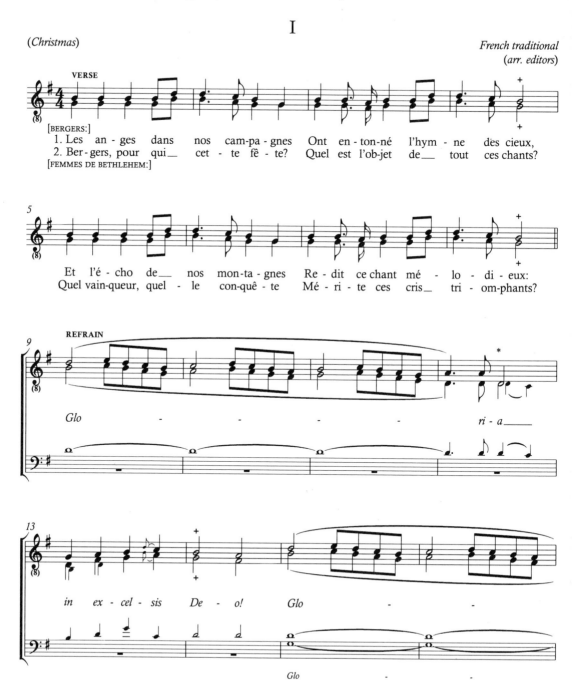

VERSE

[BERGERS:]
1. Les an - ges dans nos cam-pa - gnes Ont en - ton-né l'hym - ne des cieux,
2. Ber - gers, pour qui_ cet - te fê - te? Quel est l'ob-jet de_ tout ces chants?
[FEMMES DE BETHLEHEM:]

Et l'é - cho de_ nos mon-ta - gnes Re - dit ce chant mé - lo - di - eux:
Quel vain-queur, quel - le con-quê - te Mé - ri - te ces cris_ tri - om-phants?

REFRAIN

Glo - - - ri - a_

in ex - cel - sis De - o! Glo - -

Glo - -

*See performance note.

- - - ri - a____ in ex - cel - sis De - o!
- ria, glo - ri - a____

[BERGERS:]

3 Ils annoncent la naissance

Du Libérateur d'Israël;

Et, pleins de reconnaissance,

Chantent en ce jour solennel:

[FEMMES:]

4 Cherchons tous l'heureux village

Qui l'a vu naître sous ses toits;

Offrons-lui le tendre hommage

Et de nos cœurs et de nos voix:

[TOUS:]

5 Dans l'humilité profonde

Où vous paraissez à nos yeux,

Pour vous louer, Dieu du monde,

Nous redirons ce chant joyeux:

[BERGERS:]

*6 Déjà, par la bouche de l'ange,

Par les hymnes des chérubins,

Les hommes savent les louanges

Qui se chantent aux parvis divins:

[FEMMES:]

*7 Bergers, quittez vos retraites,

Unissez-vous à leurs concerts,

Et que vos tendres musettes

Fassent retentir les airs.

[TOUS:]

*8 Dociles à leur exemple,

Seigneur, nous viendrons désormais

Au milieu de votre temple,

Chanter avec eux vos bienfaits:

French traditional
(Smidt, 1932)

TRANSLATION 1 [SHEPHERDS:] The angels have sung the celestial hymn on our plains, and the echo of our mountains repeats this melodious song: Glory to God in the highest!

2 [WOMEN OF BETHLEHEM:] Shepherds, what do you celebrate? Why all these songs? What victor, what conquest, inspires these triumphant cries? Glory to God in the highest!

3 [SHEPHERDS:] They [the angels] announce the birth of the Saviour of Israel; and, full of gratitude, they sing on this solemn day: Glory to God in the highest!

4 [WOMEN:] Let us all seek the fortunate village which has seen him born beneath its roofs! Let us offer to him the loving homage of both our hearts and our voices: Glory to God in the highest!

5 [ALL:] In the deep humility in which you appear to our eyes, to praise you, God of all the world, we repeat this joyful song: Glory to God in the highest!

6 [SHEPHERDS:] Already, from the mouth of the angel, from the hymns of the cherubim, men know the praises which are sung in the courts of heaven: Glory to God in the highest!

7 [WOMEN:] Shepherds, forsake your haunts: join with their concerts, and let your sweet bagpipes make melodies resound! Glory to God in the highest!

8 [ALL:] Obedient to their [the angels'] example, O Lord, we shall come henceforth into the midst of your temple, to sing with them your blessings: Glory to God in the highest!

II

(*Christmas*)

French traditional
(*arr. Edward Shippen Barnes, 1887–1958*)

VERSE

1. An-gels we have heard on high, Sing-ing sweet-ly o'er the plains,
2. Shep-herds, why this ju-bi-lee? Why these joy-ous strains pro-long?

And the moun-tains in re-ply E-cho-ing their joy-ous strains:
What the glad-some ti-dings be Which in-spire your heaven-ly song?

REFRAIN

Glo - - - ri-a___

in ex-cel-sis De - o! De - o!

3 Come to Bethlehem and see
   Him whose birth the angels sing;
  Come, adore on bended knee
    Christ the Lord, the new-born King!

4 See him in a manger laid,
   Whom the choirs of angels praise;
  Mary, Joseph, lend your aid,
    While our hearts in love we raise.

H. F. Hémy (1818–88),
after James Chadwick (1813–82)

III

(Christmas)

*French traditional
(arr. Edward Shippen Barnes, 1887–1958)*

VERSE

1. An - gels, we have heard your voi - ces, Sweet - ly sing - ing o'er the plains;
2. Shep-herds, why this ju - bi - la - tion? Why this ec - sta - sy of song?

(Refrain as setting II)

Mount and crag and hill re - ply - ing, E - cho still your joy - ous strains:
Tell us what may be the ti - dings That in - spired the heaven - ly throng?

3 Come and see in Bethlem's city
　　Him whose birth the angels sing;
　　And, on bended knee, adore him,
　　Christ the Lord, the new-born King!

4 See, within a manger lying,
　　Jesus, Lord of heaven and earth;
　　Aid us, Mary, aid us, Joseph,
　　To acclaim our Saviour's birth.

Free tr., R. R. Terry (1865–1938)

This *noël*, possibly originally from Lorraine, achieved rapid popularity in France and Quebec in the 1840s. It became known in England through the free imitation by Bishop James Chadwick which appeared in his *Holy Family Hymns* (1860), and many different adaptations of the text followed. A version of verse 4 which was adapted to avoid calling on Mary and Joseph appeared in R. R. Chope's (Anglican) *Carols for Use in Church* (1877):

　　See, within a manger laid,
　　Jesus, Lord of heaven and earth,
　　Lend your voices, lend your aid
　　To proclaim the Saviour's birth!

Chadwick and his adapters made no attempt to retain the feminine endings of lines 2 and 4 in the French, and the carol was sung to a clipped version of the tune (II) which is still current in the US. In England this was displaced by Martin Shaw's harmonization in the *Oxford Book of Carols* (1928), set to James Montgomery's hymn 'Angels, from the realms of glory' (51:1). English Catholics sometimes sing Terry's reworking of Chadwick's text (III), which restores

the feminine line-ends. This text may also be sung to I, slurring the second beats of bars 3 and 7.

PERFORMANCE I, four voices or four-part choir. The shepherds' verses may be taken by tenors and basses, singing the upper parts in the refrain to bar 14 (the basses taking the small notes in bars 12–13), the full choir singing the repeat of 'Gloria' (bars 15–21). The women of Bethlehem's verses may be taken by sopranos and altos in a similar fashion. In the full verses, bars 1–8 may be sung at both octaves.

Alternatively, our dialogue instructions might be ignored, and high and low voices could split each verse between them (bars 1–4, 5–8) or alternate from verse to verse.

Ornaments: see notes, 111.

II and III voices and organ. An element of dialogue might be introduced (as in I, above) in a scheme such as the following: verse 1, men's voices (choir); verse 2, upper voices (choir); verse 3, full choir; verse 4, choir and congregation. Refrains: bars 9–14, full choir; bars 15–21, choir and congregation.

117

Birjina gaztettobat zegoen
The angel Gabriel from heaven came

I

(*Annunciation; Christmas*)

Basque traditional
(*Bordes, 1895, arr. editors*)

1. Bir - ji - na gaz - te - tto - bat ze - go - en___ Kre -
2. Ain gu - ri - a sar - tzen, di - o - la - rik:___ 'A -

- a - za - le Jao - na - ren o - thoi - tzen,___ Nou -
- gour, gra - zi - az zi - ra be - ther - ik,___ Jao -

- iz et' ain - gu - ru - bat le - hi - a - tu - ki___ Bei -
- na da zou - re - kin, be - ne - di - ka - tu___ Zi -

- tzen ze - lu - tik jai - tchi Min - tza - tze - ra___ ha - ren.___
- ra e - ta___ hai - ta - tu E - ma - tzen ga - ñe - tik.'___

3 Maria ordian duluratu,
   Eta bere beithan gogaratu
   Zeren zian ouste gabe entzuten
   Houra agour erraiten,
   Hanbat zen lotsatu.

4 'Etzitela, ez, lotza, Maria:
   Jinkoatan bathu' zu grazia:
   Zuk duzu sabelian ernaturen,
   Eta haorbat sorthuren
   Jesus datiana.'

5 Harek, duluraturik, harzara:
  'Bena noula izan daite hola,
  Etzu danaz gizounik ezagutzen,
  Ez eta ezaguturen
  Batere sekula?'

6 'Ezpiritu saintiak hountia
  Izanen duzu hori, Maria.'
  Zu zirateke, ber ordian, ama
  Bai et'ere birjina,
  Mundian bakhoitza.

7 Mariak arrapostu ordian:
  'Hao naizu Jinkoren zerbutchian,
  Zuk errana nitan biz konplitu.'
  Jaona aragitu
  Heren sabelian.

8 O Jinkoaren ama saintia,
  Bekhatugilen urgaitzarria,
  Zuk gitzatzu lagunt, bai Jinkoaren,
  Baita berthutiaren
  Bihotzez mait hatzen.

Eighteenth-century (?) Basque
(Bordes, 1895)

TRANSLATION 1 A young maiden was worshipping the Lord of Creation when an angel descended precipitously from the heavens to speak with her.

2 The angel entered, saying: 'Hail! thou who art full of grace; the Lord is with thee; thou art blessed and elect above all women.'

3 Mary was troubled, and wondered why she was hearing the angel greet her in this fashion; she was sore afraid.

4 'Be not afraid, Mary! Thou hast found grace with God; thou shalt conceive in thy womb and shalt bring forth a Son who shall be Jesus.'

5 She, troubled once more, [replied]: 'But how may this come to pass, since I know not a man, nor shall know one—no, not one?'

6 'The Holy Spirit will take care of all that, Mary. Thou shalt be at the same time a mother and also a maiden: thou alone of all the world.'

7 Mary replied thus: 'Behold the handmaid of God! May what you speak of come to pass in me!' And the Word was made flesh within her womb.

8 O Mary, blessed saint of God, refuge of sinners, teach us to love with all our heart both the Saviour and virtue.

Bordes's collection *Douze Noëls populaires* (1895) was part of the series *Archives de la tradition basque*, commissioned by a government department. The tunes are unharmonized and accompanied by the Basque texts and French prose translations. The manner of the present text (like that of 118) suggests the hand of an eighteenth-century clerical poet. Baring-Gould's version of the text was made expressly for Edgar Pettman's characterful setting (II), now standard in England, with its quasi-archaic flattened leading notes in bars 4 and 8. The small notes in the penultimate bar are alternatives: Pettman published both readings.

PERFORMANCE I, one or two voices, at any suitable pitch, with instrumental or vocal drone; II, choir.

In the Basque text all pairs of vowels except 'ia', 'oa', and 'oe' are to be treated as a single syllable.

II

(Annunciation; Christmas)

Basque traditional (Bordes, 1895,
arr. Edgar Pettman, 1866–1943)

1. The an-gel Ga-bri-el from hea-ven came,__ His wings as drift-ed snow, his
2. 'For known a bless-ed Mo-ther thou shalt be;__ All ge-ne-ra-tions laud and
3. Then gen-tle Ma-ry meek-ly bowed her head;__ 'To me be as it pleas-eth

eyes as flame:__ 'All hail,' said he, 'thou low-ly maid-en
ho-nour thee:__ Thy son shall be Em-ma-nu-el, by
God!' she said.__ 'My soul shall laud and mag-ni-fy his

Ma - ry,__ Most high-ly fa-voured la-dy!' Glo - ri - a!__
seers fore-told.__ ho-ly Name.'

† See notes.

4 Of her Emmanuel, the Christ, was born,
   In Bethlehem, all on a Christmas morn;
   And Christian folk throughout the world
      will ever say:
   Most highly favoured lady! Gloria!

English version by
Sabine Baring-Gould (1834–1924)

118

Oi Betleem!
Sing lullaby!

I

(Christmas)

Basque traditional
(Bordes, 1895, arr. editors)

1. Oi Bet - le - em! A - la e - gun zou - re glo - ri - ak, Oi Bet - le -
2. Zer ou - hou - re! A - la bei - zi - ra go - ra - ti - a, Zer ou - hou -
3. As - ke - ne - koz Hor helt - zen da Je - sus mai - ti - a, As - ke - ne -

- em! Ha - nitch bei - tu___ dis - ti - at - zen! Zou - re ga - nik___ hel - tu___ ar -
- re! Zer gra - zi - a,___ zer fa - bo - re! Ze - li - ak zi - ra hai - ta -
- koz. Ou - gun lai - da___ bi - hotz___ o - roz; Her - si na - hi___ du i - fer -

- gi - ak, Be - that - zen tu___ baz - ter___ gu - zi - ak, Oi Bet - le - em!
- ti - a Je - sus hao - rra - ren sor - le - khi - a, Zer ou - hou - re!
- ni - a, Et' i - re - ki___ gou - ri___ ze - li - a As - ke - ne - koz.

4 Gouregatik
    Jinkobat photerez bethia,
Gouregatik
Jaichten da zelu goratik:
    Bai sortzen da Jinko Semia,
    Bitima thonarik gabia,
Gouregatik.

5 Manjateran
    Dago haorrik aberatsena,
Manjateran.
Nourk othe zukian erran
    Zeru lurren jabia dena
    Ikhousiren zela etzana
Manjateran?

6 Artzañekin
    Jiten niz lehiaz zugana
Artzañekin.
Haien antzo nahiz egin;
    Adoratzen zutut, Mesia,
    Zouri' maiten bihotz guzia
Artzañekin.

7 Eztut deusik
    O Jesus! zouri eskeutzeko,
Eztut deusik,
Bihotz ogendunbat baizik:
    Eskerren zouri buhurtzeko
    Hanbat dohanen phakatzeko,
Eztut deusik.

Basque traditional
(Bordes, 1895)

TRANSLATION 1 O Bethlehem! Ah! how your glory today shines out brightly! The light that comes from you fills every corner.

2 What honour! for you are raised up on high. What grace! What favour! You are chosen of God as the birthplace of the child Jesus.

3 At last we see there the beloved Jesus. Let us praise him with all our heart; he has closed up hell and has opened up heaven for us.

4 For us an all-powerful God comes down from the heights of heaven; yes, he is born the Son of God, the spotless victim.

5 In the manger is the richest of children. Who would ever have predicted that the Lord of heaven and earth would be found lying in a manger?

6 With the shepherds I am impelled to come to you, wishing to do as they do; I worship you, the Messiah, give you all my heart, with the shepherds.

7 I have nothing, O Jesu, to offer you but a guilty heart, to show you my gratitude for all my benefits.

II

(Christmas)

Basque traditional (Bordes, 1895, arr. Edgar Pettman, 1866–1943)

VERSES 3 & 4

3. Sing lul - la - by! Lul - la - by ba - by, now a - do - zing, Sing lul - la -
4. Sing lul - la - by! Lul - la - by, is the Babe a - wa - king? Sing lul - la -

- by! Hush! do not wake the in - fant King!___ Soon comes the Cross, the nails, the
- by! Hush! do not wake the in - fant King!___ Dream - ing of Eas - ter, glad - some

pier - cing, Then in the grave at last__ re - po - sing;
morn - ing, Con - quer - ing death, its bond - age break - ing;

Sing___ lul - la - by!

Sing lul - la - by!

Sabine Baring-Gould
(1834–1924)

From the same source as 117. Pettman's only alteration in setting II is to stretch out the final cadence. In this case, Baring-Gould provided not a translation or an English version but an entirely new text, seemingly modelled on such German folk carols as no. 100 in its mingling of a lull-aby for the infant Christ with anticipation of his Passion, Crucifixion, and Resurrection.

PERFORMANCE   I, two voices, at any suitable pitch, with instrumental or vocal drone *ad lib.*; II, choir.

In the Basque text all pairs of vowels except 'ia', 'oa', and 'oe' are to be treated as a single syllable.

119

El desembre congelat
Cold December's winds were stilled

(Catalan)

(Christmas)

Catalan traditional
(arr. editors)

1. El de-sem-bre con-ge-lat, Con-fús es re-ti- ra.
2. El pri-mer Pa- re cau-sá La nit te-ne-vro- sa
3. El més de maig ha flo- rit, Sen-se ser en-ca- ra,

A - bril de flors co - ro - nat, Tot el món ad - mi - ra,
Que a tot el mon o - fus - ca La vis-ta pe - no - sa
Un lli - ri blanc y po - lit De fra-grán-cia ra - ra,

Quan en un jar - di d'a - mor Neix u - na di - vi - na flor. D'u-na
Mes en u - na mit - ja nit Bri - lla el sol que n'és eix - it D'u-na
Que per to el món se sent, De Lle - vant fins a Po-nent, To - ta

Catalan traditional

We have been unable to trace a Spanish source for this folk carol, which is popular in both the United States and Britain. The flowering rose-tree features in innumerable medieval legends (see notes for *NOBC* nos. 66 and 176): here the rose-flower is Christ. The star in verse 2 is the Star of Bethlehem; the lily in verse 3 is the traditional emblem of Mary, to whom the month of May is dedicated.

The melody derives from an old drinking-song, 'C'est notre grand pèr Noé', and was also sung as a *noël* to a variety of texts, including 'Bon Joseph, écoute moi' and 'Quand Dieu naquit à Noël'.

PERFORMANCE Choir.

(English)

(Christmas)

Catalan traditional
(arr. editors)

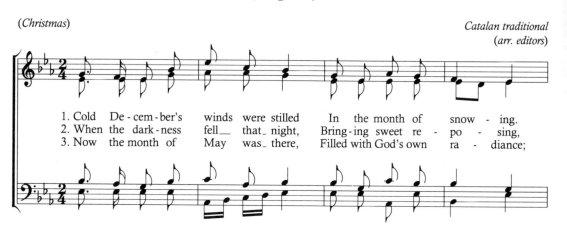

1. Cold De-cem-ber's winds were stilled In the month of snow - ing.
2. When the dark-ness fell__ that_ night, Bring-ing sweet re - po - sing,
3. Now the month of May was_ there, Filled with God's own ra - diance;

Though the world with dark_ was_ filled, Spring-time's hope was grow - ing.
All the world was hid__ from sight, Sleep men's eyes was clo - sing.
Bloomed a li - ly, white and_ fair, Flower of sweet-est fra - grance;

Then a rose - tree blos - somed new: One sweet flower up - on_ it grew; On the
All at once there came a__ gleam From the_ sky: a__ won - drous beam Of a
To the peo - ple, far_ and_ near, Came a__ breath of__ heaven-ly cheer. O the

tree once bare Grew a rose so fair, Ah! the rose, ah! the rose, Ah! the
heaven - ly star Gi-ving light a - far. Ah! the star, ah! the star, Ah! the
in - cense rare Of the li - ly there! Ah! the scent, ah! the scent Of the

rose - tree bloom - ing, Sweet the air___ per - fu - ming.
star - beam glow - ing, Bright - ness e - ver - grow - ing.
li - ly bloom - ing, All the air___ per - fu - ming!

vv. 1, 2 anon., v. 3 tr. George K. Evans,
both adapted

120

Veinticinco de diciembre
Twenty-fifth day of December

(Spanish)

(Christmas)

Spanish traditional
(arr. editors)

1. Vein - ti - cin - co de di - ciem-bre, ¡Fum, fum, fum! fum! Na - ci -
2. Pa - ja - ri - tos de los bos-ques, Vues-tros
3. Es - tre - lli - tas de los cie - los, Que a Je -

- do ha por nues-tro a - mor, El Ni - ño Dios, el Ni - ño Dios; Hoy de
hi - jos de co - ral A - ban - do - nad, a - ban - do - nad, Y for -
- sús mi - ráis llo - rar Y no llo - ráis, y no llo - ráis, A - lum -

la Vír-gen Ma - rí - a En es - ta no - che tan frí - a,
- mad un mue - lle ni - do A Je - sús re - cién na - ci - do, ¡Fum, fum, fum!
- brad la no - che os-cu - ra Con vues-tra luz cla - ra y pu - ra,

Spanish traditional

(English)

(*Christmas*)

Spanish traditional
(arr. editors)

tr. George K. Evans

In the English-speaking countries this is perhaps the most popular of all Spanish folk carols. It sounds like a dance-song, and the recurring 'Fum, fum, fum!' may imitate the sound of a drum (or perhaps the strumming of a guitar).

PERFORMANCE (*i*) Voice and guitar; (*ii*) choir.

121

El Noi de la Mare
The Son of the Virgin

(Catalan)

(*Christmas*)

Catalan traditional
(*arr. editors*)

1. Qué li da - rem a n'el Noi de la Ma - re? Qué li da - rem que li
2. Qué li da - rem el fi - llet de Ma - ri - a, Qué li da - rem a l'her -
3. Tam pa-tan-tam, que les fi - gues son ver - des, Tam pa-tan-tam, que ja

Ah! _____ Ah! _____

sá - pi - ga bon? ___ Li da-rem pan - ses en u - nes ba - lan - ces,
-mós In-fan - tó? ___ Pan - ses i fi - gues i nuez i o - li - ves,
ma - du - ra - rán. ___ Si no ma - du - ren el di - a de Pas - qua,

Li da - rem fi - gues en un pa - ne - ró. _____ un pa - ne - ró.
Pan - ses i fi - gues i mel i ma - tó. _____ mel i ma - tó.
Ma - du - ra - rán en el di - a del Ram. _____ di - a del Ram.

Catalan traditional

(English)

(*Christmas*)

Catalan traditional
(*arr. editors*)

1. What shall we give to the Son of the Virgin? What can we give him that
2. What shall we give the be-lov-ed of Ma-ry? What can we give to her
3. What shall we do if the figs are not ri-pened? What shall we do if the

Ah!

Ah!

he will en-joy?___ First, we shall give him a tray full of rai-sins,
beau-ti-ful Child?___ Rai-sins and o-lives and figs and sweet ho-ney,
figs are still green?___ If by Palm Sun-day they still have not ri-pened,

1.
Then we shall of-fer sweet figs to the boy.___
Can-dy and figs and a cheese that is mild.___
Yet shall that ripe-ness at Eas-ter be seen.___

2.
figs to the boy.
cheese that is mild.
Eas-ter be seen.

tr. George K. Evans, adapted

A song of the shepherds. In the third verse the green fig is the innocent Child, its ripening his work of redemption.

PERFORMANCE (*i*) Solo voice or unison voices, with instrumental or vocal drone (on E♭, or E♭ and B♭, throughout); (*ii*) two voices or two-part choir with drone (in this case the first two alto E♭s in the last bar should be sung as Ds); (*iii*) choir.

122

Quando nascette Ninno
When Christ, the Son of Mary

(Neapolitan)

(Christmas)

Neapolitan traditional
(arr. editors)

1. Quan - do nas - cet - te Nin - no a Bet - te - lem -
2. Non' ce - ra - no ne - mi - ce ppe la ter -
3. Guar - da - va - no le pe - co - re lu pas - tu -

- me, E - ra not - te a pa - re - a
- ra, La pe - co - ra pa - sci - a co
- re; E l'an - ge - lo, sbren - nen - te

mmie - zo juor - no! Ma - je le stel - le Lus - te - re
lo li - o - ne, Co le cra - pet - te Se - ve -
chiù de lu su - le, Com - pa - ret - te, E le di -

Neapolitan traditional

For many centuries, during the period before Christmas mountain shepherds have descended on Rome, Naples, and other cities in southern Italy and Sicily, clad in sheepskin cloaks and wide-brimmed hats and singing and playing pastoral music such as this carol. They accompany each other on the *ciaramella* (a small shawm) and the *zampogna*, a large, sweet-toned bagpipe with two drones and two chanters, which is played mostly in thirds and sixths with some embellishment.

Many eighteenth-century composers used the pastoral *siciliana* rhythm of the Italian shepherds to suggest Christmas: the aria 'He shall feed his flock' in Handel's *Messiah* is remarkably similar to the melody of 'Quando nascette Ninno', and it is possible that Handel heard it during his time in Rome as a young man, in 1707–9.

PERFORMANCE (*i*) Two voices, or two-part choir, with vocal or instrumental drone; (*ii*) choir; (*iii*) two voices with *zampogna* and *ciaramella*.

(English)

(*Christmas*)

Neapolitan traditional
(arr. editors)

1. When Christ, the Son of Ma - ry, in Beth - le - hem was born,__ 'Twas night, and yet the
2. When Christ, the Son of Ma - ry, with - in her arms was laid,__ The li - on with the
3. When Christ, the Son of Ma - ry, with - in the crib_ did lie,__ There came to shep-herds

light_____ was bright as sum-mer's morn! Stars__ were gleam-ing, Bright - ly
lamb,_____ the bear with fat - ling strayed. Close to the shep - herd Wan-dered the
drows - y a voice which sang on high: 'Peace on the earth_ Is come with this

beam - ing O'er__ the town__ of Beth - le - hem;__ A bright - er star__ there
leo - pard, E - very crea - ture was_ at peace;__ The great and small were
birth;__ Go, seek the Babe_ in yon - der stall,__ Your King, though weak_ and

shone__ For ma - gi far, a gui - ding star that led them on.__
one;__ For calf or lamb that night_____ no fright, but joy, did come.__
small;_ The world's true light is come_____ this night to save you all.'__

tr. Gordon Hitchcock, adapted

INDEXES

INDEX OF FEASTS AND SEASONS

This list comprises specific feasts and seasons other than Christmas. Since carols appropriate for use at Christmas constitute the bulk of the contents, they are not listed here. Each carol is followed by its item number.

INDEX OF SOURCES FOR MUSIC AND TEXT

This index incorporates details of authors, translators, composers, and arrangers as found in the music and text ascriptions to the carols. Supplementary references to printed and manuscript sources are also included (entered under both title and author, where the latter is known), and for more information about these readers are referred to the notes on individual carols and the bibliography in *NOBC*. Editorial arrangements, adaptations, and translations (and authors of prose translations) are not given. References are to carol numbers throughout.

INDEX OF FIRST LINES AND TITLES

Where titles differ from first lines, they are shown in *italic*. Each carol is followed by its item number.

Index of First Lines and Titles